DAYLIGHTING
PERFORMANCE
AND DESIGN

DAYLIGHTING

PERFORMANCE AND DESIGN

Second Edition

Gregg D. Ander, FAIA

WILEY

John Wiley & Sons, Inc.

Library of Congress Cataloging-in-Publication Data:

Ander, Gregg D.
    Daylighting performance and design / Gregg D. Ander.— 2nd ed.
        p. cm.
    Includes bibliographical references and index.
    ISBN 0-471-26299-4 (cloth)
        1. Daylighting. 2. Architectural design. 3. Light in architecture. I. Title.

NA2794 .A53 2002
729'.28—dc21
                            2002033187

Printed in the United States of America

10 9 8 7 6 5 4 3 2 1

To Lisa, Jason, Jesse, and Erik

CONTENTS

FOREWORD

The first decade of the 21st century begins with a revitalized interest in the subject of sustainable design practice and green buildings. Owners and design professionals alike seem to agree that daylighting strategies are an important element of these building design solutions.

However, while interest in daylighting continues to grow, actual building performance is often uncertain. The creation of well-daylighted buildings that are comfortable and energy efficient remains a challenge that is surprisingly difficult to meet. Flooding a building with daylight requires no particular architectural skill. A more appropriate response must balance the needs of owners, occupants, and society by integrating concerns for aesthetics, amenity, comfort, energy efficiency, and cost effectiveness. Great architectural designs have not always been environmentally friendly, and elegantly engineered solutions sometimes fail to meet basic human needs. Design teams need better and more relevant information to address this problem.

The *Second Edition of Daylighting Performance and Design* should prove useful to design professionals who are striving to satisfy the human preference for view and daylight while meeting our responsibilities to energy efficiency and sustainable development. It establishes realistic performance potentials for good daylighting designs, balanced with practical information on what has been accomplished to date with the use of updated case studies and revised information on new glazing and fenestration systems. The data and guidelines provided within the book are complemented with pointers to other useful information resources.

The *Second Edition of Daylighting Performance and Design* will be a valuable resource for architects, engineers, lighting designers, and energy consultants. It will stimulate the uninitiated to explore the potentials of daylighting, guide the novice to tools and techniques that will help explore alternative design options, and assist the experienced designer in stretching the boundaries of past design solutions.

Stephen Selkowitz
Berkeley, California
Head, Building
    Technologies Department
Lawrence Berkeley National Laboratory

FOREWORD

Daylighting is the greatest design tool available to an architect. It is the very magic that enlivens a building's interior. What would the Pantheon be without an oculus or the Kimball without the clerestory that brilliantly lights its vaulted ceiling? Great architectural spaces are created through the masterful use of daylight. It is the one universal element that can be applied to all buildings, and it's free! Daylight gives us a sense of place in an otherwise homogenized world, as light changes depending on the building's orientation, time of day, season of the year, and local weather conditions.

Study after study has shown that people relate to daylight in very positive ways: their productivity increases and their sense of well-being improves. (One would hope that there will never be another windowless office or classroom.) If used properly, daylighting increases the energy efficiency of a building. It allows one to turn off the lights! There is no reason not to celebrate the great benefits of daylighting now that high-performance glazing is commonplace and affordable. The designer in today's world has every tool available to use daylight to create memorable spaces that perform well and meet the criteria of the user. *Daylighting Performance and Design, Second Edition,* is a marvelous resource for all who want to responsibly use daylight to enhance their spaces, and in so doing "tread more lightly on this earth."

Susan Maxman, FAIA
Philadelphia, Pennsylvania
Past President
American Institute of Architects

PREFACE

The relationship among people, daylight, and architectural form is intimate. Daylight has the potential to introduce life, variation, and drama into otherwise banal spaces. Throughout the history of civilization, our buildings have often articulated this relationship. Daylight as a design variable can profoundly influence building orientation, form, scale, the character of interior spaces, and the way that interior space is perceived. Building occupants are also affected by the presence of daylight, often resulting in an increase in standardized test scores by students, improved productivity by office workers, and additional product sales in retail spaces.

This manual has been designed and assembled to address pragmatic issues of daylighting and provide resources to help solve a myriad of design issues. Understanding and integrating solutions throughout the design/build/operate phases will yield buildings and spaces with superior performance and spatial qualities. The building designer can add to the design palette technical performance and operational intelligence about daylight with which cost-effective decisions can be applied throughout the process.

Gregg D. Ander, FAIA

ACKNOWLEDGMENTS

The following individuals are recognized for their contributions in preparing this book: Bill Anton, Anthony Bernhiem, Stephen Dent, Deane Evens, Greg Franta, Lisa Heschong, Janith Johnson, Stephen Lesourd, Donald Mauritz, Fuller Moore, Paki Muthig, Dan Ritey, Steve Selkowitz, Jonathan Starr, Barry Wasserman, and Joe Wilcox. Kelly J. Andereck made significant contributions with graphic support and background research.

DAYLIGHTING
PERFORMANCE AND DESIGN

I use light abundantly, as you may have suspected; Light for me is the fundamental basis of architecture. I compose with light.

—Le Corbusier

Without a glass palace
Life becomes a burden.
Glass opens up a new age
Brick building only does harm.

—Scheerbart

A room is not a room without natural light. Natural light gives the time of day and the mood of the seasons to enter.

—L. Kahn

Fundamentals of Daylighting

As a design feature, the use of daylighting within a building creates a more pleasing and productive atmosphere for the people within. Daylight provides a direct link to the outdoor environment and natural light delivers a dynamic evolving distribution of light. The moderation of light levels is often subtle and usually unnoticed, and the result is one of visual richness, creating an environment that is stimulating and more comfortable.

Successful daylighting is more than simply adding large windows or skylights. It involves thoughtful integration of design strategies, which address heat gain, glare, variations in light availability, and direct-beam penetration into a building. Design considerations will often address details such as shading devices, aperture size and spacing, glazing materials, interior finishes, and reflectance. In large measure, the art and science of daylighting is not so much about how to provide enough daylighting as how to do so without its possible undesirable effects.

As an efficiency measure, daylighting is most effective during bright sunny afternoons when it can supplant the need for electric lighting entirely. Because an electric utility must provide enough generating capacity to serve the highest demand predicted for its service territory, daylighting has the potential not only to reduce the building's overall energy consumption but also to lower the peak demand.

Electric lighting directly accounts for approximately 20% to 25% of the total electrical energy used in the United States. In the commercial sector, lighting accounts for 37% (34% interior, 3% exterior) of electrical energy consumption (see Figure 1.1). Lighting also has an indirect impact on the total energy use because the heat generated by electric fixtures alters the loads imposed on the mechanical cooling equipment. As a rule of thumb, each unit of electric lighting contributes to an additional one-half unit of electricity for space conditioning because of the contributions from the heat generated by electric lighting. The energy savings from reduced lighting loads can directly reduce air-conditioning energy usage by an additional 10% to 20%.

There seems to be a strong interest in efficiency issues not only from a technical standpoint but also as they relate to social and

Architecture is the masterly, correct and magnificent play of volumes brought together in light. Our eyes are made to see forms in light . . . cubes, cones, spheres, cylinders or pyramids are the great primary forms that light reveals to advantage. . . . It is of the very nature of the plastic arts.
LE CORBUSIER

1

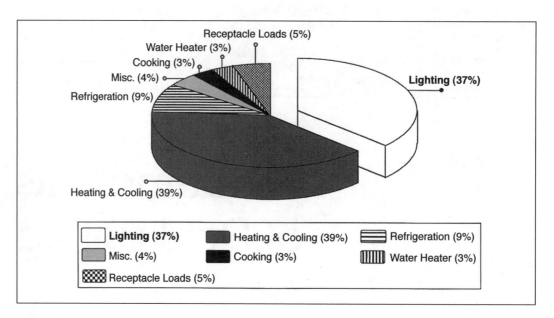

Figure 1.1 Commercial electricity use in the United States. *(Courtesy of the Electric Power Research Institute of Palo Alto, California.)*

behavioral issues. These issues often involve enhanced comfort, satisfaction, and productivity and may even have a relationship to the number of workers' compensation claims filed against an employer. The Center for Building Performance and Diagnostics (CBPD) at Carnegie Mellon has conducted many building surveys and postoccupancy evaluations to better understand the effect of design features on occupants. Appendix G contains a survey form developed to assess the impacts of perceived comfort for a series of postoccupancy evaluations conducted at the College of Environmental Design at California Polytechnic State University at Pomona.

Daylighting may potentially play a key role in supporting "sustainable" development. As clients begin to demand sustainable solutions and the design community embraces these challenges to produce buildings that reduce environmental impacts, daylighting solutions have the opportunity to play a significant role through pollution avoidance. By virtue of improving a building's efficiency, you would expect to see a reduction in annual kilowatt-hours so the amount of pollutants emitted at a utility generating station will reduce the amount of airborne pollutants, including nitrogen oxide (NO_x), carbon dioxide (CO_2), and sulfur dioxide (SO_2), all of which contribute to reductions in air quality. The Environmental Protection Agency and most utilities have data on the relationship between kilowatt-hours and pollution avoidance values. Table 1.1 represents the latest conversion values for the United States.

A key concern the design team confronts is visualizing various design solutions and quantifying the impacts of fenestration-related decisions. Some design firms regularly perform this type of service as a "basic service," whereas other firms consider it an additional service and obtain additional compensation to cover any added design and analysis time and sell the client based on anticipated reductions in operating costs. Many utilities offer design assistance or incentives to optimize buildings, and these may include assistance to solve for daylighting-related issues. It is important to remember that the daylighting design process involves the ideas of many disciplines, including architectural, mechanical, electrical, and lighting (see Figure 1.2). These design team members need to be brought into the process early to ensure that the concepts and ideas are carried through the entire design, construction, and operating process (see Figure 1.3). Ample opportunity exists for

TABLE 1.1 Emission Factors

STATES	CO_2 (lb/kWh)	SO_2 (g/kWh)	NO_X (g/kWh)
CT, ME, MA, NH, RI, VT	1.1	4.0	1.4
NJ, NY	1.1	3.4	1.3
DE, DC, MD, PA, VA, WV	1.6	8.2	2.6
AL, FL, GA, KY, MS, NC, SC, TN	1.5	6.9	2.5
IL, IN, MI, MN, OH, WI	1.8	10.4	3.5
AR, LA, NM, OK, TX	1.7	2.2	2.5
IA, KS, MO, NE	2.0	8.5	3.9
CO, MT, ND, SD, UT, WY	2.2	3.3	3.2
AZ, CA, HI, NV	1.0	1.1	1.5
AK, ID, OR, WA	0.1	0.5	0.3
National average	1.5	5.8	2.5

miscommunication throughout the daylighting system design process. The way a building is designed versus how it is built versus how it is operated is important to integrate. Building commissioning is often a critical function to ensure a building performs as designed. See Appendix B for a commissioning specification and prefunctional test protocols.

DESIGN ISSUES

Architects and designers who are sensitive to basic daylighting fundamentals can achieve an aesthetically pleasing space without sacrificing cost or creativity. An awareness of certain issues that can occur when daylighting is employed will assist in the success of an effective design.

VEILING REFLECTIONS

Veiling reflections obscure the details seen by reducing the contrast. Thus, avoid creating conditions within the building where disabling veiling reflections may occur, particularly in spaces where there are critical tasks.

There are many types of visual tasks with various degrees of criticality (see Figure 1.4). A receptionist may not require the same level of illumination as a graphic designer. Many spaces in a building can be lighted that do not require a high degree of illuminance. The Illuminating Engineering Society of North

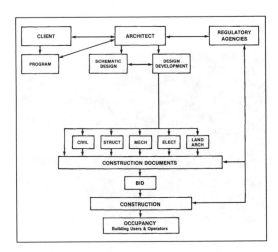

Figure 1.2 Standard design process.

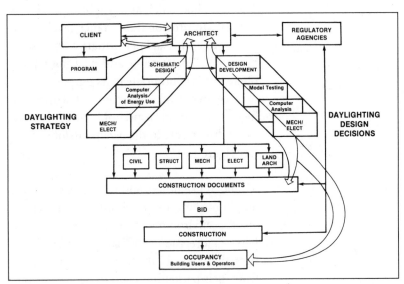

Figure 1.3 Integrated daylighting design process. *(Courtesy of Scott Ellinwood, FAIA.)*

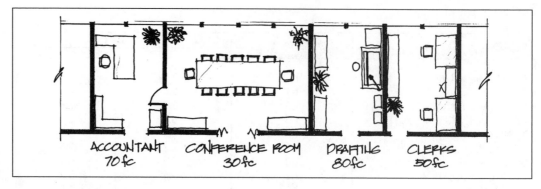

Figure 1.4 Plan showing room-specific illumination requirements.

America publishes illumination guidelines for various types of spaces.

QUANTITY

Introduce as much controlled daylight as possible, and as deeply as possible, into the building interior. Generally, the human eye can adjust to high levels of luminance without producing discomfort. In fact, the more light available, the better people can see. Veiling reflections and excessive brightness differences are often problematic and should be addressed.

GLARE

The aim of an efficient daylighting design is not only to provide illuminance levels sufficient for good visual performance but also to maintain a comfortable and pleasing atmosphere that is appropriate to its purpose. Glare, or excessive brightness contrast within the field of view, is one aspect of lighting that can cause discomfort to the occupants of a space (see Figure 1.5).

Although brightness and brightness contrast are important in providing a stimulating visual environment, excessive contrast between foreground and background may disrupt the eye's ability to distinguish objects from their background and to perceive detail. The human eye can function quite well over a wide range of luminous environments, but it cannot function well if extreme levels of brightness are present in the field of view at the same time.

Some contrast in brightness levels may not be undesirable. Dull uniformity in lighting, although never harmful, can lead to tiredness and lack of attention—neither of which is compatible with a productive environment. However, it is necessary to ensure that glare is kept under control and that extreme levels of brightness are not present in the field of view at the same time.

Glare is not a design issue most of the time; it is critical only when certain viewing conditions occur. In this regard, understanding the conditions that might cause glare is the first step toward finding a design solution to deal with it or to avoid the problem altogether.

Figure 1.5 Typical office glare.

Glare is a subjective phenomenon and as such is difficult to quantify. Nonetheless, a generalized form of glare quantification can be derived by studying changes in the contrast ratio. The study quantifies the average response of a large number of people to the same glare situation. This type of analysis is used to determine a glare constant for individual apertures and a glare index for all light sources in the field of view.

However, assessments of the physical factors can be correlated to the magnitude of the described sensation so that glare discomfort can be estimated. Studies of these factors have resulted in the development of glare indices, which can be utilized at the design stage to address glare discomfort and are integral to many computer-based design tools.

DESIGN VARIABLES

SITE ELEMENTS

Sky conditions vary the nature and quantity of the light entering a building. Three types of sky conditions are utilized to estimate illumination levels within a space.

The *overcast sky* is the most uniform type of sky condition and generally tends to change more slowly than the other types. It is defined as being a sky in which at least 80% of the sky dome is obscured by clouds. The overcast sky has a general luminance distribution that is about three times brighter at the zenith than at the horizon. The illumination produced by the overcast sky on the earth's surface may vary from several hundred footcandles to several thousand, depending on the density of the clouds (see Figure 1.6).

The *clear sky* is less bright than the overcast sky and tends to be brighter at the horizon than at the zenith. It tends to be fairly stable in luminance except for the area surrounding the sun, which changes as the sun moves. The clear sky is defined as being a sky in which no more than 30% of the sky dome is obscured by clouds. The total level of illumination produced by a clear sky varies constantly but slowly throughout the day. The illumination

> *The choice of a structure is synonymous with the light which gives image to that space. . . . A plan of a building should read like a harmony of spaces in light.*
> L. KAHN

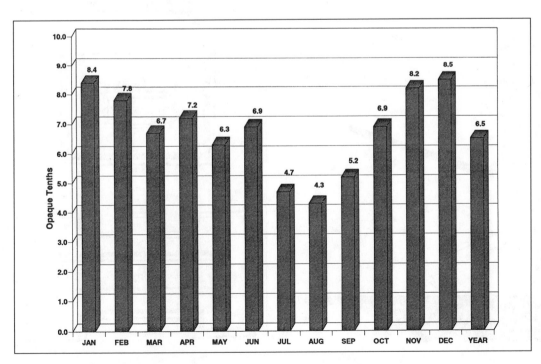

Figure 1.6 Typical bar graph indicating cloud cover measured in tenths. *(Additional climatic data are provided in Appendix C.)*

levels produced can range from 5,000 to 12,000 footcandles.

The *cloudy sky* has a cloud cover that may range from quite heavy to very light. The cloudy sky is defined as being a sky in which 30% to 80% of the sky dome is obscured by clouds. It usually includes widely varying luminance from one area of the sky to another and tends to change quite rapidly. The cloudy sky may provide periods when direct sun reaches the building site and some periods when, for all practical purposes, the sky appears overcast.

Appendix C gives weather data for a variety of climate zones, including average clear-cloudy conditions. It is quite valuable to perform a climatic analysis to formulate proper design responses.

External obstructions surrounding a window will affect the amount of daylighting entering a space. Many of these conditions, such as cloud cover and sun position, are purely a function of the climate. External obstructions, on the other hand, such as trees and other buildings, can permanently alter the amount of daylight allowed to enter a window opening (see Figure 1.7). The patterns of obstruction will normally vary for each window. They can have different shapes, different positions relative to the window, and different light-blocking or reflecting characteristics.

DESIGN STRATEGIES

INCREASE PERIMETER DAYLIGHT ZONES

Extending the perimeter form of a building may improve the building's performance by increasing the total daylighting area. The trade-offs between an increased perimeter exposure and a compact building form are shown in Figure 1.8. The thermal impact of

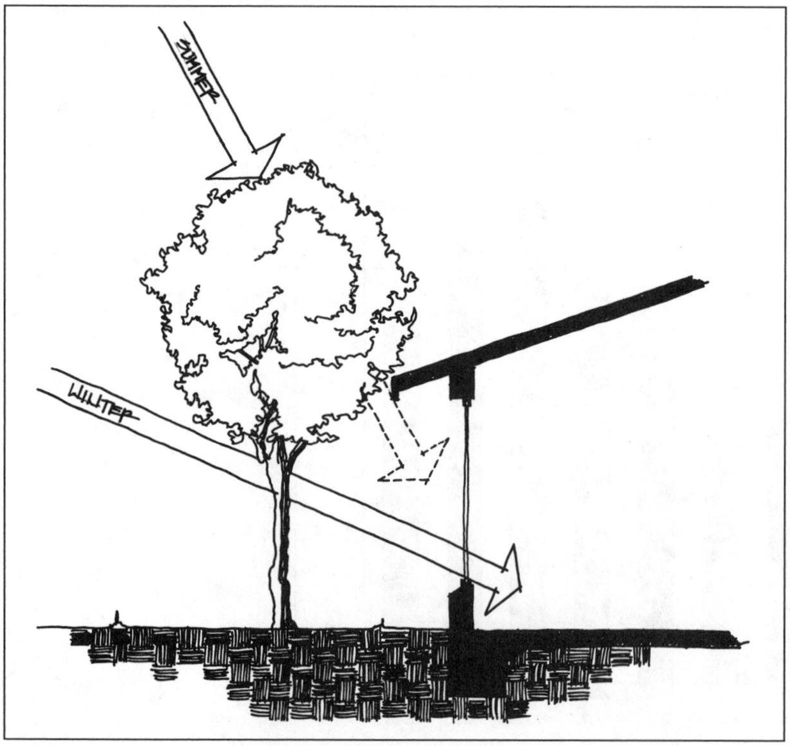

Figure 1.7 External obstruction that may impact available illuminance and solar heat gain.

Figure 1.8 Articulated plans showing increased daylighting zones.

electric lights and the increased linear footage of window wall should be given careful attention when these strategies are considered.

ALLOW DAYLIGHT PENETRATION HIGH IN A SPACE

With the location of an aperture high in a wall, deeper penetration will result. There will be less likelihood of excessive brightness in the field of view by reflecting and scattering light before it gets to task level.

USE THE IDEA OF "EFFECTIVE APERTURE" FOR INITIAL ESTIMATES OF THE OPTIMUM GLAZING AREA

When the effective aperture, the product of the window-to-wall ratio and the visible transmittance of the glazing, is around 0.18, daylighting saturation will be achieved. Additional glazing area or light will be counterproductive because it will increase the cooling loads more than it will reduce the lighting loads.

REFLECT DAYLIGHT WITHIN A SPACE TO INCREASE ROOM BRIGHTNESS

Although the source of daylight is the sun, surfaces and objects within a space reflect and scatter daylight. An increase in visibility and comfort can be achieved through increasing room brightness by spreading and evening out brightness patterns. A reduction in intensity occurs from reflecting and partially absorbing light throughout a space. A light shelf, if properly designed, has the potential to increase room brightness and decrease window brightness (see Figure 1.9 and 1.10).

SLOPE CEILINGS TO DIRECT MORE LIGHT INTO A SPACE

Sloping the ceiling away from the fenestration area will help increase the brightness

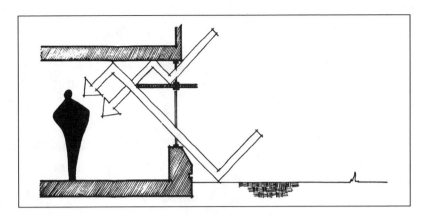

Figure 1.9 Section through typical light shelf.

of the ceiling farther into a space (see Figure 1.11).

AVOID DIRECT-BEAM DAYLIGHT ON CRITICAL VISUAL TASKS

Poor visibility and discomfort will result if excessive brightness differences occur in the vicinity of critical visual tasks. It is a fallacy to believe that good daylighting design entails merely adding large apertures of glazing to a building design. Fenestration controls should be considered if direct-beam illumination is undesirable (see Figure 1.12).

Figure 1.10 Detail of fenestration control. (*Photograph courtesy of Olson/Sundberg Architects.*)

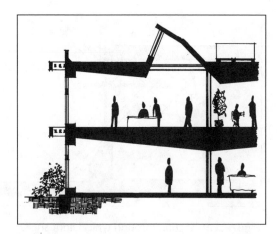

Figure 1.11 Building section showing sloped ceiling treatment.

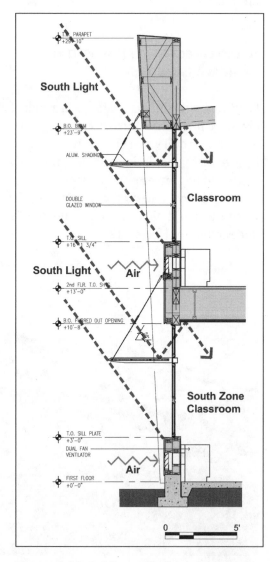

Figure 1.12 Building section showing fenestration treatments to reduce window brightness and increase room brightness. *(Courtesy of VBN Architects.)*

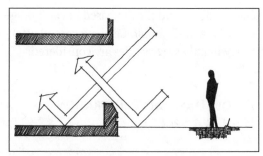

Figure 1.13 Section showing uncontrolled fenestration.

USE DIRECT SUN CAUTIOUSLY IN AREAS WHERE NONCRITICAL TASKS OCCUR

Patterns of light and shadows from the sun tracking across the sky can add an exciting and dynamic feature to a space. A feeling of well-being and a sense of time and orientation often impact the occupants of such a space. However, if they are integrated poorly, the occupants may have difficulty in seeing, and, in addition, unwanted heat gain may result (see Figures 1.13 and 1.14).

FILTER DAYLIGHT

When harshness of direct light is a potential problem, filtering can be accomplished by vegetation, curtains, or louvers. This will help soften and distribute light more uniformly (see Figures 1.15 and 1.16 and 1.17).

Figure 1.14 Section showing overhang to control direct beam.

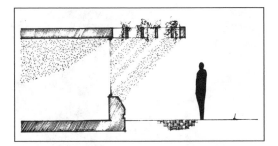

Figure 1.15 Section showing vegetation and lattice to filter daylight.

CONSIDER OTHER ENVIRONMENTAL CONTROL SYSTEMS

Fenestration systems can potentially allow light, heat, air, and sounds into a space. Ventilation; acoustics; views; electric lighting systems; and heating, ventilating, and air-conditioning (HVAC) systems all need to be considered during the design process (see Figure 1.18).

Figure 1.17 Interior of a university bookstore showing suspended fabric diffusing elements below the aperture.

DESIGN ELEMENTS

Several design considerations impacting light affect a building in terms of form and shape. Probably the most significant design determinant when implementing daylighting strategies is the geometry of a building's walls, ceiling, floors, windows, and how each relates to the other. An understanding of the effects of the various building elements will provide the basis for manipulating form to achieve adequate lighting levels. It is also important to understand geometric relationships in terms

of lighting functions, as well as to comprehend the quantitative relationships that accompany various geometric forms. A review of measured or calculated illumination levels for various design functions will be helpful, as will the experience. Designers need to manipulate the configurations and measure the

Figure 1.16 Exterior facade with lattice system.

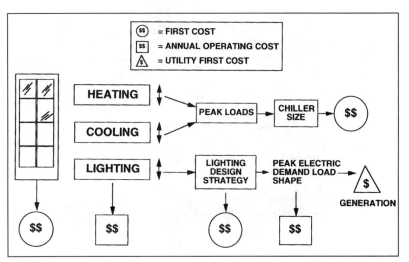

Figure 1.18 Glazing-related decision point diagram. *(Courtesy of Steve Selkowitz.)*

results before they can properly understand the quantitative relationships. This can be accomplished through physical model tests, computer simulations, or both.

EXTERIOR ELEMENTS

Overhangs can be useful controls for fenestration. In addition to blocking the direct beam from the sun, they will also reduce the amount of sky seen from within a room, thus reducing the amount of diffuse skylight admitted through the opening.

Reflected light from the ground or other surfaces can also be caught by an overhang and directed back into the interior of a room (see Figure 1.19). The result will be a slightly higher illuminance level and a more even distribution of light in the space.

Light shelves are typically horizontal devices located near the window area. Successful fenestration systems have integrated both exterior and interior light shelves. They are used primarily to reduce window brightness by blocking direct-beam sunlight from entering

Figure 1.20 Elevation showing light shelf.

the conditioned space. Light shelves also have the potential to increase room brightness by reflecting light into the building. As a design element, light shelves often introduce a strong horizontality to the building facade (see Figure 1.20). Fenestration systems may have exterior or interior light shelves. These devices may be combined so both exterior and interior work together.

Horizontal louvers are an effective method of blocking direct-beam light during the summer when sun angles are high while allowing some sunlight penetration during the milder seasons. Movable louvers can be controlled electronically or mechanically to respond to changing sky and weather conditions.

Vertical louvers or *fins* are advantageous for east and west orientations to block direct-beam light and to reflect light into the interior (see Figure 1.21). The louvers or fins can be fixed or movable (see Figure 1.22).

Figure 1.19 Wall section showing light shelf.

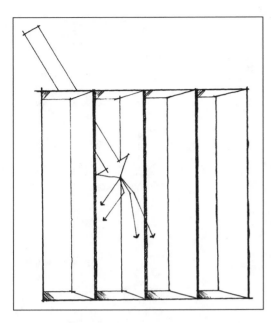

Figure 1.21 East-west window control scheme.

Daylight tracking and reflecting systems are designed to enhance the daylighting potential of skylights by tracking and reflecting sunlight through the aperture and into the open spaces below. This type of equipment can be either dynamically controlled to follow the path of the sun or completely stationary, using strategically placed mirrors to capture the direct-beam daylight.

Because low-angle daylight can be better utilized, the use of this equipment is able to extend the hours within a day, as well as the months within a year, that natural light can effectively replace or complement electric lighting.

Figure 1.22 Movable louver system.

IN-WALL AND ROOF ELEMENTS

Glazing Materials

Historically, the simplest method to maximize the amount of available daylight within a building was to increase the total amount of glazing present in the building envelope. In many cooling-dominated climates, admitting more light has, until recently, meant admitting unwanted heat gain as well. However, recent advancements in glazing technology have specifically reduced this liability.

The physical properties of glazing materials need to be well understood (see Figures 1.23, 1.24, 1.25, and 1.26). Selective coatings or low-emissivity (low-e) window systems can be specified which are transparent to daylight and are opaque to potentially detrimental ultraviolet and/or infrared radiation. A more detailed discussion of these properties is located in Chapter 3.

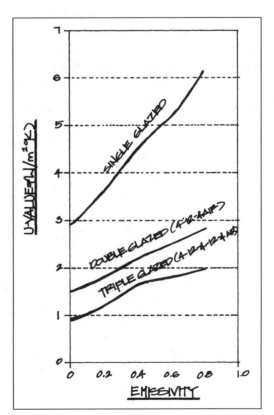

Figure 1.23 Graph illustrating emissivity as a function of *U*-value.

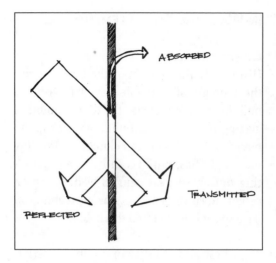

Figure 1.24 Characteristics of glazing.

Effective Aperture

In the simplest of terms, as the area of an aperture increases, the amount of daylight received in a space also increases. However, the glazing material within that aperture can effectively reduce the amount of visible light that is allowed to enter. Therefore, aperture size alone is not an effective determinant to measure illumination levels. If the glazing in an opening is a perfectly transparent material, the "effective aperture" size would be equal to the area of the opening [because the visible transmittance (VT) of the glazing would be 1.0]. If, however, the glazing has a

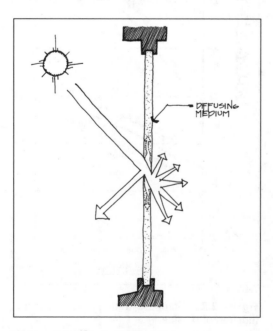

Figure 1.25 Typical diffuse transmission.

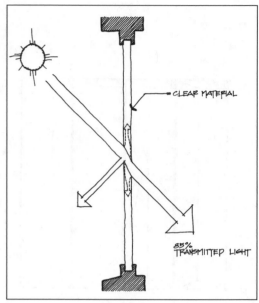

Figure 1.26 Nondiffuse transmission.

VT of 0.50, the opening will transmit only half of the light striking it, and the "effective aperture" will be half of the actual size of the opening.

The "effective aperture," or light-admitting potential of a glazing system, is determined by multiplying the visible transmittance (VT) by the window-to-wall ratio (WWR). The window-wall ratio is the ratio of the net window glazing area to the gross exterior wall area.

$$EA = WWR \times VT$$

This attribute can be useful in evaluating the cost effectiveness and the daylighting potential of a schematic building configuration.

Aperture Location

The location of an aperture will affect the distribution of the light admitted through the aperture.

The height of a window from the finished floor will dictate the depth of penetration. The higher the window, the deeper the daylight will penetrate. One rule of thumb states that the depth of daylight penetration is about $2\frac{1}{2}$ times the distance between the top of a window and the windowsill (see Figure 1.27).

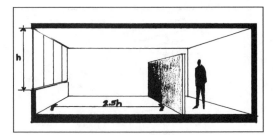

Figure 1.27 Rule of thumb for window configuration.

INTERIOR ELEMENTS

Room Geometry

The depth that daylight will penetrate is dependent on the ceiling height relative to the top of the window. A high window height will allow entering daylight to strike the ceiling plane and be reflected into the interior of the space.

The depth of the room has a direct effect on the intensity of illumination as well. If a space is modeled, keeping the floor-to-ceiling height and the area and location of the window constant, changing the room depth will cause a change in light intensity. With deeper rooms, the same quantity of incoming light is distributed over a larger area (see Figure 1.28).

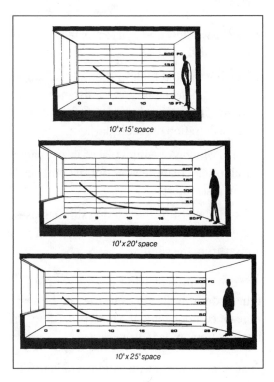

Figure 1.28 Light intensity as a function of room depth.

Reflectances of Room Surfaces

The reflectance values of room surfaces will greatly impact the performance of a daylit space (see Figure 1.29). The ceiling is the most important surface in reflecting the daylight coming into a space onto the work plane. The next most important surface is the back wall, followed by the side walls, and finally, the floor.

As the designer, keep the ceiling as light as possible and use only the floor for patterns or deep colors. Dark colors on a floor will have the least impact on the daylit space.

Interior Shading Controls

Several types of manual interior control devices can be used to eliminate excessive

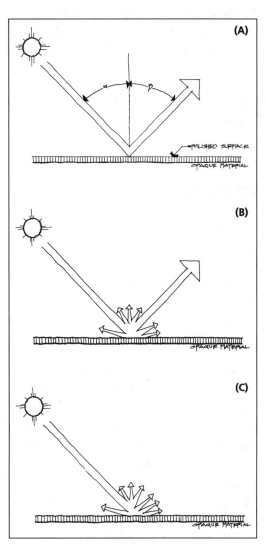

Figure 1.29 Reflectance properties. Specular reflection (A), combined specular and diffuse reflection (B), and diffuse reflection (C).

bright spots and also get daylight where it is needed.

Venetian blinds are effective because they can be fixed to block direct-beam sunshine or can be partially closed to reflect in the space while still allowing a view to the outdoors. Blinds offer versatility and tend to increase the ratio of ground-reflected light to direct sky contribution.

Draperies are often used as control devices because they can add texture, color, and flexibility to a space. Fabrics are available in a range of weaves with varying shading coefficients. An appropriate weave pattern can soften the light to necessary levels.

Roller shades of various degrees of opaqueness can be an effective control device for reducing glare and direct-beam penetration. One benefit of the interior controls is that they can be easily and completely retracted during those times that sunlight and daylight are desirable.

DESIGN OPTIONS

SIDELIGHTING

Sidelighting concepts use the walls of a building as the location of apertures to admit daylight (see Figure 1.30). The apertures can also serve by incorporating view and ventilation as a design dynamic.

Sidelighting provides illumination with a strong directionality due to the diminishing light levels as the distance from the aperture increases. Daylight admitted through wall apertures is ideal for illuminating horizontal surfaces and work planes.

As a disadvantage, sidelighting may cause glare because of the high contrast between the aperture and the surrounding wall surfaces. Proper shading devices, either exterior or interior, can largely mitigate this liability.

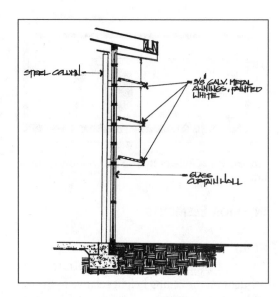

Figure 1.30 Sidelighting with direct-beam control. *(Detail courtesy of IBI Group, Irvine, California.)*

Vertical windows have long been used by designers to introduce natural light, bring in fresh air, and establish a connection with the outdoors. The dimensions, location, and spacing of windows are important variables. A basic understanding of some of the relationships among these factors will help the designer. Direct ample amounts of light where it is desired.

• Larger window areas yield greater amounts of daylight.

• Glazing located high in the wall will allow daylight to penetrate greater distances into a room. The higher the aperture, the deeper the penetration of usable daylight.

• Small window openings placed in an opaque wall often create severe contrast and occupant discomfort.

• As the height of the windowsill increases, the point of maximum illumination moves away from the window.

The contribution of light from the ground and other exterior reflecting surfaces can be a significant component of the total penetration of illumination on clear days.

Spaces can be daylit with windows unilaterally, bilaterally, and multilaterally with varying

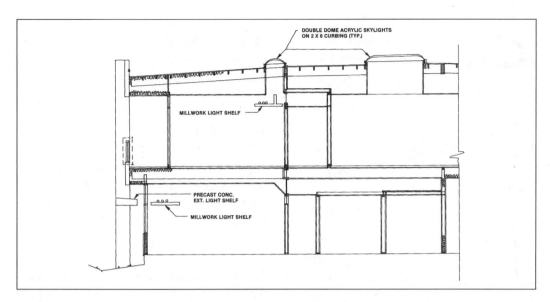

DOUBLE DOME ACRYLIC SKYLIGHTS
ON 2 X 6 CURBING (TYP.)

MILLWORK LIGHT SHELF

PRECAST CONC.
EXT. LIGHT SHELF

MILLWORK LIGHT SHELF

Figure 1.31 Bilateral daylight contribution.

effects. Unilaterally lit rooms receive light entering through windows in one wall only. Bilaterally lit spaces are illuminated by light entering through apertures in opposing walls (see Figure 1.31), and multilaterally lit areas receive light entering through fenestration in at least two nonopposing walls.

Clerestories are vertical or near-vertical windows whose sill height is above eye level but below ceiling height (see Figure 1.32). They are therefore not necessarily view apertures and so may easily incorporate glazings that are not transparent.

The principal advantage of clerestories is that the elevated vertical glazings introduce daylight high into a space, often resulting in

broader distribution and a reduced likelihood of excessive brightness in the field of vision. In addition, because they open onto the bright part of the sky dome close to the zenith, they can allow brighter and deeper daylight penetration into a building than can a window.

Clerestories provide excellent lighting for horizontal work planes, as well as vertical display surfaces. Daylight entering through a sufficiently high clerestory will typically reach a vertical surface without striking intermediate objects, thus avoiding shadows on these areas (see Figure 1.33). Light admitted through

Figure 1.32 Clerestory aperture.

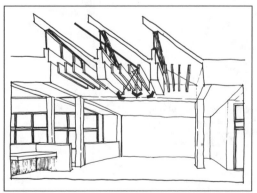

Figure 1.33 Clerestory aperture detail by Edward Mazria. *(From Fuller Moore,* Concepts and Practice of Architectural Daylighting, *VNR, New York, 1986. Used by permission.)*

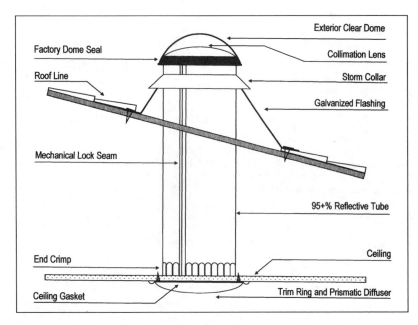

Figure 1.34A Tubular skylight section unit comes in various diameters and has a variety of optional accessories. *(Courtesy of HUVCO, LLC.)*

clerestories also exhibits less variation between maximum and minimum illuminances compared with a window and thus produces relatively even illumination.

The only major drawback to clerestories is that they require tall floor-to-ceiling heights if

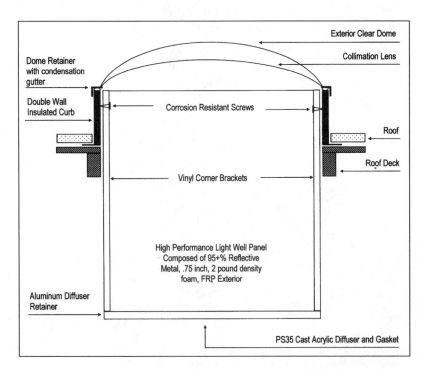

Figure 1.34B Skylight with integrated reflective light well. Skylights come in various sizes and custom light well lengths are also available. *(Courtesy of HUVCO, LLC.)*

they are to function properly. Gymnasiums, libraries, galleries, museums, and circulation spaces all are excellent spaces in which to admit natural light through clerestories.

TOPLIGHTING

Toplighting concepts allow daylight to penetrate a space from apertures that are located above the ceiling line and usually constitute part of the roof of the building (see Figures 1.34A and 1.34B).

All toplighting concepts provide interior light with distribution patterns and character significantly different from those provided by sidelighting. Lighting effects can vary dramatically, depending on the configuration and placement of roof apertures. Not only can consistent and relatively uniform daylight distribution be accomplished, but dramatic high-intensity "punch" can be introduced to strategic areas as well (see Figure 1.35).

Toplighting often restricts natural light to the upper level of the building. Another drawback of toplighting is that the penetration of direct-beam sunlight into a space usually needs to be carefully controlled to prevent occupant discomfort (see Figure 1.36). Certain spaces such as circulation areas may work well with direct-beam sunlight to add visual interest.

Skylights are defined simply as horizontal glazed roof apertures that are parallel or nearly parallel to the roof. Skylighting is an excellent toplighting strategy because large quantities of light can be admitted to all areas of single-story buildings or into the top floor of multistory buildings, with relatively small openings (see Figure 1.37).

The layout and spacing of skylights in a roof determine the light distribution characteristics of the area below the skylights. While maintaining a constant aperture area, the arrangement can vary from a single large skylight to many small skylights distributed uniformly across the roof with varying effects.

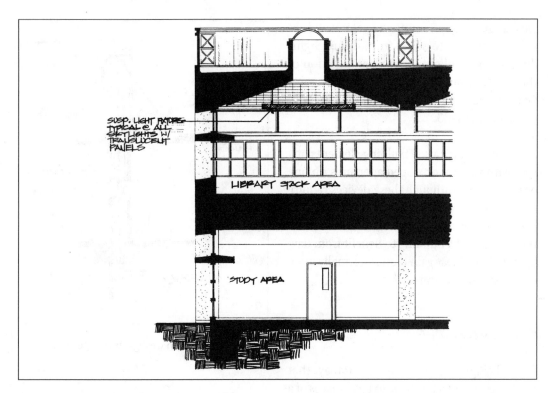

Figure 1.35 Bilateral strategy of Antelope Valley Library. *(Courtesy of Spencer Hoskins Architects.)*

Large, widely spaced skylights are usually the most economical to install but may result in uneven light distribution, reduced energy savings, and possible glare problems. Small, closely spaced skylights, on the other hand, will provide more uniform lighting conditions and greater energy savings but may be more costly to install.

The general rule of thumb is to space skylights at 1.0 to 1.5 times the ceiling height. Variations will inevitably occur because skylight placement must also be coordinated with the structural, mechanical, and lighting systems.

Figure 1.36 Toplighting through deep light well. *(Illustrated by Moshe Safdie. Courtesy of the Canadian National Gallery.)*

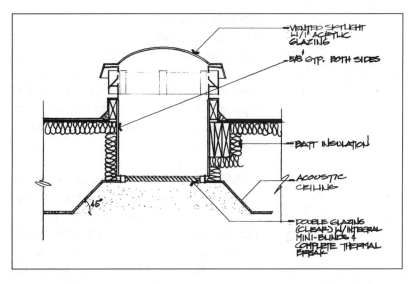

Figure 1.37 Typical skylight construction detail showing splayed ceiling treatment through plenum.

Diverse glazing options provide opportunities for the designer to select from diffuse light, direct-beam sunlight, or any combination of the two that may be appropriate to a space. Glazing characteristics are discussed in more depth in Chapter 3.

Roof monitors are raised building elements of a roof with vertical or sloped apertures on one or more sides. Although these devices require architectural coordination, proper orientation, and special drainage details, they allow the top floor of a building to benefit from daylight with less heat gain than is normally associated with other strategies.

CORE DAYLIGHTING

Core daylighting refers to a strategy that implements optical systems to light spaces of a building with sunlight that may receive both electric lighting and cooling loads. This is not a new concept because simple forms of this strategy existed in early Egyptian cultures that used mirror strategies to light deep spaces within the tombs of the Pharaohs.

There are generally three elements to core daylighting systems: the light collection system, the light transportation system, and the light distribution system.

Collection System
The core daylighting collection system captures daylight and redirects it. Collection systems may be located on the exterior of a building on the roof or at exterior walls. Two types of core daylighting light collection systems exist: active optical systems and passive optical systems.

Active optic systems use a tracking system that follows the sun as it moves across the sky and redirects the direct-beam solar into the interior of a building (see Figure 1.38). The direct-beam radiation that strikes the active mirror or lens is then directed to an input aperture of the light transportation system. This type of

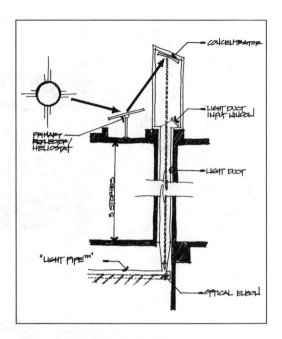

Figure 1.38 Beam daylighting system.

system is significantly disadvantaged under partly cloudy or overcast sky conditions because there is very little light input. An advantage of these types of active systems is that the visible radiation collected can be closely controlled and redirected with a high degree of certainty. On the other hand, this system can be a very complex mechanical device with fairly high associated first costs.

Passive optical systems implement fixed elements to view the most favorable or brightest portion of the sky dome and redirect the light into the light transportation system. The positioning of these types of collector systems must be tuned for a specific latitude to assure optimal performance. With no moving parts, this type of system is less costly for both first cost and maintenance-related expenses. A drawback is the reduced control of the directionality of the collected daylight.

Transportation System
The core daylighting system moves the collected daylight from the collection system to the light distribution system where the light requirement exists. New materials have been developed to overcome some of the limita-

tions associated with transporting light any significant distance. The most common types of transportation systems are either fiber optic or light ducts lined with a highly reflective material.

Distribution System

The core daylighting distribution system receives its light input from the transportation system and distributes light onto a target area or a space. This element of the system then carries light from the transportation system and emits light within the building. The devices used to accomplish this once again include both optical fibers or optical light pipes or light guides.

An example of this type of strategy has been incorporated into the design of a commercial building in Austin, Texas, for the 3M Company, which manufactured many films used in the design (see Figures 1.39 to 1.42).

The daylighting system designed and installed at 3M Company's Austin facility marks the third generation of the passive optic system pioneered at the Civil and Mineral Engineering (C/ME) building, a joint venture between BRW Architects and 3M, at the University of Minnesota. This system, designed in conjunction with the engineers at 3M to use their spreading film in the collector system, is used to light a five-story, 65-ft-tall, 50,000-ft^2 atrium connecting multiple office blocks. 3M's expertise was teamed with CRSS Architects, Inc., Houston, Texas, for the building's design. One of the major objectives for the Austin Center was to provide an integrated building campus that brought together all functions of the 3M business (laboratory, administrative, marketing, sales, etc.) into one single structure where people could move freely between locations and interact with each other on a daily basis. It was also important that interior offices have windows with access to natural daylight. Thus, the solution incorporated an enclosed atrium, located between the separate buildings, that was equipped with a daylighting system that could

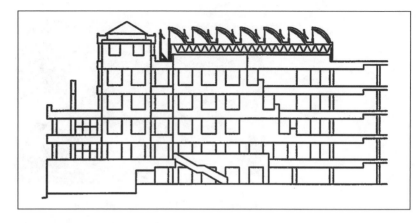

Figure 1.39 3M building section.

provide natural lighting while reducing the building's energy load.

Three Fresnel panels were used to make up the exterior primary collector and consisted of a daylighting film laminated to polystyrene panels having an acrylic exterior surface. Three similar panels were fabricated for the interior secondary reflector. The film's Fresnel grooves run horizontally on the primary collectors, spreading the light ± 5 degrees in the north-south direction, whereas the grooves run vertically on the secondary collectors, spreading the light ± 5 degrees in the east-west direction. The primary reflector spreads the light

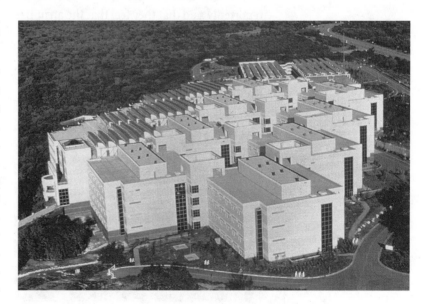

Figure 1.40 3M building complex showing roof layout.

Figure 1.41 3M building roof detail.

10 degrees in the north-south (vertical) direction, and the secondary reflectors spread the light 10 degrees in the east-west (horizontal) direction. With this film orientation, the harsh solar images would not be cast on the atrium floor 65 feet below. The finished panels were mounted on a metal frame fastened to the adjacent roof structure or dormer. The exterior collectors and vertical glazings between the primary and secondary collectors are easily accessible from the building's roof. The total fenestration of glazed area, consisting of the north-facing vertical windows, is approximately 28% of the atrium's total floor space. The system also performs well on cloudy days; for the average overcast day, unusually high light levels are produced within the atrium space. Occupants have reportedly said that they feel that the atrium is

brighter on these days than the outside appears to be. The 3M system also significantly reduces the solar heat gains that would normally be associated with a glazed atrium daylighting system. This heat reduction results from the fact that the lenses are made of a material that is an excellent reflector of the visible spectrum but is much less reflective of the infrared wavelengths. With this Austin daylighting system, nearly 58% of the infrared radiation is removed from the light entering the space.

ATRIUM

The atrium building finds its origins in the ancient Greek and Roman courtyard house where the courtyard performed as the social center of the house. Today, the atrium behaves in a similar fashion (see Figure 1.43). Typically, the centroidial placement of the atrium allows it to serve as both an element for circu-

Figure 1.42 3M building atrium.

Figure 1.43 Atrium of Brown Derby Hotel. *(Photograph courtesy of Susan Ryan Colletta, Denver.)*

lation and an element for spatial order. An atrium enjoys numerous functions that can effectively provide pleasant and comfortable environments while allowing opportunities for significant energy savings. Recent changes in glazing and system technologies have allowed large-scale atrium spaces to function with more reliability, fewer water leaks, less maintenance, and fewer other related problems displayed in the past.

Just as the ancient Roman and Greek courtyard house benefited from shade, thermal heat storage and transfer, ventilation, and evaporative cooling, the atrium performs similarly. An atrium designed for maximum energy savings and efficiency should incorporate daylighting, ventilation, and passive heating and cooling techniques as design features. Because the atrium is a centroidally located space protected by glazing, it effectively creates a second perimeter zone within a building. Daylight is able to penetrate into the large interior space while the intervening surfaces reflect the light to adjacent spaces on lower floors. Aspect ratios determine the quantity and location of solar radiation on and within the atrium.

Section Aspect Ratio

The section aspect ratio (SAR) affects daylighting, passive heating, and cooling factors within the atrium. A high SAR effectively reduces or eliminates the amount of solar radiation that will reach the lower portions of the space. However, a high SAR does contribute to passive cooling by thermal convective means. A low SAR is ideal for daylighting, passive heating, and radiative cooling.

The orientation, size, and geometry of the space, size, and placement of apertures, in addition to facade reflection properties, play important roles in the ability of daylight to penetrate into the interior spaces of a building. However, among the numerous issues considered during the design process, climate presents the greatest potential influence. Local climate conditions affect heating, cooling, and daylighting design strategies. In daylighting, design strategies need to address predominant sky conditions to maximize daylight. For example, predominantly cloudy sky conditions will maximize its daylighting potential with a stepped atrium section. In general, an overhead daylighting source enables the most daylight to penetrate the space because the sky dome is brightest at the zenith. Vertically glazed atrium spaces may enhance exterior views, but the quantity of daylight is not ideal under cloudy sky conditions, and the quality can prove to be too severe if fenestration controls are not used. In hot climate zones where solar heat gain is prohibitive, clerestories are effective, especially with exterior fenestration controls.

An atrium design can allow the intervening floors to be open to it. However, this approach brings with it a number of acoustic and fire safety considerations to which the designer must be responsive.

An atrium can also be thermally separated from the rest of the building by transparent or translucent materials. This allows the total amount of glazing area on partition surfaces to be increased because the atrium effectively serves as a buffer zone between the conditioned spaces and the outside environment.

Occupant Productivity and Performance

Without lighting—natural and electric—there simply would be no life on earth, or living, as we know it. *Daylight*, sunlight and/or degrees of cloudiness, provides warmth, heat, illumination, and the essential ingredient for photosynthesis, the process by which plants convert carbon dioxide into the oxygen we all breathe. Lighting enables people to function in society: It provides vision at home, work, school, or play; makes us feel safe and secure; and changes nighttime into a rainbow of color and shape.

Clearly, we cannot accomplish much without adequate lighting. Beyond that, however, proper and well-designed lighting systems are essential for employee morale and productivity, student learning and achievement, and personal enjoyment and mood. It is fitting, perhaps, that the first spoken words in *Genesis* are, "Let there be light." It is equally fitting, then, that light and lighting are basic for teaching and instruction, as well as for design and construction. Light is the foundation for everything.

MECHANICS OF SIGHT*

Human beings—and most animals—have an amazingly detailed and effective visual system. Using a complex system of intricate muscles, lenses, photoreceptors, neural pathways, and the mental interpretation provided by our brain, this remarkable synthesis of form and function has enormous capabilities, along with some limitations.

Light coming from any object passes through the transparent protective layer of the cornea. The iris, which is the muscular ring that determines eye color, reacts to the light, expanding or contracting to control the amount of light entering the eye (a mechanical version of this process is the aperture control on a camera). Light passes through the eye's lens, which alters shape through the working of the ciliary muscle to modify the eye's focal length. This

---

*Excerpts reprinted from the Advanced Lighting Guidelines; 2001 Edition copyright 2001, New Buildings Institute, 2001.

produces a sharp visual image on the retina, at the back of the eyeball, where the rods and cones create nerve impulses in response to the light's stimulus. Once light reaches the retina, the rest of the visual process—*seeing*—is bio-chemical and mental: nerves and processing by the brain. This entire process occurs liter-ally at the speed of light, the fastest-known velocity in the universe.

VISION

Our remarkable vision system perceives the luminance (brightness) of any given object, which is the amount of light emitted by, or reflected off, that particular body. One of the very few limitations to our visual ability is the range of luminance that we can see or, more accurately, that the eye and brain can process; but even that range is somewhat broad. Essen-tially, the range of human vision falls into three categories, or orders, of illumination: night outdoor, indoor low to indoor high, and daytime outdoor. Scientifically, this range is expressed in *lux*. The human eye can see well enough to process information in a spectrum consisting of three magnitudes (ranges) from less than 1.0 to 100,000 lux.

These magnitudes are, roughly, 0.1 to 10 lux, 1 to 1,000 lux, and 100 to 100,000 lux. Dark night outdoor light is measured at about 0.1 lux, with moonlight providing a low-end human reading (processing) of about 0.5 to 1.0 lux. Generally, indoor lighting ranges from a low of around 10 lux up to a very bright 1,000 lux. Typical office environments, for example, range from about 100 to 1,000 lux. Daytime outdoor lighting (sunlight and vary-ing cloud covers) runs the gamut from a com-paratively bright 10,000 lux all the way up to a brilliant 100,000 lux in full sunlight.

There are three processes involved in adapting to varying levels of illumination. First, the pupil constricts (narrows) in response to increased or intense light. Second, it dilates

(expands) when reacting to a drop in light lev-els—again, think of the aperture setting on a camera (see Figure 2.1). It is interesting to note that the pupil constricts in response to brightness *five times faster* than it dilates in response to dimmer illumination, although both processes take place quickly. Finally, there is photochemical adaptation, which involves the bleaching and regeneration of the pigments in the rods and cones under more extreme ranges of illumination. The cones regenerate within 10 to 12 minutes, while the rods may take up to an *hour* for full regenera-tion. Thus, adapting to darker or very low light environments (where the rods are active) takes considerably longer than adapting to brighter ones (where the cones predominate). Think about entering a movie theater on a very bright, sunny day.

The human eye, remarkable as it is, is *not* a particularly good judge of absolute illumina-tion levels; the mechanical light meter, for example, is far more accurate in measuring absolute light values. The human brain auto-matically compares *relative* brightness values (ranging from the darkest to the most illumi-nated surfaces/areas within view). Adaptation is especially important when moving from the outdoors to the indoors. During the day, for example, interior light levels may seem very dark to people who have adapted to bright daylight. The reverse is true at night, when people stepping outside from bright interior lighting may be temporarily "night blinded." This is the reason that, in countless war films, we see submariners prepare in dim lighting prior to surfacing at night or that soldiers or police officers who are in action at night try never to look directly at any bright natural or electric light.

COLORS AND OTHER VISION FACTORS

The joy of the spectrum of colors truly is one of life's treasures. Imagine living without the

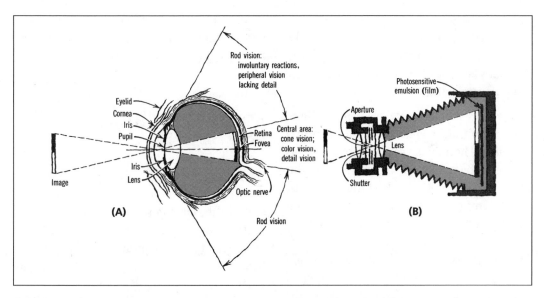

Figure 2.1 (A) The human eye and (B) the camera operate on the same optic principles. *(Reprinted with permission from* Mechanical and Electrical Equipment for Buildings, *John Wiley & Sons.)*

rainbow of colors that defines just about everything we see (even black-and-white artwork, for example, has shades of gray and may stay in our memory precisely because it *lacks* color). Colors, of course, frame our environment, indoors and outdoors, at home, work, school, or play. They allow for most of our physical (visual) work to be done, in all fields, and especially for most education to be conducted and information processed. Color even guarantees our health, from skin pallor during an examination to the glowing hues seen on sophisticated scanners.

Our eyes can visualize and interpret colors across most of the visible-light spectrum; vision "fails" gradually with age in the short-wavelength range, and it is interesting to note that children often see within the ultraviolet wavelength. Natural light provides illumination across the entire color spectrum, but can shift on an almost moment-to-moment basis because of varying cloud covers and the time of day, from morning to early evening. Electric lighting affects the colors we see in a wide variety of ways, enhancing some, subduing others, and sometimes even causing certain colors to "disappear"—all as information that our brains can process.

The ability to see color is not only a function of the eye's sensitivity and the intrinsic colors of objects, but is also a result of the brain's adaptive process and the spectral quality of the light. The brain's interpretation of colors is a *relative*, not a constant (absolute), function. The brain compares one color to another, looking for the "bluer" or "greener" of the two. It attempts to use the whitest object in sight as a reference point; thus, subtly altering white from bluish-white to pinkish-white may influence the brain's interpretation of other colors. Colors in an area are not only a function of the light source, but also all the other nearby colors that may be reflecting light. A large area of red in a room, for example, will make the light and other objects there seem redder.

• The *visual size* of an object is an important determinate of how easy it is to perceive that particular object. Obviously, the larger an object, the easier it is to see. It follows, then, that the closer we are to an object, the bigger it appears and the more detail we see on it. The focal precision of our eyes determines the extent of detail we can see on an object. With more light, we see smaller details, and those more precisely. Visual acuity is based on the diameter of the cone that is intercepted. Therefore, humans can perceive *very* small or faraway objects, especially if they stand out against sharply contrasting backgrounds (a speck of dirt on a white backdrop, or stars at night).

- *Contrast* is a fundamental element of vision; lack of contrast can reduce visibility to nearly nothing. The human visual system interprets three different kinds of contrast: brightness, pattern, and color. Brightness contrast results from variations in the amount of light that is reflected or emitted from a surface (because of shadows, surface shapes, or texture, or gradual changes in dark against light colors). Pattern contrast is the perception of changes in a regular pattern, as when the stars and stripes on a flag change perspective as the flag waves in a breeze. Color contrast is based on the juxtaposition (clashing) of different colors next to each other; color pairs that are complementary (e.g., red-green or blue-yellow) are likely to produce the greatest visual contrast.

- Typically, our eyes are in a state of constant motion, rapidly scanning the scene before us with our central vision. The brain automatically fills in the "picture" of what we see from previous information that it has received moments earlier. When we focus on a moving object, we must concentrate on that object, thus sacrificing much or all of the general (wider or peripheral) scanning process for that period of time. Motion that is more predictable or slower allows us easier focus on the object in question. Naturally, motion almost always attracts our attention and redirects our central vision to it. Similarly, changes in the *illumination* of an object—such as flashes or flickering—attract our attention and usually make that object stand out and demand a reaction (consider an ambulance behind you or a flashing warning sign of danger).

There are other factors that can—and do—have a significant effect on what we see, such as aging, a lack or abundance of peripheral vision, a diminution of depth perception due to the loss of an eye, and other considerations. For the sake of this discussion, however, we can leave those conditions aside.

ADEQUATE LIGHTING AND HEALTH

Daylight is a tremendously important component of living, profoundly affecting human life and health. During the last part of the 20th century, scientists have made a major effort to understand the biological effects of light and lighting on people. No longer is our "luminous environment" being considered merely a *visual* issue. The kind of light we are exposed to—during the day or night, both natural and electric—interacts with, and affects, some of the most fundamental biological processes of our body (see Figure 2.2). Light and health are intricately intertwined.

- Human exposure to light, particularly exposure of the skin to ultraviolet (UV) wavelengths in daylight, contributes to the manufacture of melanin in the skin. Such exposure results in a tan for fair-skinned people. Additionally, skin exposure to light results in the increased manufacture of vitamin D and an accompanying absorption of calcium. It is well known that calcium strengthens bone structure; increased manufacture of this element from exposure to the sun can help prevent diseases such as rickets and osteoporosis. Exposure to lighting, especially *blue colors,* has been found to reduce instances of jaundice in infants.

- Recently, biologists have discovered vast new information concerning the immunological effects of visible light and UV radiation on the human immune system. Medical researchers have been learning to use exposure to light (some visible, but mostly UV) in combination with specific drugs to induce cell death in some types of cancer tumors. Along those lines, we are learning that a combination of certain drugs and nutrients can alter the sensitivity of people to sunlight

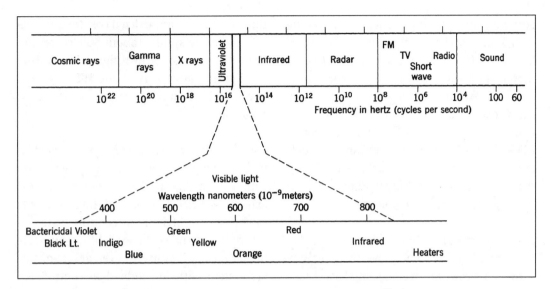

Figure 2.2 Electromagnetic spectrum. *(Reprinted with permission from* Mechanical and Electrical Equipment for Buildings, *John Wiley & Sons.)*

or certain wavelengths, consequently altering (improving) their risk factors for some diseases.

- We now know that light is one of the external cues that our biological systems use to set their "internal clocks" (*circadian rhythms*). We are beginning to understand how and why this is so. One of the earliest advances in this field came with the understanding and successful treatment of seasonal affective disorder (SAD). With SAD, some people become depressed as winter approaches and the days (and daylight) grow shorter. Treatment by exposure to bright light in the morning (before 10:00 A.M.), from either natural daylight or bright electrical (fluorescent) lighting, has helped some victims "reset" their biological clocks.

- Building on the success of treating SAD patients with effective bright lighting, researchers are now experimenting with resetting circadian rhythms in people who experience jet lag or who work on the night shift. Bright lights have been found to suppress the body's manufacture of *melatonin*, a hormone that is secreted at night, in the brain. Using lighting to reset the melatonin cycle will hopefully prove effective in resetting the overall circadian rhythms (body

clock). Information from these and similar experiments should lead to ways to combat restlessness at night, as well as other sleep-related disorders.

Much remains to be understood about how light interacts with the biological mechanisms of human circadian rhythms. For example, we are now only learning that the eye may *not* be the only biological system that receives light and responds to it. We now know that the physiology of circadian photoreceptors is different from that of their visual counterparts. Whatever we still have to learn about the relationship between lighting and life, we already know about the significance of different types of light, why the duration of exposure matters, and the effects of specific wavelengths on people and their health.

LIGHT, WORKPLACE PRODUCTIVITY, AND COST EFFECTIVENESS

Architects, lighting experts, and industrial designers have long maintained that good lighting yields benefits for an employer, both in increased productivity and in enhanced employee morale. These professionals, along with health specialists and economic analysts, have demonstrated conclusively that even a marginal improvement in employee productivity due to better lighting *far* outweighs any extra costs incurred in installing such a system. Recent studies have found that corporate CEOs and facility managers unanimously point to adequate lighting as a prime factor that contributes to a quality workplace staffed by satisfied, productive employees.

A recent definitive study relating quality of workplace lighting to employee productivity showed a clear improvement in clerical task performance after the installation of improved and brighter lighting. The key here is *improved and brighter lighting,* because a number of studies have failed to prove a correlation between improved work and morale and any particular *kind* of lighting, or its placement—just as long as the provided illumination was adequately bright and nonintrusive. It is worth noting that a number of studies have demonstrated that the ability of an employee to *control to a degree* the daylight and electric light directly around his or her work area has led to even better production and morale. This is because, while overall good lighting is important, individuals often have their own particular preferences for brightness and the angle from which light hits their work area. Clearly, personal preferences, and the ability to make those choices, further enhance the benefits of a good office lighting system.

ECONOMICS

Lighting system improvements that increase worker productivity often yield a high return on investment. Let us assume that a particular employee "costs" an employer $50,000 a year, including all wages, taxes, and benefits. That employee is paid about $24/hour, extrapolated over a year. A modern lighting system, factoring in standard energy consumption and operating-time values, costs an employer about $35/worker/year. Add to this number the annualized cost for a typical office lighting system (about $30/year), and the total expense of owning and operating the lighting system is about $65/year—or about 2.7 hours of employee labor at $24/hour.

Based on those values, an employer realizes that by improving an office lighting system—and with it enhancing employee productivity—the expense is quickly amortized. Improvements can include use of dimming controls, better fixture options to prevent poor lighting and create higher quality lighting, or even a state-of-the-art system with full individual control. For example, just a *1%* increase in an employee's productivity throughout the year can mean a benefit of *$500* to the employer. To broaden this example, if an employer invested $500 per employee in improved lighting that provided even a small boost in productivity, this would result in an impressive *100%* return on investment in perpetuity. By way of reference, *one* good office chair can cost over $500.

DAYLIGHTING STUDIES

While up to the mid-20th century almost all schools and workplaces used daylight as their primary source of lighting, the advent of inexpensive energy and the proliferation of fluorescent lights in the 1950s and 1960s made daylight as an illumination source almost irrelevant. When energy costs began soaring in the 1970s, the "glazed skin" look of many buildings became an expensive, though popular and attractive, liability that often increased the costs of both heating and cooling. Cooling, in particular, was a major cost, leading to the elimination of solar gain—the heat generated by direct natural sunlight through windows. New construction deemphasized direct sunlight and brought forth lower ceilings and lower building skin-to-volume ratios. Dropped ceilings, heavily tinted glass, and insulating panels, designed to reduce heat from windows, gained widespread acceptance.

The net result of this change in architectural and design priorities (and realities) for public buildings of all types has been a dramatic *reduction* in the amount of daylight available to students in schools and working people at their jobs. Recently, this trend is being reversed for two reasons. First is the cost. Along with heating and cooling expenses, the use of electricity to provide workplace/school lighting adds considerable overhead to the overall cost of operating a building. Not only is daylighting cheaper (a net energy benefit), it is intrinsically more efficient than any electric source because it provides greater amounts of brightness per unit of heat content (lumen per watt).

Second, a growing interest in the influence of the indoor environment on health, productivity, and scholastic achievement has resulted in growing interest in the potential benefits that daylighting can bring toward reaching these goals. Strictly *anecdotal* evidence has offered encouraging possibilities: A reduction in employee absenteeism, higher retail sales, and improved student health and academic performance all *appeared* to be the result of enhanced daylighting. Because anecdotal evidence is not enough per se to make building decision-makers demand high-performance daylighting systems, a scientific, widespread, and comprehensive study was deemed necessary to confirm that better daylighting yielded higher sales and office productivity and improved academic achievement.

HESCHONG MAHONE STUDY

The Heschong Mahone Group (HMG) directed a study in 1999, along with a small group of outside consultants/experts. Their goal was to try to quantify the effect of daylighting on human performance. The Heschong Mahone Group focused on two different areas: student improvement and retail sales. Although they might sound like mutually exclusive fields for study, the two actually are closely linked. Both groups of people are trying to do their best within their indoor environment: students learning and scoring higher on tests, and retailers hoping that an attractive setting will draw in customers and increase sales.

In setting out to look at the effect of daylighting on human performance, HMG, in both cases, focused on skylighting as an effective (and attractive) way to isolate daylight as an illumination source and a way to differentiate among all other factors involved with window-based sidelighting strategies. In sum, the study found a positive correlation between increased daylighting and better scholastic performance, and the use of skylighting as a boost for retail sales.

STUDENT PERFORMANCE

The Heschong Mahone Group analyzed student performance data from three widely separated school districts: one urban (Seattle, Washington), one suburban (San Juan Capistrano, Orange County, California), and one smaller town (Fort Collins, Colorado). Researchers obtained data from the schools (focusing on grades 2 through 5), looking for a link between the amount of daylight provided by each student's classroom environment and scholastic achievement. The researchers used grades 2 through 5 because there are already extensive data available from highly standardized tests administered to those students and because elementary students are generally assigned to one teacher, in one classroom, for the entire school year. They reasoned that if the physical environment truly affects student performance, then they could best establish such a correlation in an elementary-school setting, with its uniform "givens" such as standardized testing and a single instructor and location.

The three school districts provided reading and mathematics test score results for more than 8,000 students each and included such other data as student body demographics and participation in special school programs. HMG studied school architectural plans throughout the districts, aerial photographs of facilities, and building maintenance records. Researchers visited a sample of the schools in each district in order to classify the daylighting conditions in more than 2,000 classrooms. Each classroom was arbitrarily assigned a daylight code based on a simple, effective 0–5 scale, indicating the size and tint of its windows, the presence and type of any skylighting, and the overall amount and balance of daylight normally expected on average days during different times of the year; in other words, the general *quality* of the daylighting.

The study employed *multivariate linear regression analysis* as a control for other influences on student performance. This control method factored in variables that might affect students' performance, including socioeconomic status, special academic programs, and school and class size. The team compiled 12 models for comparing students and test scores: First, data from mathematics and reading were gathered for each of the three districts; then each mathematics and reading model was run *separately*, using first the window and skylight codes and then the overall daylight code (thus, four models for each of the three school districts). HMG reasoned that if the daylight effects truly were strong, then the variables should perform *similarly* in all models.

The results from all three districts were quite dramatic and positive, but especially so in the San Juan Capistrano area because (a) the daylighting conditions there were the most diverse and (b) the data obtained from the district were the most comprehensive. In San Juan Capistrano, which became the most precise model for the study, researchers were able to study the changes in student test scores over the school year. This was especially valuable because the San Juan Capistrano district administers standardized tests in *both* the fall and the spring semesters. This allowed HMG to compare the changes in students' mathematics and reading test scores *while they spent the year in one classroom environment.*

The results were impressive. With all influences factored in, the team found that students with the most daylighting in their classrooms progressed 20% faster on mathematics tests and 26% faster on their reading examinations over those in classrooms with the *least* amount of daylighting (see Figure 2.3). Similarly, students in rooms with the largest window areas progressed 15% faster in mathematics and 23% faster in reading skills than those in classrooms with the *least* amount of window areas. Daylighting was not the only factor found to improve academic performance. Students in classrooms with a well-developed skylight system—one that diffused the daylight throughout the room and also allowed the teacher to control the amount

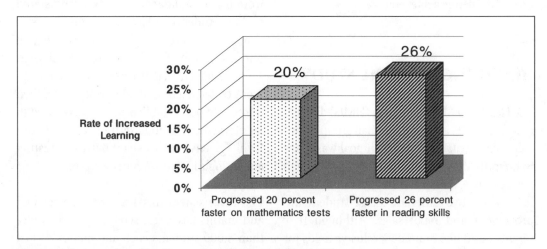

Figure 2.3 Rate of learning for mathematics and reading skills.

of daylight entering the room—also improved their test scores by a decisive 20% faster than students in rooms lacking skylights. Another interesting side result was determined when HMG found that students in classrooms with windows that *could be opened* progressed 7% to 8% faster in testing than those in rooms with fixed (nonopening) windows, regardless if the latter had air-conditioning.

The studies based in Seattle and Fort Collins used *final* (year-end) mathematics and reading test scores. This prevented the researchers from tallying the amount of change from semester to semester, as they could in San Juan Capistrano. Nevertheless, in both of these districts, HMG found significant and very positive testing improvement due to the positive effects of daylighting. Overall, students in classrooms with the most daylighting (expanded window area and/or skylighting) in the Seattle and Fort Collins districts showed 7% to 18% better reading and mathematics test scores than those in poorer lighted classrooms.

The demonstrated consistency of students' improved testing because of better and increased daylighting in their classrooms in all three districts cannot be ignored. The researchers were very careful to note that the three test districts had *very* different curricula, teaching styles, building designs, and, above all, climates. *Nevertheless, the results of these studies consistently showed a very positive and significant correlation between better and more daylighting and scholastic improvement.* There is no escaping the conclusions—and significance—of this extensive HMG study.

RETAIL SALES

Almost as compelling as HMG's study on the relationship between student performance and adequate daylight is their research into the correlation between skylighting and retail sales. The team used the sales performance of a major chain that operates nearly identical stores. The analysis incorporated 108 outlets, where *two-thirds* have skylighting and the rest do not. The layout and day-to-day operation of these stores were remarkably consistent, thus affording the researchers a model "controlled environment." The electric lighting in all was primarily fluorescent. Skylights, however, provided *far* more and better illumination, often up to twice or triple the chain's targeted illumination levels. Photosensor controls in the skylit stores turned *off* some of the fluorescent lighting when natural daylight levels exceeded the target illumination.

The Heschong Mahone Group employed gross monthly sales per store, averaged over an 18-month period, running from February 1 to August 31 of the following year. This average sales figure was transformed into a "sales index" that the researchers could manipulate statistically, but that did *not* reveal actual dollar performance. Stores used in the study sample were selected to operate within a limited geographic region that had similar climatic conditions (mostly sunny). The outlets were similar in size, age, and layout (one story). HMG used the same multivariate linear regression analysis as employed in the school district study to control the influence of other variables that might affect sales, such as hours of operation; size, layout, and age of the outlet; and economic factors consistent with the selected zip code location.

The researchers found a very consistent and positive correlation between skylighting and higher retail sales. With all other factors being equal, the average nonskylit store in the chain would be likely to enjoy an average of 40% higher sales by adding skylights (the study found a range between 31% and 49%). In fact, after the number of hours per week that the outlet was open, the presence of skylights was the *best* predictor of sales per store out of all the other variables the researchers considered. For example, if a typical nonskylit store were averaging sales of, say, $2/square foot, then its sales performance would be expected to increase to somewhere between $2.61 and $2.98/square foot with the addition of a skylighting system. If this particular chain added skylights to the remaining third of its outlets,

In a recent study conducted by Southern California Edison of a large box multinational retailer, a store with skylights designed into a facility sold approximately 26% more products than similar stores without skylights. Stores in the study included newly constructed and existing buildings within the same district. Demographics of the customers were also similar. See Figure 2.4.

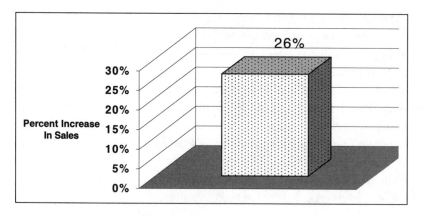

Figure 2.4 Percentage increase in sales.

its annual gross sales were predicted to increase by 11%. Even more revealing, the difference between having *none* of the stores skylit and having *all* of them so illuminated is a whopping 40% increase in gross sales across the entire retail chain. This kind of expenditure-to-benefit ratio would likely appeal to any competitive retailer.

ANCILLARY BENEFITS/POTENTIAL

In discussing the absolute necessity of lighting on human life, health, and affairs in general, and specifically the significance of ample, quality daylighting, we have focused on two broad, diverse areas: improved scholastic achievement and higher retail sales. There are, however, other important, day-to-day benefits that accrue from high-quality daylight.

- Clearly, the results of the Heschong Mahone Group study of three school districts can carry over to most, if not all, other districts in the country (and overseas). The impressive test score gains in mathematics and reading cited above likely will be found wherever and whenever other school districts reconfigure their facilities and classrooms in order to allow in more high-quality daylight. The HMG report *proves* the long-range cost effectiveness (and academic advantages) of improving schools along the lines it cites. And why stop at simply reading and mathematics performance? Educating

the next generations of youngsters for the challenges of the 21st century, here and abroad, is *far* too important a task to undertake without every available positive tool.

- There is always a shortage of qualified, dedicated teachers, at all levels of education. Better lit, more inviting classrooms and laboratories not only are attractive in themselves, they help assure prospective teachers that their school district is determined to use *every* available method to enhance the education of its students.

- In the retailing field, the driving force of the local, national, and even global economy, better, more people-friendly lighting is not only a tool for higher sales, it is a key safeguard against absenteeism, lost days due to illness, and, perhaps, a corresponding dip in workers' compensation expenses (claims). Better illumination is likely to lead to higher employee productivity and morale and to the hiring of the best available personnel. Again, we can regard ample, quality daylighting simply as another cost-effective business practice.

- The same benefits can apply, of course, to offices and production facilities anywhere in this country or around the world. Further, with an increasingly telecommunicating workforce, the benefits of good natural lighting at home are apparent, on top of the fact that good home lighting is *intrinsically* valuable.

Before the dawn of humanity, lighting was fundamental for all evolution, indeed for the creation of our world. During the *rise and advance* of civilization, adequate illumination continued to be an essential component of living and progress. At the beginning of the 21st century, light and its effects continue to profoundly affect human health, learning, commerce, and achievement—in short, *human society and existence.* In over 125 years, we have made vast strides in harnessing and improving electrical illumination; it remains for us to take the fullest advantage of abundant, *free daylight.*

Glazing Properties

Windows have long been used in buildings to introduce air and light into spaces. Studies have shown that comfort, productivity, and health are improved due to well-ventilated indoor environments and access to daylight. Window systems also have the potential to be a major source of unwanted heat transfer, condensation problems, visual discomfort, and glare.

Windows and fenestration systems have undergone a technological revolution in recent years. Glazing systems are now available that can dramatically cut energy consumption and the associated pollution sources, reduce peak demand, enhance daylighting performance, and improve occupant comfort. Other benefits include less air leakage and warmer glazing surface temperatures, which improve comfort and minimize condensation. These high-performance windows feature multiple lights of glass, specialized transparent coatings, insulating gases sandwiched between panes of glass, and improved frames.

Window systems and glazing details should be developed holistically. Once the design team and owner agree on the design problem, window and glazing options can be evaluated. Issues to consider include:

- Shading and sun control
- Visual requirements (glare, view, privacy)
- Heat gains and losses
- Thermal comfort
- Condensation control
- Ultraviolet control
- Acoustic control
- Security issues
- Color effects
- Energy requirements
- Daylight performance

The optimum choice of windows and glazing systems will ultimately depend on many factors, including the building use type, climatic issues, utility rates, and building orientation.

SPECIFYING WINDOWS AND GLAZING

A number of characteristics for glazing need to be understood to properly specify an appropriate fenestration system (see Table 3.1).

The *solar heat gain coefficient* (SHGC) is the fraction of incident solar energy transmitted through a window. Windows with low SHGC values improve comfort for building occupants near sunlit windows and also have the potential to lower the total cooling load of the building.

The *shading coefficient* (SC) is the ratio of total solar transmittance to the transmittance through $\frac{1}{8}$ inch of clear glass. The shading coefficient value is being phased out as a glazing metric; however, this value is commonly reported in the literature and in product brochures of glazing materials (see Figure 3.1). The SC value is equal to 1.15 times the solar heat gain coefficient.

The *visible transmittance* (VT) is the percentage of visible light that passes through a window. Clear, double-strength single glass typically transmits 89% of the light that strikes it and thus has a VT of 0.89.

The *luminous efficacy constant* (K_e), also referred to as the coolness index, indicates a window's relative performance in rejecting solar heat while transmitting daylight. It is the ratio of the visible transmittance (VT) to the shading coefficient (SC). Clear glass, which lets in roughly equal amounts of visible light and near-infrared solar energy, has a K_e value close to 1.0. A glazing system with a selective coating will allow visible light to pass through it while blocking all or parts of the invisible near-infrared and ultraviolet components. These types of glazing systems are highly compatible for daylighting projects and will yield K_e values greater than 1. It is generally better to have a high K_e value for daylighting systems.

$$K_e = VT/SC$$

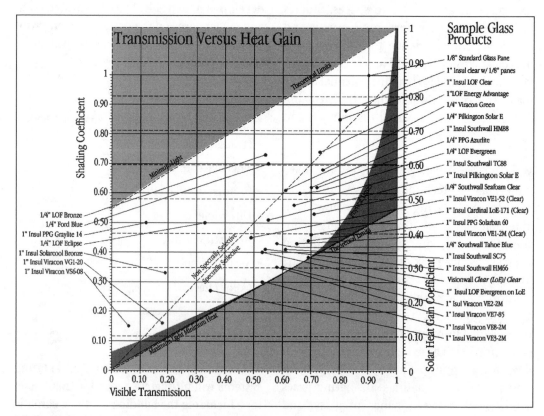

Figure 3.1 Transmission versus heat gain. *(Courtesy of Loisos + Ubbelohde.)*

The resistance to heat flow (*R-value*) is a measure of the resistance to heat flow that occurs because of the temperature difference between the two sides of the glazing. In colder climates, windows with high insulation values are significantly warmer on the inside surface than conventional windows. This provides several benefits, including moisture condensation control, increased occupant comfort, and acoustical benefits. ($R = 1/U$.)

The conductivity (*U-value*) represents the rate of heat transfer each hour through 1 square foot of material per degree of temperature difference between the two sides of that material. ($U = 1/R$.)

The performance properties of glazing can be easily altered. Combinations of the modifications can further improve the effectiveness of the glazing units. Tinted windows, also known as heat-absorbing glass, use materials dispersed throughout the glass material to reduce the amount of solar radiation transmitted through the glass and to reduce the amount of visible light passing through the material. Unfortunately, this also causes the glass temperature to rise, which will decrease comfort for occupants in the space due to the higher *mean radiant temperature* (MRT) of the surface of the glass. Common colors for tinted glass, such as bronze and gray, block light and near-infrared heat in equal proportions.

TABLE 3.1 Typical Glazing Characteristics

GLASS TYPE (PRODUCT)	GLASS THICKNESS (INCH)	VISIBLE TRANSMITTANCE (% DAYLIGHT)	*U*-VALUE (WINTER)	SHADING COEFFICIENT	SOLAR HEAT GAIN COEFFICIENT	EFFICACY FACTOR (T_{VT}/SC)
Single-pane glass (*Standard-clear*)	0.25	89	1.09	0.94	0.81	0.95
Single white laminated w/heat-rejecting coating (*Southwall California Series*)	0.25	73	1.06	0.54	0.46	1.35
Double-pane insulated glass (*Standard-clear*)	0.25	79	0.48	0.82	0.70	0.96
Double bronze reflective glass (*LOF Eclipse*)	0.25	21	0.48	0.41	0.35	0.51
Triple-pane insulated glass (*Standard-clear*)	0.125	74	0.36	0.78	0.67	0.95
Pyrolytic low-e double glass (*LOF clear low-e*)	0.125	75	0.33	0.82	0.71	0.91
Soft-coat low-e double glass w/argon (*PPG Sungate 100 clear*)	0.25	73	0.26	0.66	0.57	1.11
High-efficiency low-e (*Solarscreen 2000 VE1-2M*)	0.25	70	0.29	0.43	0.37	1.63
Suspended coated film (*Heat Mirror 66 clear*)	0.125	55	0.25	0.41	0.35	1.34
Suspended coated film w/argon (*Azurlite Heat Mirror SC75*)	0.125	53	0.19	0.32	0.27	1.66
Double suspended coated films w/krypton (*Heat Mirror 77 Superglass*)	0.125	53	0.10	0.40	0.34	1.33

Performance information was calculated using Lawrence Berkeley National Laboratories Windows 4.1 analysis program.
Azurlite® and Sungate® are registered trademarks of PPG Industries.
Heat Mirror™ and California Series® are trademarks of Southwall Technologies.
LOF Eclipse® is a registered trademark of Libbey Owens Ford Co.
Solarscreen 2000 VE1-2M™ is a trademark of Viracon.

- Gray glass transmits approximately equal amounts of visible light and infrared light.
- Bronze glass transmits less visible and more infrared light than gray glass.
- Blue and green glasses transmit more visible and less infrared light than gray glass.

Green or blue tints in glass are better for daylighting because these colors let in larger amounts of visible light while keeping heat out.

COATINGS

Translucent coatings allow for the transmission of most visible light, but disperse the light and distort the view. These coatings can be placed within the glass, embossed on the surface, or applied as a surface film. They are useful for applications where indirect daylight and privacy are needed. Translucent coatings alone may have little, if any, effect on the SC or VT of the glass. As with tinted glass, a coating can be added to a system to enhance properties or meet specific needs.

Low-emissivity (low-e) coatings were developed in the early 1970s and introduced into the market around 1980. Emissivity is the ability of a surface to emit radiant energy, where part of the energy absorbed by the glass is radiated away from the glass surface.

Most low-e coatings have high VT and reflect 40% to 70% of infrared radiation. Low-e coatings offer a reduction of 5% to 37% in ultraviolet radiation. Low-e coatings on glass or plastic films can be applied in several ways and are categorized into two major classes, depending on their application during manufacturing and their assembly within a window system.

Protective glazing is a form of coated glazing and is often used in warm climates. The surfacing, made up of metallic particles, reflects primarily visible radiation and darkens the building interior. The designer should look carefully at the SC and the SHGC of this type

of glazing before specifying. Sometimes so much solar radiation has been reflected from buildings using mirrored glass that the heat load on adjacent buildings has increased.

The installed performance of a low-e coating varies in relation to the climate and placement of the coating within the glazing unit. Low-e coatings are applied to one glazing surface facing the air gap of an insulating gas (IG) unit. The location of this surface does not affect the *U*-value, but does affect the solar heat gain properties. For cool climates, where heat must be retained, the coating is ideally on surface 3 for double glazing. For warmer climates, where heat needs to be reflected away from the building, the coating is on surface 2 (see Figure 3.2). By reflecting the heat with the first layer of glass, the second layer is prevented from absorbing it and, in turn, dissipating it to the interior. This, in effect, reduces the *U*-value.

It is important to note that these coatings are available in a wide assortment of ratings. The designer should review performance values such as SC, VT, and SHGC to determine which are the most appropriate for each particular project. Ratings provided by National Fenestration Rating Council (NFRC) may be useful in comparing overall performance values.

Some low-e coatings can be made selective to specific wavelengths of light. These are called

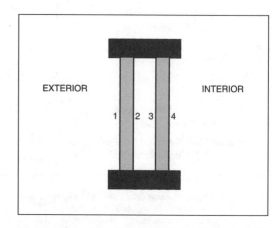

Figure 3.2 Section of typical window showing the industry standard for numbering glazing surfaces.

spectrally selective low-e coatings. Advanced forms of low-e coatings are being developed that further select the transmission of visible light and reflection of solar infrared and can block up to 99% of the ultraviolet radiation. Many are currently available and are used in assemblies called superwindows. Use of these technologies will provide greater freedom in fenestration design and glazing area and reduce the need for perimeter heating equipment.

Reflective materials can be deposited on glass in many ways and are used on clear, tinted, or otherwise treated surfaces. Apart from some higher performance versions, most reflective coatings do not require excessive protection from damage.

Reflective coatings reflect visible light and infrared radiation. They generally reduce visible-light transmission more than infrared energy, which gives them a poor daylight K_e (about 0.5). Like mirrored glazing, this can cause secondhand heat and glare and raise the cooling costs of adjacent buildings. Just as these coatings reflect light on the exterior during the day, they reflect interior light at night due to their low VT and high reflectance.

APPLICATION OF LOW-EMISSION COATINGS

The *pyrolytic coating* (hard coat) is a single layer of metallic oxide applied while the glass is still in a semimolten state. This surface is strong and durable and can be used as a single-pane unit. It has a higher SC than sputtered coatings (see below) and can sustain high temperatures. However, pyrolytic coatings may make large expanses of glass look blotchy due to color shifts away from truly "clear."

The *sputtered coating* (soft coat) is a multi-layer application of a metallic, heat-reflecting layer sandwiched between two antireflective dielectric coatings to maintain light transparency. The layers are applied to finished glass in a vacuum chamber. This system is fragile and must be protected in an IG unit.

Sputtered coatings have the lowest SC of the low-e coatings and are the most common low-e coating in current use, with roughly 80% of the market.

Suspended coated film (SCF) is a low-e system developed to provide better insulation and more K_e flexibility than typical low-e stock. Using the sputtering process, a wavelength-selective low-e coating is applied to thin plastic film, which is then suspended between two panes of glass. This creates an essentially triple-pane unit for convection and conduction. The two airspaces also provide better sound control than standard IG units. Yet what differentiates SCF units is the wavelength-selective coating on the suspended film. The coating blocks most ultraviolet radiation and varying degrees of solar radiation without blocking significant portions of visible light. The result is a unit with a low SC and high visible-light transmission. See Figure 3.3.

Several coating types are available so that the appropriate SC, amount of light transmission, and insulating value may be selected for a

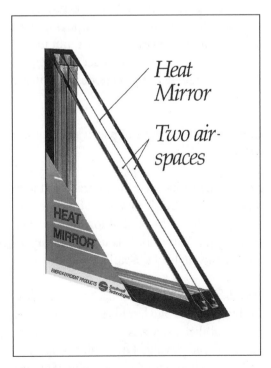

Figure 3.3 Section of a window unit with a suspended coated film. *(Courtesy of South Wall Technologies, Inc.)*

given application. Combining different glazing options is an excellent way to achieve desired performance. For example, the combination of two SCFs, low-e glass, and gas filling can achieve *R*-values as high as 10.

PLASTIC GLAZINGS

Plastic glazings were originally used as safety glass. They are less brittle and lighter in weight than glass, and they block essentially all ultraviolet radiation. Plastics are common in skylights where lighter weight, safety glazing, or molded shapes are desirable. These glazings can also be formed into structured and textured sheets. Many of the same coatings and additives discussed in this chapter can be applied to plastics as well as to glass. However, although low-e coatings can be applied to plastic suspended films, they currently cannot be applied to plastics used as the structural glazing itself.

Plastic glazing has historically had such drawbacks as flammability, low melting temperature, greater thermal expansion than glass, and degradation with time and exposure to weather. Manufacturers are studying and attempting to resolve these issues, but meanwhile, designers should consider plastic glazing very carefully in terms of design criteria and owner needs.

Currently, several types of plastic glazings are available:

Acrylic glazing has good light transmittance and longevity, but it may be soft and easily scratched. It can be frosted for translucence and privacy. Typically, it is used in skylights and is easily molded to a variety of shapes.

Polycarbonate glazing is similar to acrylic glazing but is harder and less likely to scratch. It is a UV-stabilized material for use in vertical and overhead glazing. It has added properties to optimize strength and thermal characteristics.

Insulated plastic panels consist of a double layer of plastic combined with fiberglass mesh or insulation. This material, known commercially as Kalwall®, is commonly seen as corrugated roofing panels that offer a translucent and flexible protection. Panels filled with fiberglass insulation are often used where high thermal resistance combined with translucent glazing is preferred. Exposed surfaces of some of these products may be susceptible to erosion.

GAS FILLS AND VACUUMS

Historically, double- and triple-pane windows used air to fill the voids between panes. Although it is the air fill that creates the insulating effect of multiple-glazed units, air does conduct heat and can develop convective currents within a cavity greater than 0.5 inch. By using alternative fills, such as other gases, evacuated spaces, and transparent insulation, glazing performance can be improved.

The most common fills are inert gases. Many naturally occurring and nontoxic gases have a much lower conductance value than air. By hermetically sealing these gases between two layers of glass, the conductance of the window itself can be decreased.

Currently, the most commonly used gas-filled units can achieve very high insulating values. Replacing air with argon can effectively add about *R*-1 to the unit performance of thinner units. The wider the fill space, the less advantageous alternatives to air fills become. If the airspace is too wide, convective currents can develop within an IG unit and reduce its effectiveness.

An alternative to gas fill is creating a vacuum, or evacuated space, between the panes of glass. Although not fully developed, this system theoretically has no convective heat exchange between panes of glass. Manufacturers have not yet improved the long-term integrity of the seals at the glass edges and the structural stability of the unit to make this a viable alternative. The seal must keep air density in the unit under one millionth of normal atmospheric pressure. Air density of only 10 times this amount is sufficient to reestablish conduction to normal levels.

The current technology consists of two panes of glass about a half millimeter apart with a vacuum between the panes. Tiny invisible glass spheres or silica foam within the evacuated space keeps the unit from collapsing.

DIRECTIONALLY SELECTIVE MATERIALS

Directionally selective materials reject or redirect incident solar radiation based on a geometric relationship between radiation and the material. These glazings can redirect light to a predetermined location. They include glass blocks, silk-screened glazings, prismatic devices, enclosed louvers, holographic films, and embedded structures. Figure 3.4 illustrates some common directionally selective coatings.

Frit is the most common *angle-selective coating*. It consists of a ceramic coating, either translucent or opaque, which is screen printed in small patterns on a glass surface. The pattern used on the glass controls the light based on its angle of incidence. The color of frit controls the reflection or absorption and the control of view or visual privacy. Visual transparency can also be controlled by applying frit to both sides of the glass so that at some angles it appears transparent, and at other angles it appears opaque. Angle-selective materials can be thought of as a series of fins or overhangs within a piece of glass that filter or block light.

Prismatic systems redirect light by refraction but use dielectric (nonconducting) materials. Refraction is the passing or reflection of light, which produces parallel bands of light. Fresnel lenses, made of microscopic prismatic materials embedded within the glass, are a common

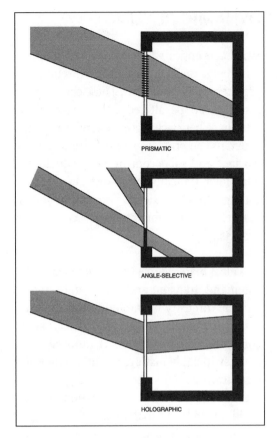

Figure 3.4 Directionally selective glazing systems.

type of prismatic device. Depending on the application, Fresnel lenses can focus light inward or outward and can work the way water appears to bend a pencil when partially immersed. Prismatic systems other than Fresnel lenses have limited commercial use.

Another type of directionally selective glazing in the research and development stage is *holographic film*. This film comprises diffractive structures of photopolymers or embossed films applied to glass that direct light deep into a space. Light is redirected and remixed as desired or as a function of the angle of incidence and wavelength of the light. Glass appears darker in areas where film is applied but visibility remains undistorted. Holographic devices function similarly to traditional light shelves but can be redirected for desired light penetration. They offer the reduced maintenance of light shelves, but do not shade lower portions of glass.

DYNAMIC GLAZING

Switchable optical windows, or smart windows, can change their physical properties based on predetermined conditions. These chromogenic glazings can be altered either passively or actively. Where a change is desired, switchable materials can provide glare reduction, privacy, daylight and solar control, and reduction of ultraviolet transmission. Most chromogenic glazings are still in the development stages and not yet available for large-scale commercial projects.

The ideal material in a hot climate would, on command, transmit only visible light, modulate the intensity of the light, and then distribute it evenly within the space. When combined with continuously dimming controls, switchable materials can provide these significant benefits and save energy in commercial buildings. Energy simulations of office buildings indicate that smart windows with lighting controls in arid climates can provide 30% to 40% energy savings over conventional windows.

Figure 3.5 illustrates several types of switchable optical materials, each characterized by the means with which occupants can control its properties.

Photochromic materials change their properties as a function of light intensity. As the metal halides in the glass are excited by light, they create a clouded appearance. As the absorptance increases, transmissivity decreases. The material reverts back to its original state in the dark. The primary benefits are visual comfort and glare control, and several skylight manufacturers now offer this option.

Two disadvantages of photochromics are (1) the threshold for change is fixed once a unit has been installed and (2) there is no seasonal selectivity to allow solar gain in the winter. Moreover, when photochromics are activated, they only reduce the visual wavelength transmittance, not the infrared, so heat gain must

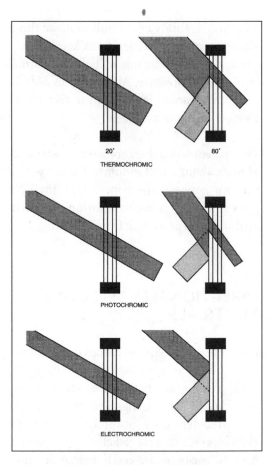

Figure 3.5 Switchable optical glazing materials.

still be addressed. Sunglass manufacturers have used this technology for some time.

Thermochromic materials change properties as a function of temperature. Optical properties are changed as liquid- and gel-based materials or thin-film solid-state devices are exposed to heat. In its exposed state, the material has a clouded appearance. The material reverts back to its original state when cooled. As with photochromics, thermochromics have the disadvantage of a fixed threshold for change.

Electrochromic materials change properties as a function of applied voltage. Properties can range from colored to bleached, or anywhere in between. These systems are more complex than thermochromic and photochromic systems, but offer the best combination of switching properties for chromogenic window applications. See Figure 3.6.

Figure 3.6 Interior view of electrochromatic glazing showing the bleached and unbleached state. *(Courtesy of Lawrence Berkeley National Laboratory.)*

The threshold for change can be altered in an existing unit, allowing for occupant and seasonal adjustment. Visible-light transmission in electrochromic glazings can be varied from 10% to 70%. Their switching times are relatively fast, and they use a low level of power. Electrochromic coatings can be combined with smart control systems to give constant light levels, and they can be applied to various layers of single- or double-pane units or combined with other coated or uncoated glazings.

HUMAN COMFORT CONSIDERATIONS

Glazing has a different effect on the visual and thermal properties of the surrounding walls, ceilings, floors, and ambient air. These thermal anomalies can lead to people's discomfort through several physical mechanisms, as illustrated in Figure 3.7.

When the temperature of an interior glazing surface differs from that of the surrounding air, the air may move in a natural convection flow, or draft, that can cause discomfort to

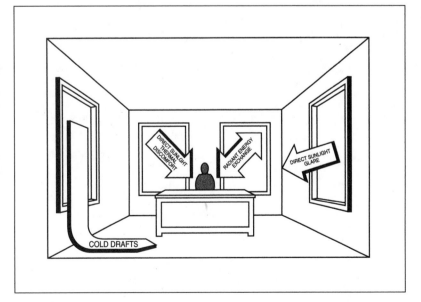

Figure 3.7 Glazing performance factors affecting human comfort.

nearby occupants. Drafts are most problematic in winter, when cool glazing temperatures cause the nearby air to cool and fall to the floor. Comfort is diminished by cooler temperatures near the floor and the drafts caused by the air motion. This problem can be alleviated by increasing the glazing R-value, decreasing the glazing area, or suppressing the convective flow through barriers.

When an occupant is near a glazing surface with a temperature different from the human body, radiant energy exchange will occur between the glazing surface and the occupant. If the temperature difference is great enough, the surface area large enough, or both, the occupant will feel discomfort from excessive radiant energy loss or gain. This phenomenon will occur even if the ambient air temperature is comfortable. For example, if one stands next to a single-glazed window in a warm room in the winter, the occupant will "feel" the cold of the window. The person really feels warmth from the body radiating toward the window. A measure of an occupant's radiative environment is the mean radiant temperature (MRT), which can be thought of as the average temperature an occupant feels from radiant exchange with his or her surroundings. As with drafts, the mean radiant temperature can be decreased by increasing the glazing R-value or by decreasing the area of the glazing. Another solution is to "block" the radiant exchange with a curtain or glazing insulation.

Integration with Electric Lighting

A complete daylighting system involves a variety of architectural elements used to capture and control natural light and also incorporates automatic photocontrols on the electric lighting system to control those fixtures. This control strategy is essential for the system inasmuch as significant energy savings are likely to occur with a well-integrated system (see Figure 4.1). Automated photocontrols are normally made up of two components: a device that senses the amount of available daylight (see Figure 4.2) and a controller that either dims the electric lights or switches them off.

SWITCHING CONTROLS

Controls that switch electric lamps are often referred to as on/off controls. They are very simple control devices that turn lamps off when the photocontrol senses enough daylight is present in the space (see Figure 4.3). When the illumination in the space falls below the required design level, the electric light will be automatically switched to the on position. Although these types of controls are typically the most economical, they frequently have the least amount of energy savings. This is because lamps and ballasts are typically energized until the available daylight threshold is reached, at which time the controller will switch those devices off.

Switching controls may result in significant variation in illumination levels, which can be disconcerting to occupants within a space due to sudden variations in light levels. These types of controls may be effective in building types such as large warehouses where light quality and variations may not be as significant as in spaces such as offices and libraries.

STEPPED CONTROLS

Stepped controls offer intermediate levels of electric lighting and integrate better with daylight availability. Stepped controls have the

Figure 4.1 Control system with relays.

capability of integrating individual lamps within a luminaire to allow a variety of combinations of lamps to operate. For example, with a three-lamp fixture, the intermediate steps would consist of one lamp on, two lamps on, and all lamps on.

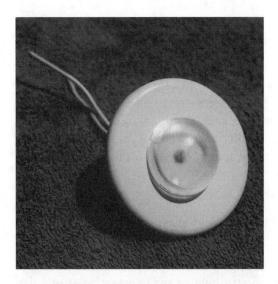

Figure 4.2 Ceiling-mounted light sensor. *(Photograph courtesy of Jason Ander.)*

With this type of system, the building occupants may be less aware of the turning on/off of electric lights because the incremental level of illumination is less perceptible and less distracting to the occupants.

In addition, stepped controls can provide more comfortably lit spaces because at least one lamp can be allowed to remain on at all times. This will avoid a darkened ceiling, which creates an uncomfortable cavelike environment for the occupants.

DIMMING CONTROLS

Dimming controls are often preferred by lighting designers because they continuously adjust the electric lights by modulating the power input to complement or enhance the level of illumination provided by daylight (see Figure 4.4). This type of control has the potential to achieve the greatest degree of energy savings because it will continuously adjust the amount of light required to meet the design level within a space. Dimming controls do not function properly with all lamp-and-ballast combinations. The designer should carefully select and specify equipment that is compatible to ensure the control system works properly.

SELECTION CONSIDERATIONS

The characteristics and quality of the space should be assessed when selecting daylighting controls (see Figure 4.5). Considerations include:

- Type of space (retail, industrial, office)
- Types of lamps and ballasts
- Fixture layout
- Shape and size of the space

The optimal control system will modulate the electric lights without adversely impacting the

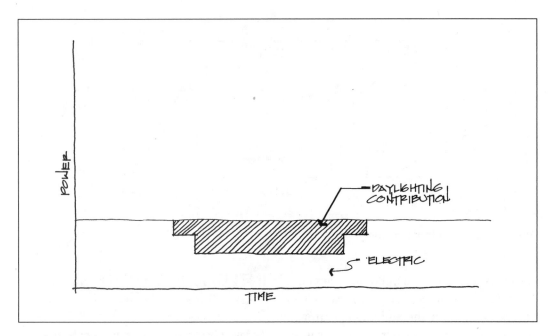

Figure 4.3 Typical on/off profile with a stepped function.

quality of illumination in the space. Time delays are typically integrated into the controls to reduce the response time to varying light intensity changes that occur on days when there are partly cloudy skies.

The photorelay should also incorporate a deadband for the lighting to be switched off when the daylight illuminance on the photo-cell exceeds some level. However, it will not be restored until the daylight drops considerably below the switch-off threshold.

Many lighting control systems can also be interfaced with existing energy management systems (EMSs) to provide additional control possibilities. An energy management system can, for example, schedule the operation of

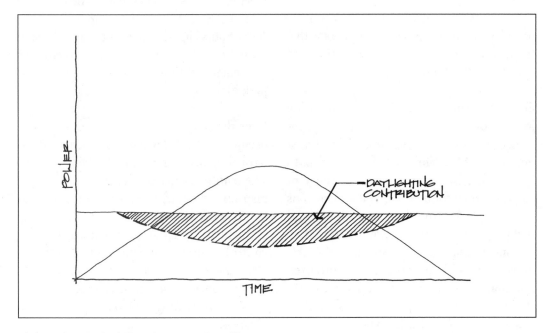

Figure 4.4 Typical dimming control profile.

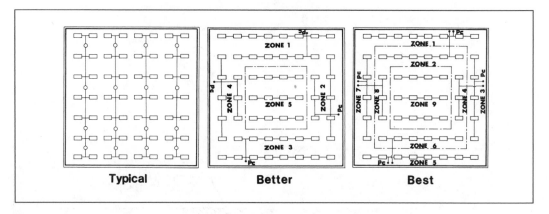

Figure 4.5 Control zoning schemes.

the lights to conform to building occupancy. In addition, the extra intelligence available in an EMS may allow the building operator to prevent the control system from reacting in an undesirable manner.

INTEGRATION WITH THE EMS

The EMS industry has advanced rapidly over the past decade. Today's EMSs are intelligent, microprocessor-based building monitoring and control systems that are an integral part of most commercial buildings.

This EMS technology and market penetration provide building owners and designers with a tremendous opportunity for innovation and operational flexibility.

EMSs are generally building- and site-wide installations composed of numerous controllers residing on a distributed local area network (LAN). This distribution of EMS "processor power" permits a wide range of control options for both *stand-alone* functions (i.e., simple thermostatic operations) and building-wide *supervisory* applications (i.e., demand limiting). In either situation, the LAN provides the additional benefit of centralized information access from any operator workstation. Figure 4.6 presents a simplified schematic of a typical EMS architecture.

INTEGRATING THE EMS AND LIGHTING CONTROLS

Today, it is common for an EMS to be used for scheduling both interior and exterior lighting systems. The EMS is typically implemented at the circuit breaker level. For example, a large office area may include several dozen individual lighting zones (i.e., light switches), even though electrical power is supplied via only a few circuits of an electrical panel. In this situation, the EMS will typically be used as a master schedule for the overall building's lighting, whereas zone level control remains dependent on the manual occupant actions. In addition, several override switches may be incorporated into the EMS to permit occupant-initiated "after hours" lighting (e.g., a corridor-located push button that signals the EMS to activate a particular lighting circuit for a prescribed period).

Over the past several years, more extensive occupancy- and daylighting-based controls have been incorporated into building designs. The controls increase energy savings by respectively tailoring lighting schedules to a building's zone level occupancy and by using ambient light. These new types of lighting controls can be implemented in either a *stand-alone* (EMS-independent) or a *supervised* manner. A schematic representation of the various lighting controls is presented in Figure 4.7.

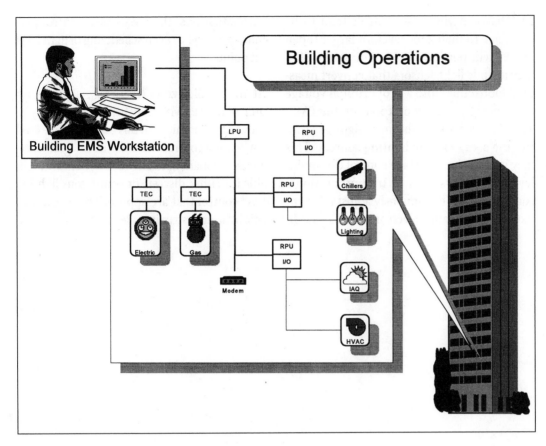

Figure 4.6 Energy management system control diagram. *(Courtesy of Energy Simulation Specialists, Inc.)*

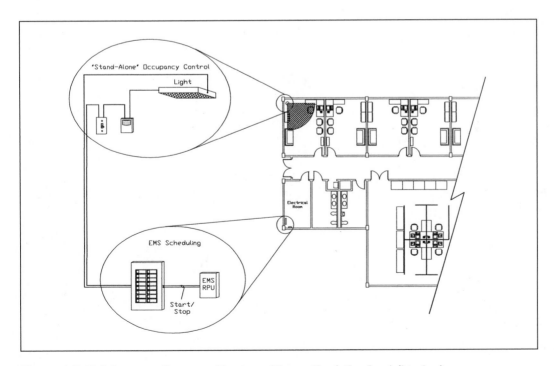

Figure 4.7 Lighting control system. *(Courtesy of Energy Simulation Specialists, Inc.)*

EMS-based daylighting controls tend to be more macro than zone level. In larger (open area) daylit portions of a building, the EMS may include light sensors that convert measured footcandles into a proportional voltage or amperage signal monitored by the EMS. The EMS then acts on the input signals to control the area's electric lighting sources. This may include discrete stage control (for multilevel lighting systems) or true proportional control through continuously adjustable light fixtures (dimmable electronic ballasts). In such situations, the EMS-based control permits easy reset or even scheduling of light level set points.

At the smaller zone level (e.g., a perimeter office), direct EMS daylighting control is typically not economical. In this case, any zone level daylighting control will likely be integral to the zone's occupancy sensor. Such devices are available for either discrete or continuous lighting level control that are appropriate for the specific lighting system installed in the zone.

Daylighting Design Tools

During the last half of the 19th century, methods for calculating illumination from natural sources first became available. Since then, the literature on daylight calculation methods has become extensive. The following section provides an introduction to daylighting calculation methods. The methodologies will help reinforce the intuitive feeling the designer has for natural illumination. The calculation tools are most useful during the design process to help resolve both the quantitative and the qualitative issues.

5.1 HAND CALCULATION METHODS

LUMEN METHOD

The lumen method closely parallels the methods used in electric lighting calculations, both of which require the "coefficient of utilization." The coefficient of utilization is defined as the ratio of light incident on a reference point to the light entering a space. This approach was first taken in the late 1920s when an empirically based method was initiated to determine the coefficient of utilization. In this method, rooms were measured with varying dimensions, window sizes, and interior surface reflectances. The results found that coefficients of utilization varied within a moderate range; however, to avoid complexity, a single value of 0.4 was adopted that limited the accuracy. Much of the complexity associated with empirically based data was eliminated in the early 1950s by Bill Griffith and his colleagues, who developed coefficient of utilization tables from a series of measurements conducted in both experimental rooms and physical models (see Figure 5.1.1). Fund-

Figure 5.1.1 Coefficient of utilization values. (*Source: IESNA Lighting Handbook. Published with permission by the Illuminating Engineering Society of North America, 120 Wall Street, New York, NY 10005.*)

Coefficient of Utilization from Window Without Blinds.
Sky Component $E_{xvsky}/E_{xhsky} = 0.75$.

ROOM DEPTH/WINDOW HEIGHT PERCENT						WINDOW WIDTH/WINDOW HEIGHT			
D		0.5	1	2	3	4	6	8	Infinite
1	10	0.824	0.864	0.870	0.873	0.875	0.879	0.880	0.883
	30	0.547	0.711	0.777	0.789	0.793	0.798	0.799	0.801
	50	0.355	0.526	0.635	0.659	0.666	0.669	0.670	0.672
	70	0.243	0.386	0.505	0.538	0.548	0.544	0.545	0.547
	90	0.185	0.304	0.418	0.451	0.464	0.444	0.446	0.447
2	10	0.667	0.781	0.809	0.812	0.813	0.815	0.816	0.824
	30	0.269	0.416	0.519	0.544	0.551	0.556	0.557	0.563
	50	0.122	0.204	0.287	0.319	0.331	0.339	0.341	0.345
	70	0.068	0.116	0.173	0.201	0.214	0.223	0.226	0.229
	90	0.050	0.084	0.127	0.151	0.164	0.167	0.171	0.172
3	10	0.522	0.681	0.739	0.746	0.747	0.749	0.747	0.766
	30	0.139	0.232	0.320	0.350	0.360	0.366	0.364	0.373
	50	0.053	0.092	0.139	0.163	0.174	0.183	0.182	0.187
	70	0.031	0.053	0.081	0.097	0.106	0.116	0.116	0.119
	90	0.025	0.041	0.061	0.074	0.082	0.089	0.090	0.092
4	10	0.405	0.576	0.658	0.670	0.673	0.675	0.674	0.707
	30	0.075	0.134	0.197	0.224	0.235	0.243	0.243	0.255
	50	0.028	0.050	0.078	0.094	0.104	0.112	0.114	0.119
	70	0.018	0.031	0.048	0.059	0.065	0.073	0.074	0.078
	90	0.016	0.026	0.040	0.048	0.053	0.059	0.061	0.064
6	10	0.242	0.392	0.494	0.516	0.521	0.524	0.523	0.588
	30	0.027	0.054	0.086	0.102	0.111	0.119	0.120	0.135
	50	0.011	0.023	0.036	0.044	0.049	0.055	0.056	0.063
	70	0.009	0.018	0.027	0.032	0.035	0.040	0.041	0.046
	90	0.008	0.016	0.023	0.028	0.031	0.034	0.035	0.040
8	10	0.147	0.257	0.352	0.380	0.387	0.391	0.392	0.482
	30	0.012	0.026	0.043	0.054	0.060	0.067	0.070	0.086
	50	0.006	0.013	0.021	0.026	0.029	0.033	0.035	0.043
	70	0.005	0.011	0.017	0.021	0.023	0.026	0.027	0.034
	90	0.004	0.010	0.015	0.019	0.021	0.023	0.025	0.030
10	10	0.092	0.168	0.248	0.275	0.284	0.290	0.291	0.395
	30	0.006	0.014	0.026	0.032	0.036	0.041	0.044	0.059
	50	0.003	0.008	0.014	0.017	0.019	0.022	0.024	0.032
	70	0.003	0.007	0.012	0.014	0.016	0.018	0.019	0.026
	90	0.003	0.006	0.011	0.013	0.015	0.016	0.017	0.024

ing for Griffith's work, as well as the publication of his results, was provided by the Libbey-Owens-Ford Company, which is the reason Griffith's method is referred as the LOF method. The lumen method, as refined by Griffith, has also been adopted by the Illuminating Engineering Society (IES) of North America as part of its Recommended Practice of Daylighting. The following calculation process best summarizes the lumen method and is described in greater detail in the IES's most recent Recommended Practice of Daylighting.

When developing a preliminary building design, the architect must first establish a variety of interior visual criteria and basic lighting performance requirements for each project. Then the designer must determine the parameters of the available daylight for the particular location and select the appropriate daylight data utilized as a basis for the design purposes. He or she is ready to calculate daylight contributions for various design schemes.

Due to varying sky conditions, the amount of available daylight is extremely variable for almost all localities. From sunrise to sunset, from winter to summer, and from day to day, the amount of available light from the sun and sky is constantly changing.

Except in a few isolated instances, very few instrumented data on daylight are available. Thus, it is impossible to establish a single set of conditions that can be used as an "absolute" design base.

Generally, the designer will find the maximum and minimum sky conditions or the conditions considered most prevalent or typical as the most advantageous for calculating accurate measurements. If the particular locality in question has a high percentage of overcast days, the designer might choose to give more weight to the advantages and disadvantages of his or her proposed design under the overcast sky. If the locality has a high percentage of clear days, he or she might choose to ignore the overcast sky condition and design for clear sky and sun.

Figure 5.1.2 shows a typical lumen method illuminance curve as a function of solar altitude used to provide an indication of the illumination that may be expected for a particular sky, solar altitude, and building orientation. It should be kept in mind that these charts provide only very approximate illumination levels, and their use should be replaced in the event that more accurate local data are available.

For a cloudy or overcast sky scenario, the illumination of the unobstructed horizontal plane of the ground (or roof plane) will be needed for determining the daylight contribution to the interior from toplight openings and for determining reflected light from the ground. The illumination on the vertical plane of the fenestration will be needed for determining sidelighting contributions.

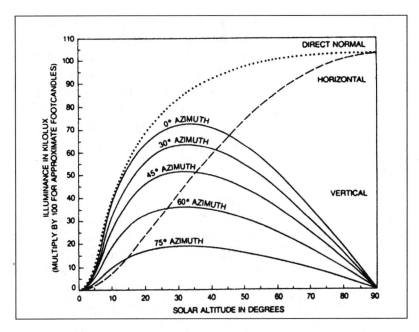

Figure 5.1.2 Illuminance from the sun under clear sky conditions as a function of solar altitude and azimuth. *(Source: IESNA Lighting Handbook. Published with permission by the Illuminating Engineering Society of North America, 120 Wall Street, New York, NY 10005.)*

The illumination from a clear sky condition will be needed only for determining the daylight contribution from sidelighting where direct sun is not falling incident on that wall. The illumination from both clear sky and direct sun is required for determining the daylight contributions from toplight openings, for side wall lighting where the wall is exposed to direct sun, and for determining reflected ground light.

After the designer has determined the illumination on the horizontal or vertical surface from the sky selected, the illumination contribution from the sun can be determined on the illuminance curve and added to the illumination contribution from the sky.

The percentage of time that any sky condition is likely to occur is another factor used in selecting design sky conditions. The National Oceanic and Atmospheric Administration (NOAA) or simulation weather files may provide a basis for estimating the number of hours per month when illumination levels or solar radiation will be above or below certain thresholds.

The data in the lumen method charts are taken from these types of sources citing measurements at numerous weather stations throughout the country. Data are based on hourly observations of the "percentage cloud cover," that is, the degree of cloudiness, in tenths of the entire sky, zero to $3/10$ being considered clear, $4/10$ to $7/10$ partly cloudy, and $8/10$ to $10/10$ overcast.

A completely overcast sky might be thin and bright or dense and dark, resulting in different illumination levels on the ground. Although the illuminance data are derived from weather bureau instrumentation, extensive local information may not be available and may be a limiting factor for this methodology.

PREDICTING INTERIOR DAYLIGHTING

Interior illumination is determined for each of several conditions and then added together for final results. For instance, illumination from windows and skylights can be determined separately and then added together for final results.

The calculation process used for the lumen method for determining interior daylighting is based on a process of interpolation of test data from actual testing. There are inherent limitations to the general type of room, fenestration, openings, and controls tested. However, with the use of a little common sense, these parameters can be expanded to fit a wide variety of building and fenestration designs.

BRS DAYLIGHT PROTRACTORS

The BRS Daylight Protractors were devised primarily to simplify the calculation of the sky factor and sky component and to enable daylight measurements to be made from the delineation of a design of buildings.

In this respect, they are not design methods but merely an aid to design and are used to test the adequacy of a design at the stage at which scale drawings are available. This type of procedure is very suitable in the early stages of a design to determine the approximate dimensions and positions of fenestration as it relates to the daylight factor.

The components of the daylight factor in a building consist not only of the light that reaches the point directly from the sky but also the light reaching the point after reflection from external surfaces and from surfaces within the room—the ceiling, walls, floor, and furnishings. The daylight factor can therefore be considered to comprise three distinct components: the sky component, the externally reflected component, and the internally reflected component.

All three components are functions of the fenestration area, but the relative values of each vary with the particular conditions to which each is subject. In other words, the distance from the fenestration, degree of external obstruction, reflectances of external and internal surfaces all will impact this value. Building codes exist in certain parts of the world that require a minimum daylight factor within spaces.

The distinction among the components of the daylight factor is made primarily to facilitate the calculation of interior daylight and to enable methods best suited to the calculation of direct and reflected light to be used where appropriate, but it has advantages when the relative amounts of direct and diffused light are required, as in the determination of modeling effects.

The daylight factor and its components are defined by the Commission Internationale de l'Eclairage (CIE) as follows:

> The daylight factor is the ratio of the daylight illumination at a point on a given plane due to the light received directly or indirectly from a sky of

assumed or known luminance distribution, to the illumination on a horizontal plane due to an unobstructed hemisphere of this sky. Direct sunlight is excluded for both values of illumination [see Figure 5.1.3].

The BRS Daylight Protractors are composed of a set of circular protractors that resemble in appearance and mode of operation the ordinary angular protractor (see Figure 5.1.4). The use of the Protractors in elementary daylight situations is simple and straightforward, although refinements in technique are possible that allow the Protractors to be used in the determination of direct daylight in more complex situations. The complete set of BRS Day-

light Protractors is composed of two sets of five, corresponding to uniform sky and CIE overcast sky conditions. Each Protractor within each set applies to a particular slope of glazing and, in one case, to unglazed openings.

The Protractors are designed to be used with designer-scaled drawings, but any other drawings to scale that show the glazing in section and plan can be employed if detailed drawings are not available. Care should be taken so that the drawings show the thicknesses of window walls and include internal and external projections such as sills, blind boxes, and overhangs, and external obstructions and other details such as louvers known to interfere with the admission of daylight to the interior.

In most cases, the scaled drawings prepared in standard production of architectural design work will work for determining sky components. Although the scale of the drawings is not critical, the Protractor can be laid conveniently over the section or plan, sight lines drawn accurately, and the intercepts read off without difficulty. A large scale helps in the accurate location of sight lines to the operative

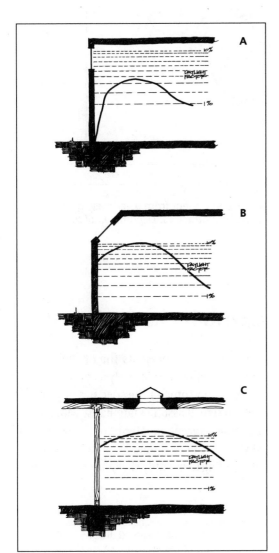

Figure 5.1.3 Daylight factor for various apertures.

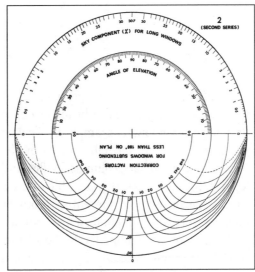

Figure 5.1.4 BRS Sky Component Protractor for vertical glazing (CIE overcast sky). *(Source: Building Research Establishment,* B.R.S. Daylight Protractors, *Department of the Environment, United Kingdom.)*

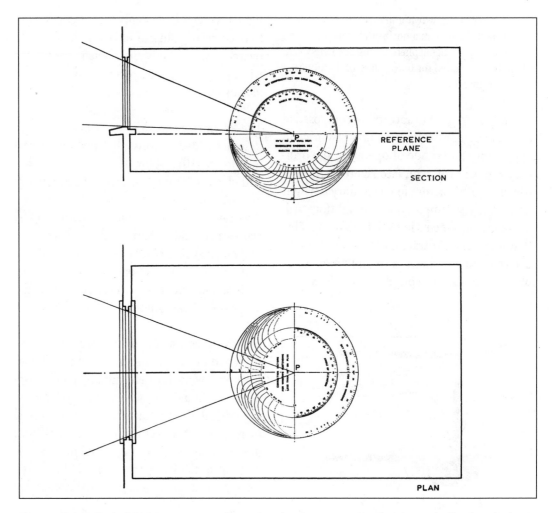

Figure 5.1.5 Typical BRS Protractor to determine the sky component from a vertically glazed window. *(Source: Building Research Establishment,* B.R.S. Daylight Protractors, *Department of the Environment, United Kingdom.)*

edges of window openings and is essential when accurate readings must be made for the detailing of a window, for example, in allowing for the reduction in daylight caused by the window frame and bars, columns, baffles, and louvers. In some cases, it is possible to use a small-scale drawing of the entire room or building from which to obtain a first estimate of the probable daylighting levels and a large-scale drawing of the window itself from which to assess the effective area of the glazing.

The process of taking the sight line from the edges of the fenestration to the point in the interior is shown in Figure 5.1.5.

SKYLIGHT CALCULATIONS*

This discussion presents the Skylight Work-sheets, a set of simple analysis procedures for focusing on some of the specifics of your skylight design. It assumes familiarity with many of the basic concepts and terms of daylighting and skylights. These should be understood before attempting to quantify skylight energy savings.

*Excerpted with permission from the *American Architectural Manufacturers Association Skylight Handbook—Design Guidelines* (SHDG-1-88) with PC disk. Available: $100.00 (book only $52.00). Write to AAMA, 1827 Walden Office Square, Suite 550, Schaumburg, IL 60173. Call (847) 303-5664. E-mail: aamanet.org.

The Skylight Worksheets are used for optimizing the basic physical parameters of the skylight system:

- Skylight size and shape
- Glazing material
- Light well size and shape

The overall goal of this analysis is to maximize lighting energy and cost savings. Saving energy is not the only, or even primary, reason for using skylights, but controlling energy costs is a real concern for building owners, and reducing energy consumption is an increasing concern in building codes and regulations. The Skylight Worksheets provide an easy way to address this complex issue. They are based on years of research, practical experience, and computer analysis, and are useful for establishing the basic parameters of your skylight design. . . .

The basic sequence of the Worksheets is illustrated on the flowchart [shown in Figure 5.1.6]. The Worksheets assume that you are starting early in the design sequence, and know very little as yet about the specifics of your skylight design. They help you answer basic questions about the skylight design likely to be best for your situation.

There are other ways the Worksheets can be used, depending on your style as a designer and the nature of the problem you are addressing. As you become familiar with their structure, you will adapt them to your needs, as you would with any tool.

There are 5 Skylight Worksheets that guide you step-by-step through the analysis. You will need to provide some basic information about your building design. . . . If you are not far enough along in your design process to provide all the information required, the Worksheets will suggest default values that can be used in the interim. As the Worksheets are presented, there are sample Worksheets, filled in with an example to illustrate the process.

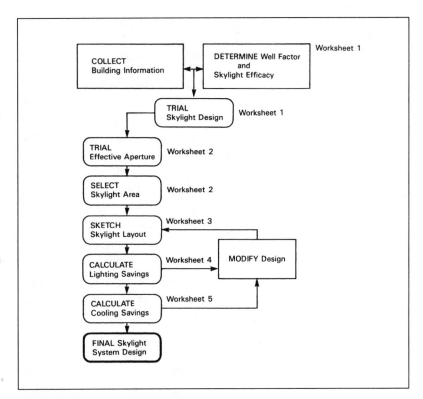

Figure 5.1.6 Worksheet flowchart.

The Worksheets are organized into "Steps." As you get further along, you will notice references to numbers developed in earlier steps. For example, when you are asked for the Gross Floor Area, you will be referred to Step 2, where that information is recorded. There are five Worksheets, but the numbering of steps is continuous from beginning to end; there is only one Step 4, and it is found on Worksheet 1.

The following sections explain in detail what is required for each Step of each Worksheet. It is recommended that you read through this discussion step-by-step the first time you go through the Worksheets, and refer back to it if you have questions later on.

Skylighting design is an iterative process. After you have the basic parameters of your design, you can refine that information in the context of your building and your design goals, and you can repeat some of the calculations. This will yield a more accurate picture of the energy and cost performance of your design.

WORKSHEET 1

Trial Design Worksheet

As with many design analyses, you need a trial design to begin. This includes information about the size and configuration of your skylighting system, and provides a basis for the initial analysis. It is used as a starting point in further developing and refining the system. Your trial design should be based on some reasonable assumptions about the kind of skylight system you might use in your building. You do not need to spend a great deal of effort in choosing a trial design, however, because the analysis is quick and simple enough that you can easily start over with a different trial design at a later time.

If you wish, you can use the trial skylight design represented by the default values on the Worksheets and illustrated in the examples. This is an ordinary square, 4' × 4' skylight with tinted glazing and a simple, rectangular light well.

Instructions

Step 1: Choose Representative Location

There are six skylighting zones, and seven representative cities used in the Worksheets. Worksheet 1 shows the zones and the names of these cities. Each zone represents approximately constant daylight availability.

Choose the zone that includes your own location. Check off the representative city for that zone.

Step 2: Find Basic Building Information

This information will be used in various parts of the Worksheets. It applies to the portion of your building that is skylit and had daylighting controls. If only part of the building has skylights, treat it as a discrete building throughout this analysis and ignore the non-daylit parts. If there are different daylit areas containing different occupancies, for example separate office and warehouse areas, you should analyze them separately.

List the Occupancy type; this is primarily for reference.

List the Desired Average Illuminance, which should correspond to the control setting of the daylighting system; e.g., if the control system is designed to maintain 50 footcandles, that would be the Desired Average Illuminance. This should also correspond to the illuminance required for the visual task to be performed.

List the Gross Floor Area, in square feet, for the daylit area in question. This should include only the floor area of building with skylighting and daylight controls for the electric lights. Gross floor area means that you should ignore the floor area taken up by partitions and other obstructions, and use the overall area of the space.

List the Lighting Power Density (LPD), in Watts/square foot (W/sf). . . . This calculation basically involves summing the lamp and ballast wattage for all luminaires, and dividing by the gross floor area. Refer to the IES Handbook for a more detailed description of the calculation.

Check off the applicable daylighting control system type. If you are using a step control system with more than two steps, use the continuous dimming choice. See [Chapter 4] for a discussion of daylighting controls.

Step 3: Select Trial Skylight

Consult manufacturers' literature for skylight sizes and glazing options. Select a skylight unit that is close to what you will want in your design, to use on a trial basis. As mentioned above, the default value is for an ordinary, 4' × 4' skylight.

List skylight opening area, in square feet, for a single skylight unit. This number will be used later to derive the number of skylights.

List glazing characteristics: visible transmittance and shading coefficient. These are decimal fractions, such as 0.82. They are discussed more fully in [Chapter 1, and Appendix D] contains a table of representative values for typical glazing materials. Refer to manufacturer's literature, when available, for actual numbers. The shading coefficient should be for glazing in a horizontal position, if available.

Step 4: Determine Trial Well Factor

If there will be a light well, you should sketch a trial configuration for it. It should be consistent with the trial skylight and with what you know about ceiling thickness and other building design characteristics. . . . If none of the typical well configurations apply to your design, calculate the well factor using the defaults.

List the well height, as measured from the bottom of the glazing to the ceiling plane, in inches. If it is not a constant value, use the maximum height.

List the well length, in feet. If there are splayed walls to the well, calculate the maximum length of the well at the ceiling plane.

List the well width, in feet. Again, use the maximum width.

List the reflectance of the well walls, as a decimal fraction. [Manufacturers' literature may have these values for many products.]

Calculate the Well Index (WI), as shown on the worksheet.

Use the graph to find the Well Factor (WF), based on reflectance and WI. Start with the Well Index you just calculated. Draw a vertical up to the sloped line corresponding to the well wall reflectance (interpolate as necessary). From that intersection, draw a horizontal line to find the Efficiency of Well, or Well Factor (WF).

Step 5: Determine Skylight Efficacy

[Refer to the table on this page for representative values.]

Calculate SE, using the visible transmittance (VT) and shading coefficient (SC) from Step 3, and the well factor (WF) from Step 4, above.

GLAZING TABLE

	VISIBLE TRANSMITTANCE* (VT)	SHADING COEFFICIENT* (SC)	SKYLIGHT EFFICACY* (SE)
Single Glazing			
Clear glass (colorless)	0.88	0.94	0.94
Clear acrylic (colorless)	0.92	0.98	0.94
Clear polycarbonate (colorless)	0.83	0.99	0.84
Diffusing acrylic	0.17–0.72	0.20–0.87	0.80–0.85
Diffusing polycarbonate	0.43	0.72	0.60
Tinted glass (¼" bronze)	0.49	0.67	0.73
Tinted glass (¼" blue/green)	0.75	0.67	1.12
Tinted glass (bronze)	0.49	0.75	0.65
Double Glazing			
Polycarbonate			
Clear/clear	0.69	0.93	0.74
Diffusing/clear	0.36	0.66	0.55
Bronze/clear	0.43	0.72	0.60
Bronze/diffusing	0.22	0.56	0.39
Acrylic			
Clear/clear	0.85	0.89	0.96
Diffusing/clear	0.48	0.58	0.83
Bronze/clear	0.25	0.43	0.58
Bronze/diffusing	0.17	0.32	0.53

*All numbers are average and will vary with material thickness, degree of tint, and skylight design.

WORKSHEET 1

(Note: See [Trial Design Worksheet, pages 56–57] for more information and an example of the use of the form.)

Step 1: Choose Representative Location

The map shows zones of roughly equal daylight availability. Each has a representative city. Choose the zone that contains your own location. Note: For Zone 2, data is provided for both Madison, WI and Washington, DC. Choose the location whose climate, especially for cooling, is most similar to that of your location.

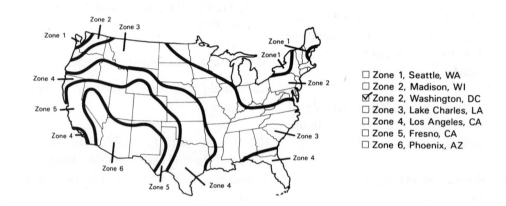

☐ Zone 1, Seattle, WA
☐ Zone 2, Madison, WI
☑ Zone 2, Washington, DC
☐ Zone 3, Lake Charles, LA
☐ Zone 4, Los Angeles, CA
☐ Zone 5, Fresno, CA
☐ Zone 6, Phoenix, AZ

Step 2: Find Basic Building Information

Occupancy   _office_
(office, retail, etc.)

Desired Average Illuminance (default: 50 fc)   50   fc

Gross Floor Area   10,000   sf
(with daylighting)

Lighting Power Density (default: 1.5)   1.5   W/sf

Daylighting Control System: (Continuous Dimming) ☐   1-Step ☐   2-Step ☑
(Note: Ceiling height does not enter into this calculation. It is assumed that skylight spacing is less than or equal to 1.5 times ceiling height. . . .)

Step 3: Select Trial Skylight

If possible, list the following details for a trial skylight. If not, enter the default values and skip to end of Step 4.

Area of typical skylight opening (individual unit)   16   sf
(default: 16)

Visible transmittance, VT =   0.50
(default: .50)

Shading coefficient, SC =   0.44
(default: .44)

Step 4: Determine Trial Well Factor (WF)

If possible, perform this analysis with a trial light well design. If not, use [the following] default well factor. . . .

Sketch trial design below:

List the well dimensions:

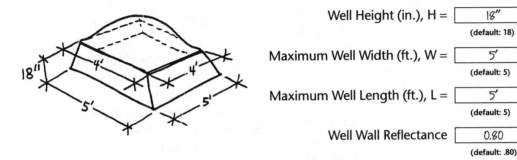

Well Height (in.), H = $\boxed{18''}$
(default: 18)

Maximum Well Width (ft.), W = $\boxed{5'}$
(default: 5)

Maximum Well Length (ft.), L = $\boxed{5'}$
(default: 5)

Well Wall Reflectance $\boxed{0.80}$
(default: .80)

Calculate Well Index, using well dimensions listed above:

$$\text{Well Index} = \frac{H \times (L + W)}{24 \times W \times L} = \frac{\boxed{18''} \times \left(\boxed{5'} + \boxed{5'}\right)}{24 \times \boxed{5'} \times \boxed{5'}} = \boxed{0.30} \quad \text{(default: .3)}$$

Use the graph to find Well Factor, using values listed above. Start at Well Index. Draw up to appropriate wall reflectance curve, and across to find Well Factor; enter result below.

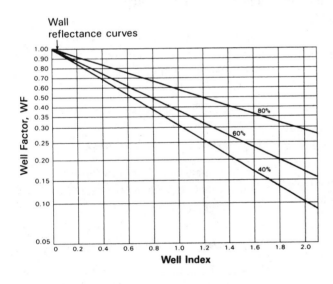

Well Factor, WF = $\boxed{0.90}$
(default: .90)

Step 5: Determine Skylight Efficacy (SE)

Use values listed above in Steps 3 and 4 to calculate SE. . . .

$$\text{Skylight Efficacy} = \frac{WF \times VT}{SC} = \frac{\boxed{0.90} \times \boxed{0.50}}{\boxed{0.44}} = \boxed{1.02} \quad \text{(default: 1.02)}$$

WORKSHEET 2

Skylight Area Worksheet

Once the basic skylight parameters are determined on Worksheet 1, you are ready to find the target skylight area for your building. The numbering of steps continues on Worksheet 2 from where it left off on Worksheet 1.

Step 6 presents a method for determining a target range of Effective Apertures (EA) to use in initial skylight system sizing. The target ranges are based on optimum EAs which produce minimum peak electricity demands for the building. This usually means the skylighting system is not causing increases in the cooling system size, and that peak demand charges from the electric utility will be reduced. . . .

If your design is far enough along that you know the number of skylights, the well factor, and the visible transmittance of your skylight system, you should skip directly to Steps 10–12, and work out the actual EA.

You can then compare this to the Trial EA that is found in Step 6 for your location. If your actual EA is larger than the maximum EA or smaller than the minimum EA, you should consider adjusting your design. You can also proceed to Worksheets 4 and 5 to explore the cost savings of your design.

Instructions

Step 6: Find the Trial Effective Aperture (EA)

[The figures shown after Step 12 contain] seven sets of graphs, one for each of the representative locations. Within each set there are three graphs, corresponding to three different levels of required illuminance. The graphs indicate bands of EAs that yield maximum savings from skylighting. The graphs are used to find the range of EAs to target in your design. In general, the ranges are broad, because there is not a sharp optimum point on skylight performance curves. There are many design options within the range of EAs, which allows you flexibility in designing your skylight system.

Choose the [Effective Aperture (EA) graph] that matches your Representative Location (Step 1), and Desired Average Illuminance (Step 2). There are solid line curves for maximum EA, and dashed line curves for minimum EA. Follow the directions on the form for finding the maximum and minimum values of EA. These should be entered in the appropriate blanks under Step 7 below.

Step 7: Determine Skylight-to-Floor Ratio (SFR)

There are two calculations here, one for the maximum and one for the minimum SFR. They use the maximum and minimum EAs found in the previous step.

For each calculation, use the glazing visible transmittance (VT, from Step 3) and the well factor (WF, from Step 4).

Calculate SFR as shown on the form.

Step 8: Determine Skylight Area

For both maximum SFR and minimum SFR, multiply by Gross Floor Area (from Step 2), to find skylight area in square feet.

Step 9: Determine Number of Skylights

For the minimum and maximum skylight areas, divide by the size of the trial skylight (from Step 3) and round up to arrive at the number of skylights that correspond to each case. These numbers set upper and lower limits for your trial skylight design. The Trial Design Worksheet helps you to relate these numbers to your building design.

At this point, skip to the beginning of Worksheet 3. Steps 10–12 are only to be used when you are working with a known skylight design.

Step 10: Determine Total Skylight Area

This calculation starts with the number and size of skylights, and gives the total skylight area (in square feet). The Unit Area is the opening area of a single skylight unit, and is taken from Step 3.

Step 11: Determine Skylight-to-Floor Ratio (SFR)

This calculation finds the SFR. Again, the calculation should only include the floor area of the building with skylighting and daylight controls for the electric lights. Gross floor area means that you should ignore the floor area taken up by partitions and use the overall area of the space.

Step 12: Determine Effective Aperture (EA)

. . . The EA that results may be used in other parts of the Worksheets. It may be compared to the EAs for your location found in Step 7, and it may be used in the lighting and cooling savings worksheets (Worksheets 4 and 5) that follow.

Optimum Effective Area Graphs Based on Peak Demand

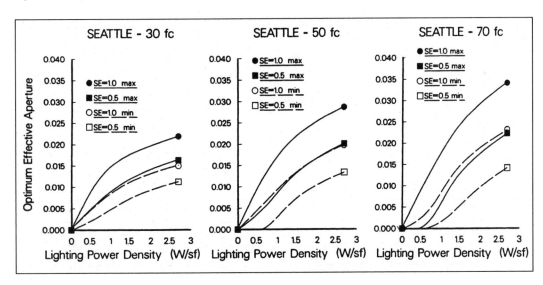

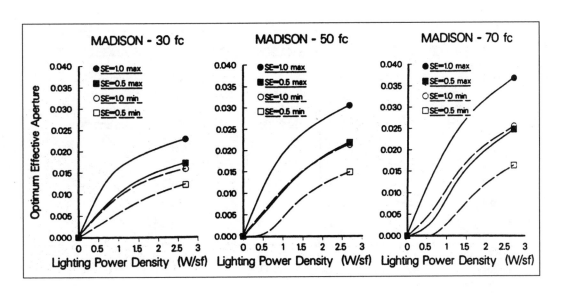

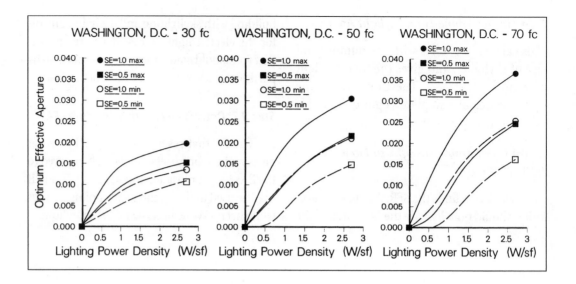

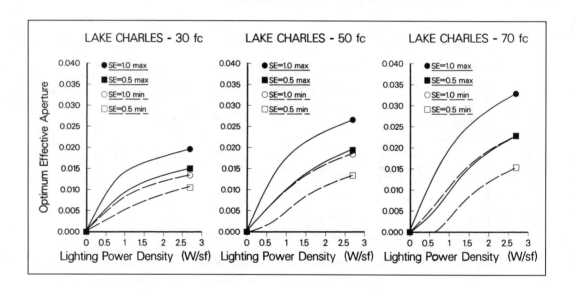

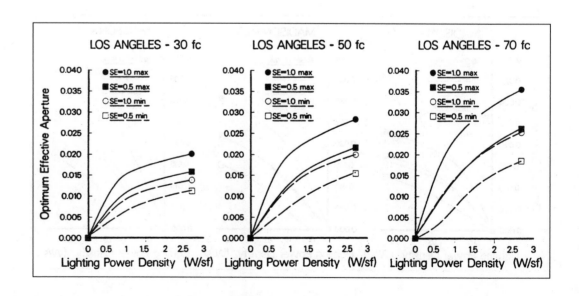

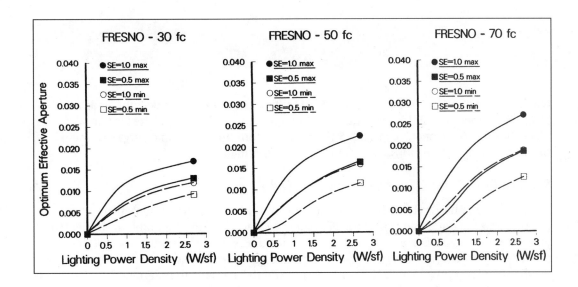

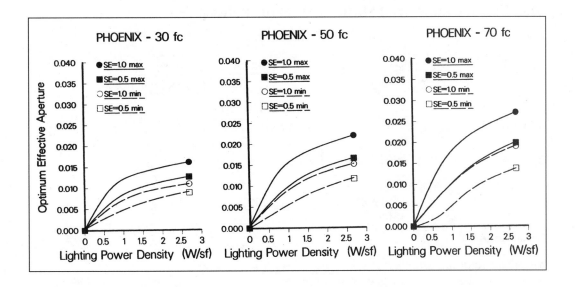

WORKSHEET 2

Note: Use [page 64] of this form (Steps 6–9) for first cut estimates of skylight area; use [page 65] (Steps 10–12) for subsequent analysis, when actual skylight sizes are known. See [Skylight Area Worksheet, pages 60–63] for more information and an example of the use of this form. Some "Step" numbers refer to Form 1 information.

Step 6: Find Trial Effective Aperture (EA)

Choose the graph from [pages 61–63 that] corresponds to your Representative Location (Step 1) and to your Desired Average Illuminance (Step 2). Enter the graph at the LPD for your design (Step 2). Draw up to the dashed line curve that is closest to your SE (Step 5); mark the intersection points (you may interpolate between dashed curves). Repeat this step for the solid line curves. Draw horizontal lines from these points to find minimum and maximum Effective Apertures (EA). Enter these numbers in Step 7 below.

Step 7: Determine Trial Skylight-to-Floor Ratio (SFR)

Minimum EA = 0.015   Maximum EA = 0.024

$$SFR = \frac{Min\ EA}{VT \times WF} = \frac{0.015}{0.50 \times 0.90}$$
(Step 3) (Step 4)

Minimum SFR = 0.033

$$SFR = \frac{Max\ EA}{VT \times WF} = \frac{0.024}{0.50 \times 0.90}$$
(Step 3) (Step 4)

Maximum SFR = 0.053

Step 8: Determine Trial Skylight Area

Minimum Total Skylight Area:
Min. Area = Min. SFR × Gross Area = 0.033 × 10,000
       (Step 7)   (Step 2)   sf

Minimum Area = 330 sf

Maximum Total Skylight Area:
Max. Area = Max. SFR × Gross Area = 0.053 × 10,000
       (Step 7)   (Step 2)   sf

Maximum Area = 530 sf

Step 9: Determine Trial Number of Skylights

Minimum Number of Skylights:
Min. Nmbr = Min. Area ÷ Unit Area = 330 ÷ 16
       (Step 8)   (Step 3)   sf

Minimum Number = 21
         (round up)

Maximum Number of Skylights:
Max. Nmbr = Max. Area ÷ Unit Area = 530 ÷ 16
       (Step 8)   (Step 3)   sf

Maximum Number = 34
         (round up)

Note: The following three steps are used to calculate Effective Aperture (EA) when the number of skylights, the well factor, and the visible transmittance of the skylight are known. . . .

Step 10: Determine Total Skylight Area

Number of Skylights × Unit Area = $\boxed{30}$ × $\boxed{16}$ × $\boxed{480}$ Total Skylight Area
    (#)   (sf each)   #   sf each   sf
               (Step 3)

Step 11: Determine Skylight-to-Floor Ratio (SFR)

Total Skylight Area ÷ Gross Floor Area = $\boxed{480}$ ÷ $\boxed{10{,}000}$ = $\boxed{0.048}$ Skylight-to-Floor Ratio (SFR)
   (Step 10)   (Step 2)   sf   sf

Step 12: Determine Effective Aperture (EA)

$\boxed{0.048}$ × $\boxed{0.50}$ × $\boxed{0.90}$ = $\boxed{0.022}$ Effective Aperture
 SFR   VT   WF   EA
(Step 11) (Step 3)   (Step 4)

WORKSHEET 3

Trial Layout Worksheets

The Trial Layout Worksheet provides two sketch areas of grids for you to do a quick layout of the maximum and minimum numbers of skylights determined on the previous worksheet.

At this point, you should go back to your building plans and look at how these trial designs relate to your other design goals. Check the following details:

- Coordination with the structural system and interior layout
- Skylight spacing
- Spacing-to-ceiling height ratio
- Lighting quality considerations
- Appropriateness of the trial skylight size and well design in light of other design considerations

Based on this analysis, you can decide if your trial skylight and well designs are acceptable, or you can modify them. Any of the parameters could be changed. For example, you may decide that you want to use a larger skylight with a lower transmittance glazing and a deeper well for reasons of lighting quality.

If you do choose a different skylight or well design, return to Step 3 on Worksheet 1 and go through the analysis again, this time using the new parameters. The major difference this time through is that you would use Steps 10–12, along with Step 6, to learn if your new design still falls within the optimum range. If it has moved out of the optimum, you should consider modifying it again to get back within that range.

WORKSHEET 3

Note: See [Trial Layout Worksheets, page 66] for more information and an example of the use of this form.

Use the following sketch areas to lay out trial skylight areas on your floor plan. Alternatively, do trial layouts on building design drawings.

If this analysis leads to a different skylight or well design, return to Step 3, Form 1, and recalculate to refine the worksheet calculations.

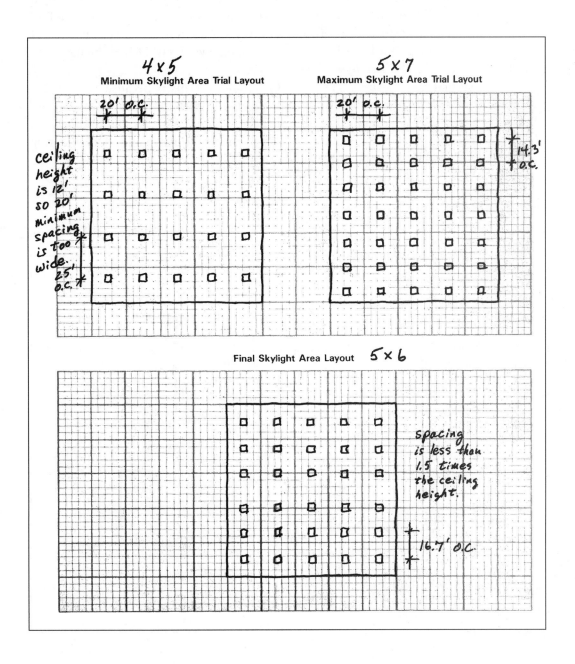

WORKSHEET 4

Lighting Savings Worksheet

This worksheet helps you to estimate the actual lighting energy and cost savings from the daylight system.

Instructions

Step 13: Find Full Load Lighting Hours

This is the number of hours of full load, or undimmed, lighting operation in a year that your building would require without the daylighting system operating (no dimming). The default value corresponds to typical office working hours, as shown in [the figure below]. This schedule was used as the basis for the savings calculations in these Guidelines. The calculations are valid as long as the occupancy schedule for your building is similar to this schedule. If, on the other hand, your building's schedule is substantially different, refer to [Appendix E] for a procedure to adjust the calculations to your actual schedule.

For example, if the building is a school that finishes operation during the afternoon and is closed on weekends, then the daylighting system will turn off lights for a larger fraction of the time than it would in an office, and the lighting energy savings would be different. Likewise, if the building is a restaurant that operates only in the afternoon and nighttime hours, its energy savings would also be different.

The default lighting schedule is shown in [the figure below]. For most hours, not all of the lights are turned on. For instance, at 10 A.M. on a weekday, 90% of the lights are turned on, while at 5:30 P.M. only 50% of the lights are on. This is because some of the occupants have left for the day and turned off lights. On Saturdays, only some of the lights are on during the morning, and fewer during the afternoon.

Default Lighting Schedule

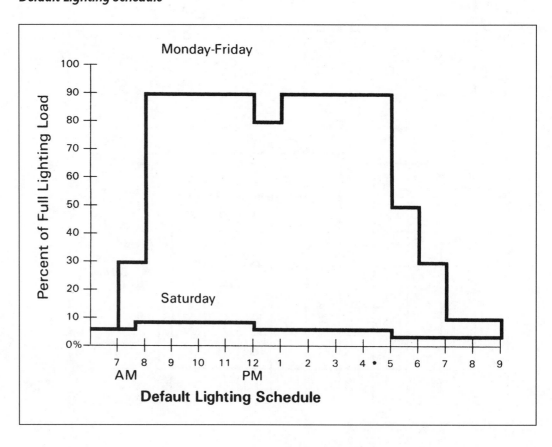

Default Lighting Schedule

Step 14: Find Fraction of Lighting Energy Saved

[From the eighteen Lighting Energy Savings] graphs: choose the graph for the Representative City you selected (Step 1) and for your Desired Average Illuminance (Step 2). Use the curve that corresponds to your control system type (Step 2). Interpolate as necessary. Follow the directions on the form to find the Fraction of Lighting Energy Saved.

Step 15: Calculate Lighting Energy Saved

This calculation yields the total number of kilowatt-hours of electricity saved per year by the daylighting system. Multiply the Lighting Power Density, by the gross floor area, and by the number of full-load lighting hours and the fraction of lighting energy saved. Division by 1000 converts to kilowatt-hours per year.

Step 16: Calculate Lighting Cost Saved

This Step calculates the dollar value of the lighting energy saved.

[Find the average cost of electricity, including demand charges, from your local utility.] Multiply the cost by the lighting energy saved to arrive at lighting cost saved.

Lighting Energy Savings Graphs

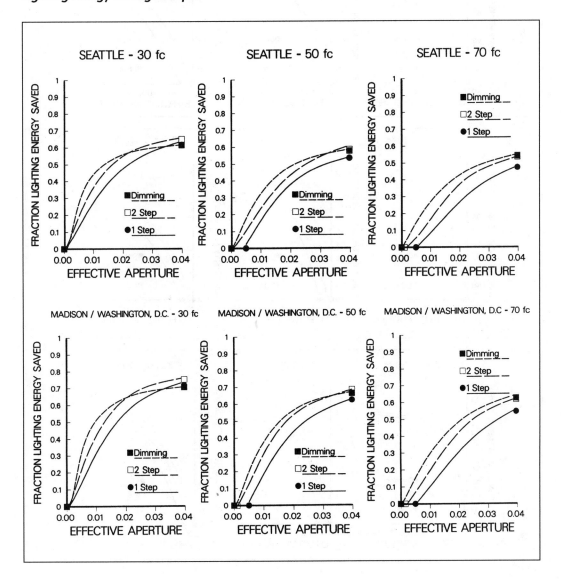

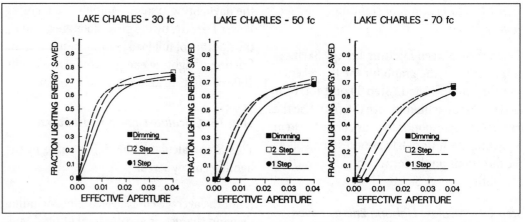

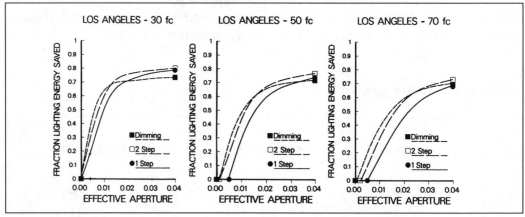

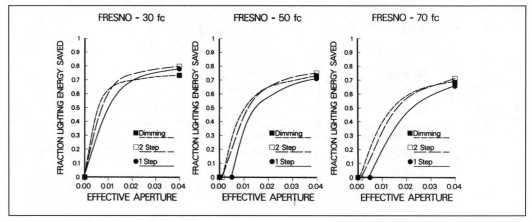

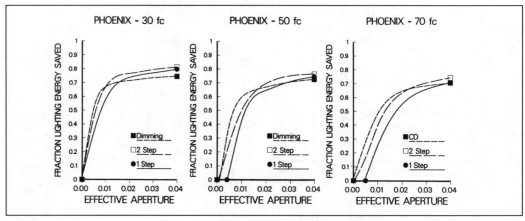

WORKSHEET 4

Note: See [Lighting Savings Worksheet, pages 68–70] for more information and an example of the use of this form. Some "Step" numbers refer to previous Form information.

STEP 13: Find Full Load Lighting Hours

The default value corresponds to typical office working hours, as shown in the schedule in [the previous section]. If that schedule differs greatly from the schedule in your building, refer to [Appendix E] for the procedure for finding your full-load operating hours. Otherwise, use the default value.

Full load lighting hours = $\boxed{\text{2600}}$ hrs.
(default: 2600)

STEP 14: Find Fraction of Lighting Energy Saved

Use the graph from [the Lighting Energy Savings Graphs, pages 69–70] corresponding to your Representative Location (Step 1) and your Desired Average Illuminance (Step 2). Enter graph at the EA value (Step 12) corresponding to your skylight design. Draw a line up to the curve for your Daylighting Control System (Step 2), then across to the fraction of lighting energy saved. Enter the fraction below.

EA = 0.022 (Step 12)
Fraction of Lighting Energy Saved $\boxed{0.55}$

STEP 15: Calculate Lighting Energy Saved

$$\frac{\text{LPD (Step 2)}}{1000} \times \underset{\text{(Step 2)}}{\text{Gross Floor Area}} \times \underset{\text{(Step 13)}}{\text{Full Load Hours}} \times \underset{\text{(Step 14)}}{\text{Fraction Saved}} = \text{Lighting Energy Saved (kWh)}$$

$$\frac{\boxed{1.5}}{1000} \times \boxed{10{,}000} \times \boxed{2{,}600} \times \boxed{0.55} = \boxed{21{,}450} \text{ kWh/yr}$$

STEP 16: Calculate Lighting Cost Saved

. . . If actual electricity costs are not known, [contact your local utility for a current rate schedule].

$$\underset{\text{(Step 15)}}{\text{Lighting Energy Saved}} \times \underset{\text{($/kWh)}}{\text{Average Electricity Cost}} = \underset{\text{kWh/yr}}{\boxed{21{,}450}} \times \underset{\text{$/kWh}}{\boxed{0.073}} = \underset{\text{$/yr}}{\boxed{\$1{,}566.}}$$

WORKSHEET 5

Cooling Calculation Worksheet

This Worksheet helps you to estimate the cooling energy and cost effects from your skylight system. These effects result primarily from reduced internal gains when the electric lighting is automatically turned off by the daylight control system, and reflect the additional solar heat gains that enter through the skylight. These effects should be added to the lighting cost savings calculated in Step 16, to arrive at the combined savings.

In general, the cooling effects will be small compared to the lighting savings. It is even possible for the cooling effects to be negative, i.e., there is an increase in cooling costs. This would indicate that the skylight system may be oversized. If, however, the combined lighting and cooling savings are still substantial, it indicates that the lighting savings far outweigh the increased cooling costs due to skylighting.

Instructions

Step 17: Note Representative City

As in the earlier calculations, a representative city is used here. Check off the representative city that you selected in Step 1. This is for reference when performing the following cooling calculations.

Step 18: Find Coefficients for Representative Cooling City

The numbers in the table are used in the next step to calculate the cooling energy effects for the representative city. Circle the numbers for the cooling city you have chosen.

Step 19: Calculate Cooling Energy and Cost Effects

Perform the calculation as shown, using the numbers circled in Step 18. The Cooling Energy Effect is found first. This is multiplied by the Average Electricity Cost to find the Cooling Cost Effect. You should use the same electricity cost as was used in Step 16. A negative value is an added cooling cost; a positive value represents a saving.

As discussed above, the Cooling Cost Effect should be added to the Lighting Cost Saved to obtain total savings.

WORKSHEET 5

Note: See [Cooling Calculation Worksheet, page 72] for more information and an example of the use of this form. Some "Step" numbers refer to previous Form information.

STEP 17: Note Representative City

This calculation makes use of the same representative cities selected in Step 1. Check off your selection again here, for reference:

☐ Seattle, WA
☐ Madison, WI
☑ Washington, DC
☐ Lake Charles, LA
☐ Los Angeles, CA
☐ Fresno, CA
☐ Phoenix, AZ

STEP 18: Find Coefficients for Representative Cooling City

	B1	B2
Seattle, WA	0.19	11.5
Madison, WI	0.31	16.6
Washington, DC	0.42	21.1
Lake Charles, LA	0.66	30.8
Los Angeles, CA	0.53	28.1
Fresno, CA	0.51	36.9
Phoenix, AZ	0.68	47.3

STEP 19: Calculate Cooling Energy and Cost Effects

B1 (Step 18)		Fraction Saved (Step 14)		LPD (Step 2)		Temporary Value #1
0.42	×	0.55	×	1.5	=	0.347

B2 (Step 18)		Effective Aperture (Step 12)		Skylight Effic. (Step 5)		Temporary Value #2
21.1	×	0.022	÷	1.02	=	0.455

Temporary Value #1		Temporary Value #2		Unit Cooling Energy Effect		Gross Floor Area		Cooling Energy Effect
0.347	−	0.455	=	−.108	×	10,000	=	−1,080.
(from above)		(from above)		kWh/yrsf		(Step 2)		kWh/yr

				Cooling Energy Effect		Average Electricity Cost		Cooling Cost Effect
				−1,080	×	0.073	=	−79.
				kWh/yr		(Step 18)		kWh/yrsf
				(from above)		$/kWh		

LIMITS OF ANALYSIS

The estimation method contained in the Worksheets and presented in this [section] was derived from an extensive body of computer analysis. (The technical basis for the work is contained in a series of papers published by Lawrence Berkeley Laboratory. . . .) As with any such analysis effort, a set of common assumptions were used to establish a base case building. From this base, the most important variables were systematically changed, such as Effective Aperture and Lighting Power Density. The results of this body of computer simulations were distilled into the graphs and procedures presented in these Guidelines.

In choosing the base case and the variables for this study, care was taken to make assumptions that are broadly applicable to typical commercial buildings. As a result, the information presented is valid for many, if not most, commercial skylighting applications. For buildings that differ significantly from the typical buildings used in this study, however, the results may be less meaningful.

These results are generally valid when the following conditions are true:

- Climate conditions similar to those in the representative cities.
- Occupancy schedules and characteristics similar to office occupancies, i.e., daytime operation, ordinary internal heat gains, ordinary lighting requirements. See [Lighting Savings Worksheet, pages 68–70] for more information.
- Generally even lighting requirements, with no major differences in task illuminance.
- Flat and low-slope roof systems (<4:12 pitch).
- Roughly even skylight distribution across roof.
- No significant shading from adjacent buildings or vegetation.

- Skylight spacing less than or equal to 1.5 times ceiling height.
- Effective aperture less than 0.05.
- Skylight glazings that are at least partially diffusing.
- Daylighting controls for lighting.

Buildings that differ greatly from these conditions may require a detailed analysis to accurately estimate their skylighting performance.

The following [section] presents additional technical information on other energy considerations for skylighting, such as heating load and peak electricity demand. That information may cause you to adjust your skylight design to a different optimum than was selected with these Worksheets. If that is the case, you can return to the Worksheets and work through your new design comparing it to the original.

DAYLIGHT ECONOMIC ANALYSIS

The preceding sections presented a set of worksheets that can be used to estimate the lighting and cooling energy and cost savings from skylighting. This savings information is important, because it shows that skylighting reduces operating costs, in addition to its other benefits to occupants. For many applications, this may be sufficient to justify using skylights. To make a complete economic evaluation, however, requires more information.

The savings estimates derived above assumed a simple, flat rate for electricity. . . . however, utility rate structures are more complicated than flat rates, and may require more detailed breakdowns of energy consumption to accurately estimate. This becomes even more so when all the energy effects of skylighting are included, such as heating energy and peak demand changes. . . . [A] complete analysis of energy and cost savings could require detailed computer simulations. . . .

In addition to cost savings, or "benefits," from skylighting, we need to know the "costs" of the skylighting system. These costs include two primary elements: the costs of the skylights and of the daylighting controls, along with the associated labor to install them. There are also other costs that may be included, such as maintenance costs or long-term replacement costs. There may also be associated savings, such as increased life of lighting equipment.

The primary costs can be accurately predicted by the building contractor or hardware supplier; the "softer" costs must be estimated as best they can.

Once the costs and benefits of skylighting have been quantified, they can be compared to each other, and also to the costs and benefits of alternative systems. The easiest comparison is the "simple payback," which is the first cost divided by the annual savings, and is a crude measure of the number of years it will take for the savings to pay back the initial investment. More sophisticated analyses take into account the time value of money, esti-mates of general inflation and energy cost inflation, and lifetime of the equipment until replacement. A complete analysis would compare the life cycle costs and benefits of a "no skylighting" design with one or more skylighting and daylight control systems. This would provide clear guidance in selecting the final skylighting system.

A complete economic analysis can quantify the dollar benefits and costs of skylighting; it cannot quantify the less tangible, but nevertheless valuable, benefits of skylights such as occupant satisfaction and delight. This is left to the judgment and sensibility of the owner, designer, contractor, and occupants. In a well-designed system, these benefits can far outweigh the straight economic benefits.

[Note: A thorough discussion of this calculation methodology is presented in the American Architectural Manufacturers Association (AAMA) Skylight Handbook. For additional information, it can be obtained from: AAMA, 1827 Walden Office Square, Suite 550, Schaumburg, IL 60173. Telephone: (847) 303-5664. E-mail: aamanet.org.]

5.2 COMPUTER PROGRAMS

Computer programs have existed for practitioners to investigate various aspects of daylighting since programmable calculators first became available. Over the years, the cost of hardware has been steadily decreasing while the speed and storage have been increasing. Several simulation programs are discussed that many practitioners who regularly design and integrate daylighting strategies into buildings implement at strategic phases of the design process.

More general information on a wide range of tools is displayed later in the text in the design tools survey section compiled by Lawrence National Berkeley Laboratory.

RADIANCE

The Windows and Lighting Program at the Lawrence Berkeley National Laboratory in Berkeley, California, is charged by the U.S. Department of Energy with developing new technologies for the energy-efficient use of daylight and electric lighting in buildings. One of the group's major thrusts is the development of design tools to help architects and engineers produce better building designs using existing technology.

One such project is the collection of lighting simulation and analysis routines called RADIANCE. RADIANCE has been developed in a

UNIX environment over a period of years and consists of more than 100 separate routines that provide numerous functions and capabilities for lighting and daylighting design and research.

RADIANCE is an advanced lighting simulation program that uses a ray-tracing methodology to accurately predict the behavior of light in spaces. Users describe the geometry of the space and the characteristics of surface materials and light sources. The program then uses the mathematics of the physical behavior of light to calculate luminances in the scene. The output is a photo-realistic color image that contains numeric predictions of light levels at any point in the scene.

The ability to view an illuminated space without having to physically construct it is of immeasurable value not only to designers but to researchers as well. The RADIANCE program has the potential to promote energy-efficient lighting design by demonstrating the visual effect of new lamp technologies, daylighting, and intelligent controls. Many innovative lighting designs have been rejected by clients who thought the modest energy consumption would result in dark, unrentable spaces. A proven tool for predicting visibility in a form everyone can understand, "a picture" could allay such doubts and clear the path to more efficient and reliable designs. As computers become faster and cheaper, and as computer-aided design becomes more common, design studies will rely increasingly on simulation to explore innovative architectural and lighting solutions.

RADIANCE can be used at any point in a design process. It needs only a single light source and a single surface to calculate an image. Of course, the more detail the user provides, the more accurate and interesting the final image. The user describes the color and other optical properties of each surface. Typically, a library of standard materials (e.g., wood, copper, glass) is maintained. Surface textures and patterns can also be applied. An easy technique to improve the realism of the final image is to digitize photos of fabrics or other patterns and apply them in a scene. Textures are defined mathematically, and patterns can be created this way as well; for example, a very realistic wood grain pattern can be created simply with a function. Next, the user adds photometric data for electric light sources and, if daylight modeling is desired, also provides time of day, latitude, longitude, and calendar day. Once the calculation of the final scene is complete, the user specifies viewpoint, exposure, and other parameters for the image and lets the software work for several hours (very complex images can take 24 hours to produce). This process can be done in batch mode in the background, keeping the machine free for other tasks. To help establish viewpoints and to spot mistakes in the model, RADIANCE has a lower grade imaging utility that is interactive. As it progressively refines an image on the screen, it allows the user to manipulate view parameters or check lighting values.

The final output is an image that can be displayed on the screen or copied onto video, paper, or film. Sequences of stills can be captured on video for animated walk-through. In addition, any kind of lighting data can be obtained, and these can be plotted or otherwise manipulated in any manner.

The RADIANCE program has been used to produce synthetic images of many indoor and outdoor lighting situations, with an emphasis on calculations that were previously considered too difficult to resolve with other methods. These include daylit office spaces with penetrating beam sunlight and venetian blinds, building atria, and rooms with many glass and metal surfaces (see Figures 5.2.1 to 5.2.2C).

COMPUTATIONAL METHODOLOGY

Accurately modeling the behavior of light in real environments with thousands of reflective surfaces is a challenge to current computational techniques. RADIANCE uses a technique called ray tracing to follow light backward from an observer to the light source(s) of a hypothetical scene. Once a path has been found, the luminance associated with each ray is computed from the candle power distribution of the light source and the reflective properties of the intervening surfaces (see Figure 5.2.3). Accuracy is obtained with a computational model that handles many types of surfaces (e.g., matte, shiny, or glass) and objects of high geometric complexity. With the use of advanced sorting techniques, scenes containing thousands of objects can be rendered efficiently. Unlike other relighting programs that are limited to calculations of illuminance in purely diffuse environments, RADIANCE accurately handles reflections from shiny surfaces, permitting the realistic rendition of highlights. The lighting model has been further enhanced with the calculation of interreflections between surfaces and contributions from spatially distributed sources such as the sky.

A synthetic image consists of thousands of pixels (picture elements), and several rays are needed to compute the luminance value at each one. A high-resolution image therefore requires millions of computations. On a microcomputer workstation, an image may take several central processing unit (CPU) hours to generate; thus, jobs are usually run overnight.

Although the real-time generation of high-resolution images is beyond the capability of today's workstations, low-resolution images can be completed interactively using a technique called "adaptive refinement." One of the RADIANCE programs uses this technique to trace rays continuously on a color workstation, progressively increasing the resolution of the displayed image while the user looks on. During the typical calculation, the display evolves at a rate of 50 pixels per second and represents far more information than could be obtained from a physical model or a hand calculator through conventional photometry. The user can interrupt the program at any time to move the viewpoint, adjust the exposure, or display individual luminance values. In a few minutes, an experienced designer can

Figure 5.2.1 Radiance output showing an interior space and the corresponding direct-beam penetration.

Figure 5.2.2A Radiance output showing an interior view with unprotected fenestration and the resulting shadow lines from window mullions.

Figure 5.2.2B Photorealistic output of a large-volume atrium space.

Figure 5.2.2C Interior space showing the window wall, direct-beam sun penetration, and room furnishings.

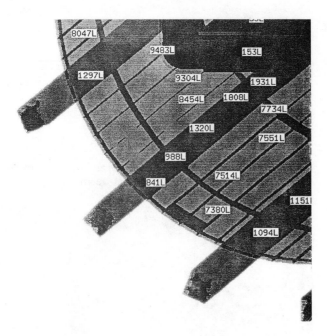

Figure 5.2.3 Floor plan showing lux without fenestration control. *(Courtesy of Greg Cunningham, AIA.)*

get a good idea of how the environment will look in a final rendering or in real life.

LIMITATIONS

RADIANCE is not a user-friendly program in its current form. The first step is creating the scene geometry. For example, walls, windows, and furniture are described. This is ideally done with a three-dimensional drawing program. However, RADIANCE works only with text files. In other words, a cube must be given to RADIANCE as a text field containing the numeric spatial coordinates of the cube's six surfaces. Technicians are currently developing software to translate commercial CAD files for RADIANCE input, and several of them are now available. Typically, a user will convert the CAD file to a text format and then translate this text to a RADIANCE text file; this does not free the user from interacting with RADIANCE text, because some fine tuning of the geometry may be desired and additional data must be added to the CAD output. Information about materials, lights, and geographic location are not included in the base CAD file. Also, many CAD packages have a limited range of geometric forms that they can easily create; RADIANCE not only handles any kind of geometry but also contains many tools to easily create complex forms. Users may find it highly desirable to leave difficult shapes for RADIANCE and not attempt them with the CAD software.

Because most CAD packages handle strictly metric data, it is necessary to manually apply optical properties to every surface drawing in CAD. (Some drawing packages allow additional attributes to be added to surfaces; this means a material code number could be included in the CAD text file to be used by RADIANCE.) Once the CAD geometry has been translated for RADIANCE, materials must be created and applied to surfaces. This requires working with the text form of a scene that the user is accustomed to viewing in three dimensions, which makes exact identification of specific parts of the scene difficult. Some vendors are working on interfaces to ease this process. A functional prototype for an interface that helps the user "map" materials onto surfaces in the three-dimensional model is available. This interface also provides a more intuitive way to create materials; for example, colors are selected from a color wheel rather than described by their red-green-blue numeric values.

Lights must also be placed in the scene. This requires describing their photometric properties and locating them correctly. There are some tools to assist in entering the data, but complex lighting conditions can require considerable lighting expertise. In terms of placing simple sources when working with a CAD program, the user can place dummy "markers" in the three-dimensional file for replacement by RADIANCE with something more appropriate.

PREREQUISITES

Because of the compelling images RADIANCE produces and because of its potential to increase one's overall understanding of the behavior of light in spaces, RADIANCE is an invaluable tool for anyone involved in architectural or lighting design. However, it takes a tremendous commitment to become a RADIANCE user, at least until significant improvement has been made in the area of program's ease of use. At a minimum, you must (1) be familiar with the UNIX operating system, (2) be familiar with a UNIX text editor, (3) have a reasonable understanding of photometries, and (4) have a UNIX-running computer available for long time periods. Designers who answer no to any of these and who want RADIANCE only for its graphic output should carefully consider the difficulties involved. It takes a lot of work to create a RADIANCE image, but the results are rich with information. If you do not need all of that information, perhaps such a complex program is not the best choice for you. On the other hand, others will find the effort is worth it.

HOW TO OBTAIN A COPY

To obtain a copy, write to:

Windows and Lighting Program
Building 90-3111
Lawrence Berkeley National Laboratory
University of California
Berkeley, CA 94720
http://radsite.lbl.gov/radiance/home.html

SUPERLITE

The SUPERLITE program is a state-of-the-art computer program for predicting illuminance in buildings. The program addresses the need to accurately model geometrically complex fenestration systems in architecturally complex building spaces.

This program's free geometric system is capable of calculating illuminance levels for virtually any building configuration that can be defined by walls and windows of trapezoidal geometry. This allows the program to model complicated building shapes, such as A-frame structures, L-shaped rooms with internal obstructions (e.g., partitions), and external obstructions such as overhangs or adjacent buildings.

In addition to calculating daylighting levels from diffuse sources of outdoor illumination, the sky and ground, SUPERLITE accounts for the effect of direct sunlight in the room. The window glazing can be either clear or diffusing glass with a diffusing sheer curtain or shade.

The solar and weather data input for the program can be supplied in three ways. The first option allows the user to supply the appropriate sky condition. The sky models available in this program are (1) the uniform sky; (2) the CIE standard overcast sky; and (3) the CIE standard clear sky, with or without direct sun. The second option involves specifying geographic data, such as latitude and longitude, and the time and date of the simulation using the stipulated sky conditions. This option allows a series of simulations to be conducted for given times of the day and year. The third option requires specifying the solar location under predetermined sky conditions.

Illuminance data are calculated for nodal points on arbitrary work planes located and oriented as specified by the user. These data can be provided numerically in terms of illuminance level or daylight factor in tabular format. Analyses are conducted for different sky conditions, different hours, and various times of the year to study the annual performance of fenestration systems combined with daylighting.

CALCULATIONAL METHODOLOGY

SUPERLITE adopts a very detailed point-by-point illumination calculation for the date, time, and sky conditions specified. The daylight illumination on any arbitrary work surface inside a room depends on three quantities: the direct illumination from the sky and sun, illumination from external reflections, and illuminance from internal reflections. To determine the contribution of each of these quantities, the luminance distribution of the sky and each internal and external reflector must be known.

The luminance distribution of the sky depends on weather conditions, the time of day, and the time of year. It is estimated from an empirical formula. The luminance distribution of any external or internal surface depends on both the quantity of light received from the sky and reflections from surrounding surfaces. For internal surfaces, this includes light from the sky and external reflections, which is attenuated on transmission through windows. By calculating light-exchange factors for each surface, one can calculate the light impinging from sky and surrounding reflectors on any surface.

LIMITATIONS

Like RADIANCE, SUPERLITE is not a user-friendly program in its current form. The entire geometry of the space to be analyzed is defined in terms of numerical coordinates. The input file is a string of numbers without any explanations. Hopefully, in the near future, several CAD interfaces will be available.

In the present stage of development, SUPERLITE has a number of limitations. The first limitation is the assumption that all reflected light is assumed to be perfectly diffuse, whereas some building surfaces may be semi-specular. A second assumption is that the luminous flux entering a room has a uniform spectral composition and that its reflection by surfaces is uniform over the entire visible spectrum. Also, the modeling of the sky is limited to the three theoretical sky distributions described previously; therefore, partly cloudy skies cannot be simulated.

Typically, these limitations are not of great concern for normal daylighting studies; however, the capabilities of the program are being expanded to allow modeling of everchanging design strategies and system technologies for which these limitations would be significant.

PREREQUISITES

SUPERLITE is a valuable tool for anyone involved in architectural or lighting design. However, it takes a significant commitment to become a SUPERLITE user, at least in the present form. At a minimum, one must (1) be familiar with the operating system, (2) be familiar with the compilation procedure for compiling FORTRAN routines, and (3) have a reasonable understanding of the three-dimensional geometrical coordinate system. Designers who require reliable lighting predictions for a complex space, without spending a lot of money, can resort to SUPERLITE. Also, SUPERLITE does not directly produce any graphic output. The user is able to take the information from SUPERLITE to any other plotting software for development of contour plotting.

HOW TO OBTAIN A COPY

To obtain a copy, write to:

Windows and Daylighting Group
Building 90-3111
Lawrence Berkeley National Laboratory
University of California
Berkeley, CA 94720
http://windows.lbl.gov/software/software.html

DOE2

DOE2 (also DOE2.2, DOE2.1E, DOE2.1D, etc.) was specifically developed for evaluating the energy performance of buildings on an hour-by-hour basis and is one of only a few detailed building energy simulation programs that incorporates detailed hourly daylighting analysis.

For many years, architects and engineers have used scaled models, hand calculator programs, and sophisticated mainframe computer programs to determine levels of interior daylight for different building configurations. However, none of these tools determines the annual energy savings from daylighting, information that could have an important effect on design decisions.

Difficulties were overcome by adding daylighting simulation algorithms to the original DOE2.1B version in about 1982. Taken into account are such factors as window size, glass transmittance, inside surface reflectances, sun control devices such as blinds and overhangs, and the luminance distribution of the sky.

DOE2 daylighting calculations are essentially used to perform energy analysis of buildings with energy savings potentials by using daylight through various types of building apertures.

When thermal zones of the building under analysis are defined, daylighting elements such as window location, glass transmittance, interior and exterior shades, other external shades, reflectances of walls, roof, floor, and so on are identified. Based on the type of visual task of the space, required illumination level is prescribed for the space. The control scheme for the lighting zone (e.g., stepped or continuously dimmed) is specified. The thermal zone can be divided into one or two lighting zones controlled by individual lighting sensors (reference points). During an hourly simulation, depending on the available daylight in the specified reference point and daylighting controls, electric lighting is either dimmed or switched off. The direct energy savings achieved by reducing the hours of operation of lights and the cooling energy savings from the reduction of the internal heat gain (from lights) is corrected and accounted by DOE2. Hence, on an annual basis, the user can predict the energy savings associated with daylighting.

COMPUTATIONAL METHODOLOGY

The DOE2 daylighting model, in conjunction with the thermal loads analysis, determines the energy impact of daylighting strategies based on hour-by-hour analysis of daylight availability, site conditions, window management in response to sun control and glare, and various lighting control strategies.

The daylighting calculation has three main stages. In the first stage, a preprocessor calculates daylight factors for later use in the hourly loads calculation. The user specifies the coordinates of one or two reference points in a space. DOE2 then integrates over the area of each window to obtain the contribution of direct light from the window to illuminance at the reference points and the contribution of light that reflects from the surfaces before reaching the reference point. Taken into account are such factors as the luminance distribution of the sky, window size, orientation, glass transmittance, and internal and external shades. The calculation is carried out for standard CIE clear and overcast sky conditions for a series of 20 different solar altitude and azimuth values covering the range of annual sun positions in the sky vault. Similarly, daylight factors for glare are also calculated and stored.

In the second stage, an hourly daylighting calculation is performed every hour that the sun is up. The illuminance from each window is found by interpolating the stored daylight factors using the current-hour exterior horizontal illuminance. If the glare control option has been specified, the program will automatically close window blinds or drapes to decrease glare below a predefined comfort level. A similar option uses window shading devices to automatically control solar heat gain.

In the last stage, the program simulates the lighting control system (which may be either stepped or continuously dimmed) to determine the electrical lighting energy needed to make up the difference between the daylighting level and the design illuminance. Finally, the zone lighting electrical requirements are passed to the thermal calculation portion of the simulation, which determines hourly heating and cooling loads.

LIMITATIONS

Because DOE2 interpolates daylight factor values from precalculated solar positions for each hour of the day, a small amount of error is associated with the interpolation. The interior reflected component of the daylight factor in DOE2 is calculated based on the split flux principle. In this method, the daylight transmitted by the windows is split into two parts: a downward flux, which falls on the floor and the portions of the walls below the imaginary horizontal plane passing through the center of the window; and an upward flux, which strikes the ceiling and portions of the walls above the window midplane. This split flux principle works well when the window geometry is simple and the reflectance variation between the surfaces is not extreme. However, this methodology cannot reliably predict the interreflected com-

ponent if the window has special devices for reflecting light, such as light shelves. Also, the luminous distribution of the sky is calculated based on the cloud cover, cloud type, and solar radiation using an empirical relationship. This calculated daylight level may be different from the actual daylight available.

PREREQUISITES

The DOE2 daylighting program is suitable for professionals who want to analyze the impact of daylighting controls on the overall energy consumption of the building. Because it is coupled with the energy analysis program, the user has to learn to use the program as a whole rather than just for the daylighting analysis portion. DOE2 has its own input syntax, and learning it might be time-consuming.

HOW TO OBTAIN A COPY

To obtain a copy, write to:

Building Energy Simulation Group
Lawrence Berkeley National Laboratory
University of California
Berkeley, CA 94720
Telephone (510) 486-5711
http://gundog.lbl.gov/

PC versions are available from several private vendors.

5.3 DAYLIGHTING DESIGN TOOL SURVEY*

Other design tools and calculation methodologies exist to evaluate daylight-related issues. Table 5.3.1 identifies many that are

available to the designer, along with a brief description of the attributes of each tool.

---

*The table in this section is reprinted with permission from Lawrence Berkeley National Laboratory.

TABLE 5.3.1 Tools Available to the Designer

TOOL	DESCRIPTION	ADDITIONAL INFORMATION
ADELINE	ADELINE is an integrated lighting design computer tool that provides architects and engineers with accurate information about the behavior and the performance of indoor lighting systems. Both natural and electric lighting problems can be solved in simple rooms or the most complex spaces.	Software request: Windows and Daylighting Group, Building 90, Room 3111, Berkeley, CA 94720 http://radsite.lbl.gov/adeline/HOME.html
ENERGY 10	ENERGY-10 software is a design tool that analyzes—and illustrates—the energy and cost savings that can be achieved through more than a dozen sustainable design strategies. Hourly energy simulations help you quantify, assess, and clearly depict the benefits of daylighting, passive solar heating, natural ventilation, well-insulated envelopes, better windows, lighting systems, mechanical equipment, and more.	Sustainable Buildings Industry Council (202) 628-7400 sbic@sbicouncil.org
Buildings Design Advisor (BDA)	A suite of tools for schematic design.	http://kmp.lbl.gov/bda
Optics	A software program for analyzing the optical properties of glazing systems.	http://windows.lbl.gov/materials/optics/default.html
Window	Analyzes window, thermal, and optical performance.	http://windows.lbl.gov/software/window/window.html
LUMEN-Micro 6	Analyzes complex interior lighting systems, including daylight, direct/indirect lighting, mixed and aimed luminaires.	Lighting Technologies (720) 891-0030 lighting.technologies.com
FORM Z	Analyzes 2D/3D forms and is useful when performing shadow studies.	formz.com

5.4 PHYSICAL MODELING

The physics of illumination is such that light behaves exactly the same way in a model as it does in a full-scale building. If a scaled model duplicates the full-scale building, and if it is tested under analogous sky conditions, the results in the model will be identical to those of the full-scale building. The technical issues surrounding daylighting design do not require the use of expensive equipment or excessive data analysis to answer a simple question (see Figure 5.4.1).

Physical models can be built and studied at all stages of the design process and on all budgets. Fundamentally, daylighting models are design tools that answer questions not only of daylighting issues but of many other aspects of building design.

Design options can be explored through physical modeling by changing one variable at a time, such as aperture size, placement, or orientation. The most desirable conditions can be recog-

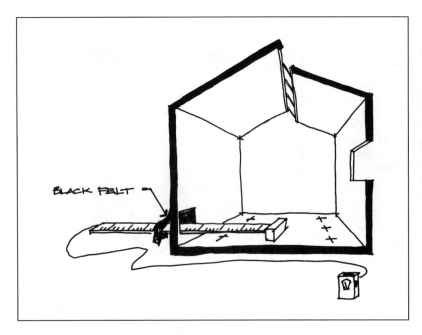

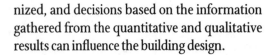

Figure 5.4.1 Model test with inexpensive hand-held light meter.

Figure 5.4.2 Sky simulator facility measuring 24 ft in diameter allows architects, researchers, and students to accurately test building models. It is located on the U.C. Berkeley campus. The facility is operated by the Building Technologies Program at Lawrence Berkeley National Laboratory. *(Photograph courtesy of Lawrence Berkeley National Laboratory, Berkeley, California.)*

nized, and decisions based on the information gathered from the quantitative and qualitative results can influence the building design.

Model simulations can be performed under an artificial sky, where conditions can be held constant, or under the actual sky. Outdoor testing is the least expensive but is often more time-consuming because of unpredictable sky conditions. Indoor testing, on the other hand, requires an artificial sky or a heliodon. The artificial sky simulator is able to produce a controlled lighting environment. The light will simulate natural sky conditions in a controlled environment. After the initial expense, testing is quite simple. Several artificial sky domes exist throughout the country. The University of California at Berkeley has one type of artificial sky dome (see Figure 5.4.2). Many designers have found it very beneficial to make use of the facility early in the design process.

Model building is a routine activity in most architectural offices. Only slight modifications to this normal practice are necessary for using these models for daylight studies. The instrumentation required to get the quantitative measurements are simple and usually inexpen-

sive. There is also an opportunity for qualitative evaluation through visual observation, photography, and video recording. The subsequent analysis of photographs typically satisfies the modeling objectives. Simple and inexpensive hand-held meters can provide adequate illuminance data for analysis. Several things can be accomplished through model studies:

- They can be constructed for visual observations and aesthetic analysis.
- Comparisons can be made between modifications of designs.
- Window areas can be changed to test impacts of usable daylight, as can different types of wall treatments.
- Illumination levels resulting from different design schemes can be compiled and used to project energy savings (see Figures 5.4.3 and 5.4.4).

SKY CONDITIONS

The type of sky conditions that will exist at a site should be understood. Appendix C graph-

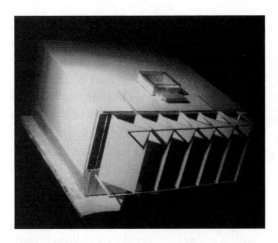

Figure 5.4.3 Direct-beam model test.

Figure 5.4.4 Direct-beam model test.

ically presents weather data, including cloud cover, for five different climate zones throughout the United States.

The illumination produced by natural sky conditions tends to change constantly. Interior illumination values will not be very meaningful if the sky changes significantly between tests. It is recommended that coincident light levels be recorded during a model testing session, both inside the model and outside the model at a horizontal surface. This will give you the opportunity to normalize illumination levels in the model relative to the instantaneous sky conditions.

Model testing under partly cloudy conditions is not recommended because of the rapid changes in sky conditions. A clear or uniformly cloudy condition is more suitable.

There are five types of sky conditions: uniform sky, overcast sky, clear sky, partly cloudy sky, and direct sunlight.

UNIFORM SKY

The uniform sky provides an equal amount of illuminance in all directions. Hand calculation or an artificial sky simulator is best suited to test under uniform sky conditions.

OVERCAST SKY

Under overcast sky conditions, water particles diffusely refract and reflect all wavelengths of sunlight. As a result, the zenith is three times brighter than the horizon.

CLEAR SKY

The light is diffuse because it is refracted and reflected as the sunlight passes through the atmosphere. Under these conditions, the sky is brighter along the horizon and less intense at the zenith.

PARTLY CLOUDY SKY

The illuminance level varies depending on the position of the clouds relative to the sun. Higher horizontal illuminance may result under a partly cloudy sky than under a clear sky.

DIRECT SUNLIGHT

Direct sunlight is perpendicular to the surface. It is largely viewed that direct sunlight is too intense for task illumination.

To simulate the effect of daylighting for various times of the day and year with the sun in a different position with respect to the window wall, a solution is to put the model on a tilt table (see Figure 5.4.5). Adjustments are made to the tilt table with respect to the sun to simulate solar penetration at various times of the year using a sundial to verify the simulated date and time. The position of the sun in the sky is measured by its "altitude" angle (angle from horizon) and its "azimuth" angle (horizontal angle east or west of south). The solar azimuth and altitude are dictated by the site latitude, day of the year, and time of the day.

Tilting a daylighting model to simulate different months and hours may cause distorted results if the window sees different portions of the sky vault and ground as it is tilted. When

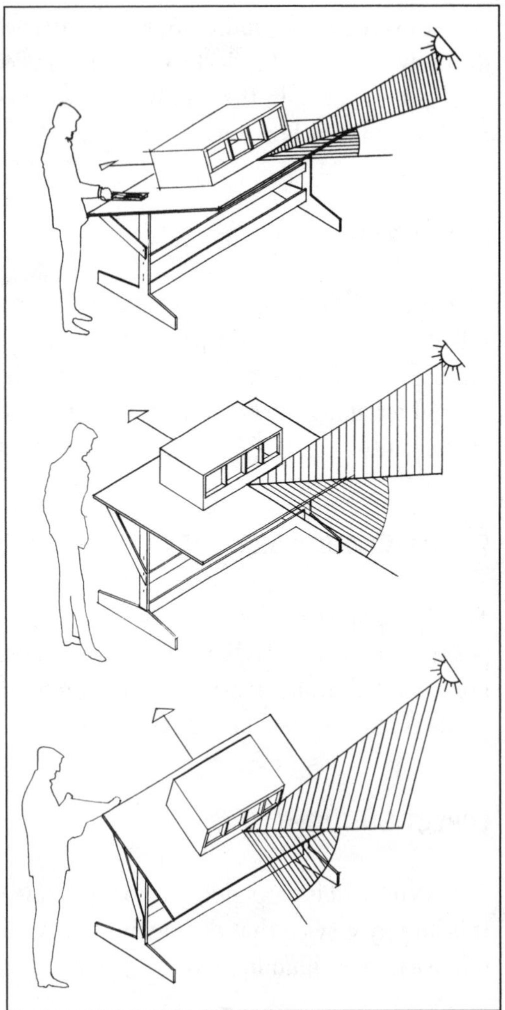

the measurements are made in the winter and the model is tilted downward to simulate a higher summer sun, the amount of error increases the more the model is tilted. This can be minimized by doing the measurements on a rooftop or in the summer when the sun is high. In this case, the model is tilted upward to simulate the low winter sun. This will be much more accurate when enough of a ground base is constructed to act as a horizon.

An advantage of simulating daylighting with models under summer sky conditions instead of during the winter is that the amount of error is not only smaller but is also constant for all of the studies. Unfortunately, models with skylights cannot be tilted to simulate the time of year, because they receive light from the entire hemispherical sky vault. In this case, tilting a skylight model decreases the available sky vault and produces incorrect results.

When windows or clerestories are facing different directions and tilting is desired, the daylighting levels can be measured separately for each orientation and the results added together. The windows or clerestories not facing the direction under study are covered with opaque black to account for light lost through the window to the outside. This is repeated for each of the building orientations with windows or clerestories. The individual results are added together. A grid system of light measurement points is necessary to do this with accuracy. After light meter readings are completed, a diagram can be plotted to illustrate the relation between the amount of light and the building cross section. Peaks and valleys of the light level can be located and altered by changes in the solar control design. By graphing the light levels of different options on the same graph, one can easily make a comparison.

Figure 5.4.5 Tilt table simulating different seasons.

SCALES

Models for studying daylight can be constructed at any convenient scale. Generally, it is difficult to reproduce details accurately in very small models, and the relative size of the illumination meter probe to be used may cause excessive absorption and reflection when inserted into a small model. However, a small-scale model is useful at an early stage of design development. Typically, 1/16 or 1/8 in. per 1 ft is a practical scale to provide a sense of massing, solar access, reflection, or obstruction of daylight. Mid- and full-scale models are used for detail refinements. At 1 in. per ft to full-scale mock-ups, effective photography analysis can be accomplished. At mid to full scale, critical daylighting details are evaluated in accordance with the building's desired performance. A scale of 1 in. per foot also produces a convenient-size model for studying a room. This scale may be too large to handle conveniently if several rooms or adjacent parts of the building must be included in the study. A scale of 1/2 or 3/8 in. may be used if care is exercised in construction. Models at lesser scales are difficult to build to scale and to measure using available light-sensing cells (see Figures 5.4.6 and 5.4.7).

Figure 5.4.6 Researchers test a scale model of a hotel atrium using light sensors linked to a data collection program. *(Photograph courtesy of Lawrence Berkeley National Laboratory, Berkeley, California.)*

MATERIALS

Materials of the model are important only in terms of their transparency or opacity (light transmitted or blocked), their reflectance (light reflected or absorbed), and their texture (glossy or diffusing).

The illuminance levels may be affected by the reflectance of the interior surfaces and furnishings. The reflectance of the surfaces and furnishings must be recognized, but the accuracy of representation should be determined at each stage of the design process. A method of approximating reflectance with a light meter is described in Figure 5.4.8.

The texture of materials affects the quality and quantity of light distributed in a space.

Color is of no significance if it is measured with a properly corrected light meter. These

Figure 5.4.7 Researchers select a series of roof shading designs in a hotel atrium to evaluate solar access properties. *(Photograph courtesy of Lawrence Berkeley National Laboratory, Berkeley, California.)*

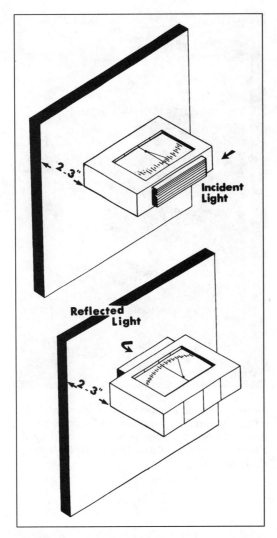

Figure 5.4.8 Method to estimate reflectance values.

instruments do not differentiate between colors but measure only the quantity of light reflected from these surfaces. Thus, gray paint or dark and light patterns can be used to simulate colored surfaces, provided a reflectometer is available for measuring and watching the paint's reflectance properties.

Walls can be built of plywood, foamboard, or cardboard and painted appropriately. Foamboards are often not completely opaque and must be painted or covered with foil or some other opaque material to prevent the penetration of unwanted light. The construction joints and material opacity are two sources of light leaks. Window glass can be simulated in the model with real glass, or for relatively simple

openings, glass may be altogether omitted from the model and a multiplication factor applied to the measured illumination levels to compensate for the light reflection and absorption of the glass. For the simulation of a glass with a transmission of 80%, for instance, the illumination levels in the model without glass may be reduced by a factor of 0.20. Although the glass does not, in fact, reduce illumination uniformly throughout the interior space, the distribution effect is relatively minor except when direct sun is on the fenestration, in which case actual glass or acetate should be used in the model to account for specular reflection off of the glass. The model builder is safe in using the actual materials where possible.

The integration of electric lighting into physical models is a difficult task. To incorporate the aspects of electric lighting, one should calculate the additional light provided from electric sources after the daylighting values have been measured.

MEASUREMENT EQUIPMENT

Illuminance meters are used to find qualitative and quantitative results in daylighting models (see Figures 5.4.9 and 5.4.10). The illuminance meter is particularly useful in calculating Daylight Factors (the amount of light inside the model versus outside the model).

When illuminance is measured, the illuminance meter's unfiltered photocells respond to the total energy spectrum differently than the human eye, which responds to the "visible" portion of the spectrum. The photocell responds to other portions of the energy spectrum as well. For comparative studies of models, this discrepancy is not significant. The relative merits of two design schemes being compared are still valid. However, for absolute measurements (actual illumination levels), the photocell must be adapted with a color corrector (often referred to as a "viscor filter"), which causes its response to match that of the average human

Figure 5.4.9 Model test with light sensors.

eye. Because the addition of the color correction device seldom alters significantly the price to the purchaser, it is recommended that it be included in any new purchase.

Photocells are also subject to the "cosine law of illumination"; that is, they are not as sensitive to light striking the cell at a low incident angle as from a high or more direct angle. This produces incorrect measurements when the instru-

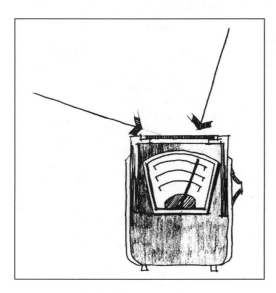

Figure 5.4.10 Typical hand-held light meter used in determining illuminance levels.

ment is used for general lighting studies. Most manufacturers of photometers can provide a cosine correction device for their photocells. It is absolutely necessary that photometers for lighting studies be equipped with a cosine correction device.

There are three types of cosine correction geometry: domed diffuser, partial cosine correction, and full cosine correction.

DOMED DIFFUSER

The meter is a hemispheric "photographic type" equally sensitive to light from all directions. However, a domed diffuser is intentionally not cosine corrected and thus is not ideal for light measurements.

PARTIAL COSINE CORRECTION

The meter is a simple flat diffuser that approximates cosine correction. However, it tends to reflect too much light at low angles. Also, the meter undermeasures light at high angles of incidence.

FULL COSINE CORRECTION

Extra light is allowed to strike the edge or side of the diffuser to compensate for higher diffuse reflectance at lower angles.

DATA ANALYSIS

Following the quantitative results, the designer must evaluate the accumulated data. Typically, the data are presented graphically to measure the quality and distribution of light. In the process, the performance of the various proposed design schemes is considered. Graphically, two formats are generally used: the Iso-Lux contour plan and the Daylight Factor graph/section.

An Iso-Lux contour is a graph that plots the contours of equal Daylight Factors over a building's floor plan. In this method, the designer can measure the distribution of illuminance throughout a space. For instance, if the contours are spaced closely together, a strong illuminance gradient exists.

The Daylight Factor graph/section is presented in a building section cut through the fenestration. The average illuminance is found in the total area under the curve. This allows the designer to compare the total illumination on the work plane. Graphically, a flatter curve indicates a uniform distribution of daylight. However, a flatter curve may result in contrast glare in the user's field of vision. The slope of the curve indicates the amount and rate of illuminance change.

MODEL PERFORMANCE

Model performance can be used for energy calculations in conjunction with hourly simulation computer programs such as DOE2, Trace, and Blast. Several methods can be implemented to accomplish this, including modifying the radiation component of the weather tape relative to daylight in the model or modifying the performance of the electric lighting system.

Most hourly simulation programs such as DOE2 have profile numbers that represent a percentage of the maximum load (see Table 5.4.1). You simply input a watts/square foot (power density) value for the building or thermal zone, and on an hourly basis, the program

TABLE 5.4.1 Electric Lighting Schedule from DOE2

Lighting Schedule for Interior Zone	
Lights: DSI = Day-schedule	
Hours = (1, 7)	Values = (0.05)
Hours = (8, 11)	Values = (.1, .9, .9, .95)
Hours = (12, 15)	Values = (.95, .8, .8, .9)
Hours = (16, 19)	Values = (.9, .95, .8, .7)
Hours = (20, 24)	Values = (.6, .4, .3, .2, .2)
Lighting Schedule for North Perimeter Daylight Zone	
Lights: DS1-N = Day-schedule	
Hours = (1, 7)	Values = (0.05)
Hours = (8, 12)	Values = (.1, .39, .39, .42, .33)
Hours = (13, 17)	Values = (.28, .28, .39, .39, .42)
Hours = (18, 24)	Values = (.8, .7, .6, .4, .3, .2, .2)
Lighting Schedule for South Perimeter Daylight Zone	
Lights: DS1-S = Day-schedule	
Hours = (1, 7)	Values = (0.05)
Hours = (8, 12)	Values = (.1, .34, .34, .37, .29)
Hours = (13, 17)	Values = (.24, .24, .34, .34, .37)
Hours = (18, 24)	Values = (.8, .7, .6, .4, .3, .2, .2)
Lighting Schedule for East Perimeter Daylight Zone	
Light: DS1 = Day-schedule	
Hours = (1, 7)	Values = (0.05)
Hours = (8, 12)	Values = (.1, .27, .27, .29, .32)
Hours = (13, 17)	Values = (.27, .27, .39, .39, .42)
Hours = (18, 24)	Values = (.8, .7, .6, .4, .3, .2, .2)
Lighting Schedule for West Perimeter Daylight Zone	
Lights: DS1 = Day-Schedule	
Hours = (1, 7)	Values = (0.05)
Hours = (8, 12)	Values = (.1, .39, .39, .42, .42)
Hours = (13, 17)	Values = (.27, .27, .27, .27, .29)
Hours = (18, 24)	Values = (.8, .7, .6, .4, .3, .2, .2)

TABLE 5.4.2 Methodology to Modify Electric Lighting Schedules in Hourly Simulation Programs[a]

For Dimming Control

$$MDL_{hr;or} = (PC_{yr} \times FC_{clr,hr,or}) + (PO_{yr} \times FC_{or,hr,or})$$

$$DRF_{hr,or} = \text{Minimum} \begin{cases} \dfrac{MDL_{hr,or}}{DL} \\ 1.00 \end{cases}$$

$$PRF_{hr,or} = \text{Maximum} \begin{cases} \dfrac{MDL_{hr,or}}{CF} \end{cases}$$

$$NPN_{hr,or} = OPN_{hr,or} \times PRF_{hr,or}$$

For an On/Off Control

$$MDL_{hr,or} = (PC_{yr} \times FC_{clr,hr,or}) + (PO_{yr} \times FC_{or,hr,or})$$

$$DRF_{hr,or} = \frac{MDL_{hr,or}}{DL}$$

$$PRF_{hr,or} = \begin{cases} CF & DRF \geq 1.00 \\ 1.00 & DRF < 1.00CF \end{cases}$$

$$NPN_{hr,or} = OPN_{hr,or} \times PRF_{hr,or}$$

where:

$PC =$ percentage of clear sky conditions (see Appendix C).

$FC_{clr/oc,hr,or} =$ average clear or overcast day footcandles level at hour and orientation (from model test).

$PO =$ percentage of overcast sky conditions (see Appendix C).

$MDL_{hr,or} =$ mean daylight level at hour and orientation.

$DL =$ design level. (This is the illumination level required in footcandles.)

$DRF_{hr,or} =$ daylight reduction factor at hour and orientation (must not exceed 1.00).

$CF =$ control factor. (This is the minimum setpoint that a dimming system will reduce to, typically around 0.50. This corresponds to a dimmer going down to 50% full load.)

$PRF_{hr,or} =$ power reduction factor at hour and orientation (must be at least equal to CF).

$OPN_{hr,or} =$ old profile number at hour and orientation.

$NPN_{hr,or} =$ new profile number at hour and orientation.

[a]clr, clear; hr, hour; or, orientation.

will take a fraction of that power density for the thermal calculations.

If you can reduce these profile numbers relative to the daylight levels in the physical model, the program will factor this electric lighting reduction into the hourly calculations.

Typically, one would take footcandle readings in the physical model at least three times during the day or simulated day when a tilt table is used. For example, 9 A.M., noon, and 3 P.M. can be used to simulate the day. Ideally, one would also like to test four seasons, which would represent the entire year. Readings during an equinox period (March 21 or September 21) will give an average condition for an annual calculation.

Actual summer performance will be better than spring or fall performance, whereas winter performance will actually be worse because of shorter days and lower sun positions. Hence, winter and summer measurements offset each other. For most cases, data for September 21 at 9 A.M., noon, and 3 P.M. can be used to modify electric lighting schedules. The methodology for modifying the profile numbers or the percentage of maximum load for dimming control and an on/off control is shown in Table 5.4.2.

CHAPTER 6

Case Studies

The sensitivity with which light is allowed to enter into a space remains a design issue. The methods of light control, its entry into spaces, and its impact on surfaces all are dependent on the designer's understanding of light.

This chapter summarizes a variety of buildings implementing daylighting strategies. Per-formance specifications are included to help evaluate each project for its energy efficiency. Each example includes a short written descrip-tion, building graphics, and images to help better understand the design team's intent.

RETAIL

Low-Energy Super Store (LESS) by Stop and Shop

Building Type:	Supermarket
Location:	Foxboro, Massachusetts
Building Area:	65,000 ft^2
Daylighting Strategies:	The main retail space has fifty-five 25-ft^2 high-performance skylights with splayed openings. The produce and checkout areas have custom linear light pipes with curved, perforated metal reflectors at the base to redirect diffuse light onto vaulted ceilings. The restrooms incorporate light pipes.
Lighting Design Levels:	40–60 fc in the retail spaces.
Electric Lighting Controls:	Automatic dimming controls responding to daylight availability.
Mechanical System:	The LESS project features electronic enhancements applied throughout the entire product refrigeration system. Variable-frequency drives (VFDs) continuously change the speed of reciprocating semihermetic motor compressors and remote air-cooled condenser fan motors.
Additional Sustainability Measures:	Recycled-content, nontoxic, and environmentally sensitive materials and equipment, locally sourced materials to the greatest extent possible, environmentally sensitive procedures, protection of the environment—both on site and off site—during demolition and construction, efficient operations, and optimum control of solid wastes.
Building Owner:	Stop and Shop, Quincy, Massachusetts
Architect:	Peterson Griffen Architects, Boston, Massachusetts
Engineers:	*Electrical:* Engineering Advantage, Inc., Boston, Massachusetts
	Mechanical: Griffith & Vary, Wareham, Massachusetts
Consultants:	*Daylighting:* ENSAR Group, Boulder, Colorado
	Electric Lighting: Clanton & Associates, Boulder, Colorado
	Green Building: McCoppin Studios, San Francisco, California
	Environmental Concepts and Charrette: Rocky Mountain Institute, Snowmass, Colorado
	Energy Analysis: CTG, Los Angeles, California
Summary:	The design strategies included a unique light pipe system that created direct/indirect daylighting over selective areas, skylighting over the main retail space, and an efficient direct/indirect electric system. The light pipe system, over both the produce and checkout

areas, was custom-made with linear, rectangular light shafts of highly reflective, specular surfaces. Sloped skylights (³⁄₁₂ pitch facing south) use high-efficacy glazing with low solar heat gains and high daylight transmittance (Clear Heat Mirror™SC75). At the bottom of the light shaft, light reflectors redirect the daylight toward the ceiling to softly provide ambient light in the produce and checkout areas. The reflector is made of white perforated metal to diffuse the light as it is reflected and allows some light to penetrate downward toward the produce.

The space over the checkout area has a similar direct/indirect daylighting system as the produce area, only smaller. A white perforated metal is used as the curved reflector. It provides the ambient light for the checkout process and is augmented with both indirect and direct electric lighting. Over the primary retail area, daylighting was achieved using a more traditional daylighting approach with high-performance skylights and splayed openings. About 5% of the roof area over the primary retail space was glazed with sloping skylights and patterned, diffusing glazing and Clear Heat Mirror™SC75.

The electric lighting system was completely revamped to support the daylighting design, produce brighter surfaces, and use lower ambient light levels that allow the accent lighting to be more effective. The ambient system of pendant-mounted direct/indirect T5 HO fluorescent luminaires is controlled through an automatic dimming system in response to daylight, as well as accent lighting in selective areas. See Figures 6.1 to 6.10.

Figure 6.1 Front elevation.

Figure 6.2 Interior over produce area showing ceiling treatment.

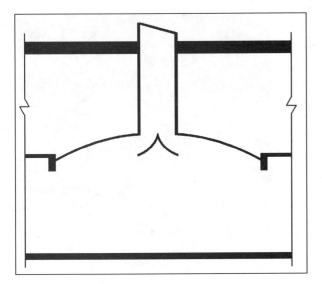

Figure 6.3 Section through curved ceiling and reflecting device.

Figure 6.4 Construction progress image.

Figure 6.5 Roof showing skylights.

Figure 6.6 Interior with splayed skylight detail.

Figure 6.7 Skylights along circulation.

Figure 6.8 Skylight detail.

Figure 6.9 Linear skylight over produce area.

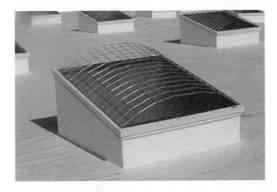

Figure 6.10 Skylight roof detail.

OFFICE BUILDINGS

Nike European Headquarters

Building Type:	Offices
Location:	Hilversum, The Netherlands
Building Area:	375,000 ft^2
Daylighting Strategies:	Narrow floor plates, four-story daylit atriums, thermal glazing.
Lighting Design Levels:	Per Dutch Standard.
Electric Lighting Controls:	Fixtures are equipped with individual sensors for dimming. Levels are controlled by sensors at work surface level. Clock timers are used.
Mechanical System:	Features closed-loop geothermal heat pump system and central air-based heating.
Additional Sustainability Measures:	The stakeholders agreed to pursue effective energy strategies, leading to a combination of architectural and technical measures that serve to make the campus the most energy-efficient office complex of its size in the Netherlands. Renewable energy sources provide 30% of the total supply, in large part owing to one of northern Europe's largest geothermal heating and cooling systems. The design also seeks to facilitate improvements in the future through its curving roof profiles, which will enable easy installation of photovoltaic panels when they become more cost-effective.

Landscape design informs the architectural plan. Buildings do not exceed the height of existing trees. Transparent lobbies connect green space and the adjacent sports park, blurring the distinction between indoors and outdoors. The design creates an urbane and secure campus environment that feels open and connected.

All wood is sustainably harvested; building is virtually polyvinyl chloride (PVC) free; biocomposite partitioning; interior and exterior sports surfaces composed of recycled sports shoes; low-VOC (volatile organic compound) paints, stains, and finishes; cisterns are native landscaping and retain all storm water on site. Nike EHQ boasts Europe's largest rainwater collection system. |
Architect:	William McDonough + Partners (Design Architect); B & D Architekten (Architect of Record)
Engineer:	Ingenieursbureau Zonneveld B.V. (Structural); DHV AIB B.V. (Mechanical)
Consultants:	Loisos + Ubbelohde (Daylighting); DHV AIB B.V. (Environmental management)
Summary:	Nike's business revolves around world-class athletic performance, and the design for its European headquarters aspires to equivalent levels of building and human performance by creating an active

habitat that promotes physical, social, and cultural health in the broadest possible senses. By combining eco-effective resource management, aesthetic appeal, and long-term flexibility, Nike European Headquarters exemplifies a model approach for 21st-century architecture. The project demonstrated the effectiveness of early discussions between all project stakeholders—municipal officials, building owner, tenant, developer, designers, and financial parties. We learned how important it is for each party to have at least one advocate for "greening" of the design.

The north-south solar orientation maximizes daylighting. Nike's office buildings do not exceed 60 ft, allowing all employees a workspace within 16 ft of an operable window with a view. Office buildings are convertible to residential use and the windows are operable. The selection of a light-colored brick helps to keep the courtyards bright. Deep overhangs serve to mitigate unwanted summer heat gain, while skylights and light monitors capture and direct sunlight indoors. The high-performance glass is as clear as possible, since sky conditions are only 17% clear in winter and 44% clear in summer. The glass has a visible transmittance of about 60% and a shading coefficient of approximately 40%. See Figures 6.11 to 6.26.

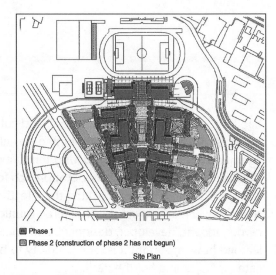

Figure 6.11 Site plan showing outline of future phases. *(Courtesy of William McDonough + Partners.)*

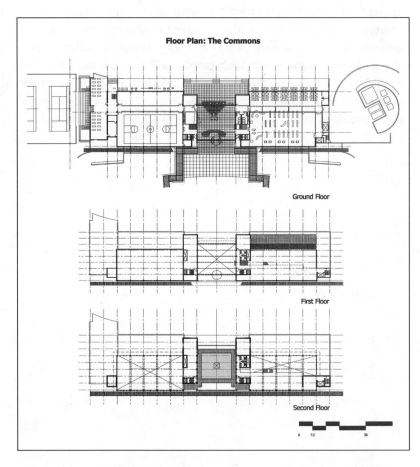

Figure 6.12 Floor plans of commons. *(Courtesy of William McDonough + Partners.)*

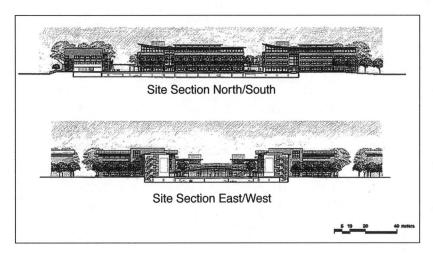

Site Section North/South

Site Section East/West

Figure 6.13 Building sections. *(Courtesy of William McDonough + Partners.)*

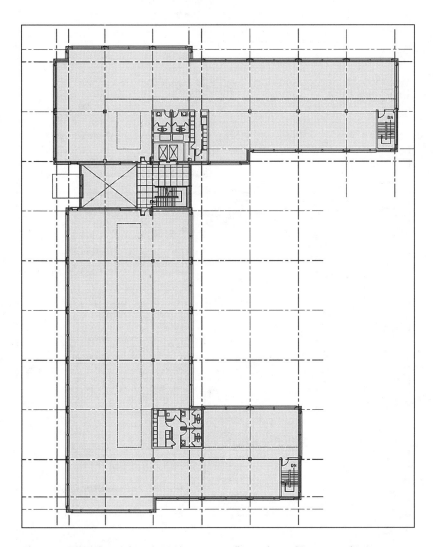

Figure 6.14 Floor plan showing narrow floor plate. *(Courtesy of Loisos + Ubbelohde.)*

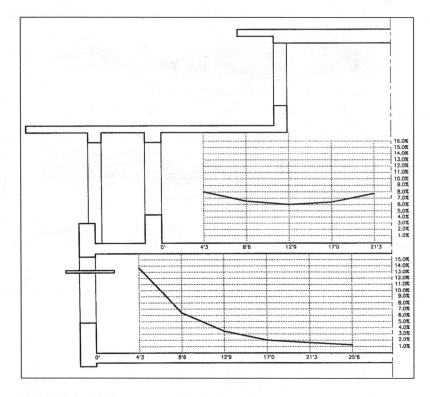

Figure 6.15 Section showing daylight factors. *(Courtesy of Loisos + Ubbelohde.)*

Figure 6.16 Building section. *(Courtesy of Loisos + Ubbelohde.)*

Figure 6.17 Elevation of typical office villa. *(Courtesy of Loisos + Ubbelohde.)*

Figure 6.18 Elevation showing entrance and reception atrium. *(Courtesy of Loisos + Ubbelohde.)*

Figure 6.19 Elevation showing garden court. *(Courtesy of Loisos + Ubbelohde.)*

Figure 6.20 Elevation showing sports court and deep upper-level overhang. *(Courtesy of Loisos + Ubbelohde.)*

Figure 6.21 Office villa showing double-height studio space and glass rain canopy. *(Courtesy of Loisos + Ubbelohde.)*

Figure 6.22 Elevation showing glass with supergraphics and skylight. *(Courtesy of Loisos + Ubbelohde.)*

Figure 6.23 Clerestory skylight at upper-floor office space showing curved ceiling treatment. *(Courtesy of Loisos + Ubbelohde.)*

Figure 6.24 North-facing double-height studio space. *(Courtesy of Loisos + Ubbelohde.)*

Figure 6.25 Skylight at office villa entry. *(Courtesy of Loisos + Ubbelohde.)*

Figure 6.26 Typical office floor looking toward window wall. *(Courtesy of Loisos + Ubbelohde.)*

United Gulf Bank

Building Type:	Commercial Office/Mixed Use
Location:	Manama, Bahrain
Building Area:	98,000 ft²
Daylighting Strategies:	Narrow footprint/orientation on site (long facade on north and south). Facade treatment follows solar movement, three window treatments—vertical glass louvers, light shelves, and CLR/open small openings—deep window wells on south facade, low-e glass, and open skylit atrium on the north side.
Lighting Design Levels:	40–50 fc.
Electric Lighting Controls:	On/off, dimming controls.
Mechanical System:	Four 125-ton chillers with cooling tower, air-conditioning split systems, and centralized facility system management.
Additional Sustainability Measures:	
Architect:	Skidmore, Owings & Merrill LLP (Adrian Smith, FAIA, Design Partner)
Engineers:	Pan Arab Consulting Engineers, Kuwait
Summary:	This 12-story office building employs several daylighting strategies to minimize solar heat gain and create a comfortable interior environment in this harsh, sunny, arid Middle-Eastern climate. The long, narrow site dictated the slender footprint and the building's northwest-southeast orientation.

The building curves in plan along the southeast, south, and southwest, and the window treatments were designed to control and/or optimize daylight along the sun's path. Vertical green glass fins intercept and diffuse the sun's direct rays during the most critical times of the day, therefore minimizing solar gain. While referencing indigenous architecture, deeply recessed windows help shield the interior from severe, direct sunlight. Light shelves block direct-beam sunlight and reflect sunlight into the space. On the west facade, where the sun's intensity hits the facade at its full force, narrow windows allow only a minimal amount of sun.

Off the northeast facade, a 10-story atrium capped by clear, insulated skylights brings natural light into the open office areas. The narrow windows of the facade form a grid pattern referencing the indigenous *mashrabiyah* (wooden lattice screen) and create interesting light effects in the atrium. In addition to the skylights and the slit windows, large open windows at the top floors of the atrium supply additional daylight to the open space. Bridges across the atrium are built of glass block to allow additional daylight to filter down into the space. These sculptural features are equipped with downlights for evening usage or to supplement the amount of light in the atrium. Otherwise, the northeast facade remains quite closed off from the sun's intensity. See Figures 6.27 to 6.38.

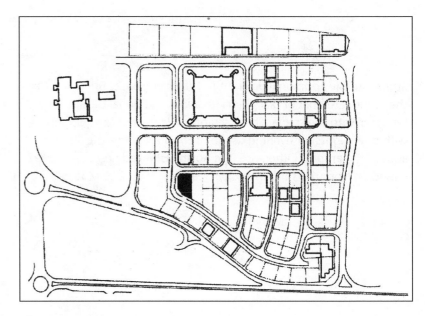

Figure 6.27 Site plan.

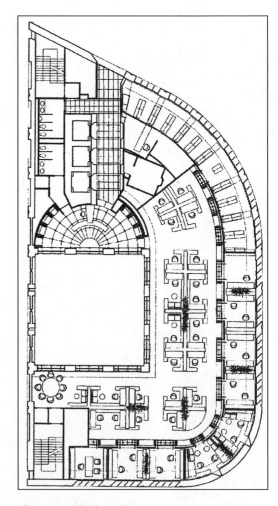

Figure 6.28 Floor plan.

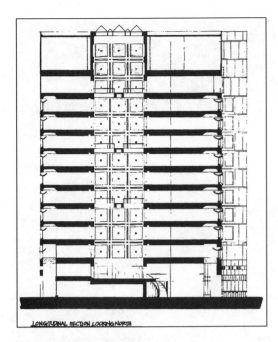

Figure 6.29 Section.

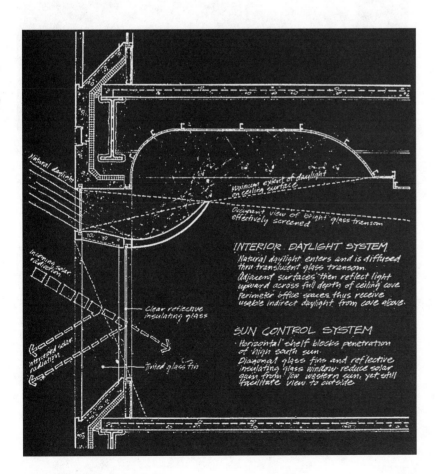

Figure 6.30 Detail section.

Figure 6.31 Interior showing light shelf.

Figure 6.32 Exterior elevation.

Figure 6.33 Exterior entrance.

Figure 6.34 Horizontal and vertical sun control.

Figure 6.35 Looking up at the atrium toward elevated walkways with translucent blocks.

Figure 6.36 Elevated walkway.

Figure 6.37 Interior curved light shelf.

Figure 6.38 Recessed and controlled windows.

Xilinx Development Center

Building Type:	Office—Research & Development
Location:	Longmont, Colorado
Building Area:	120,000 ft^2 on two floors
Daylighting Strategies:	Toplighting was implemented with translucent skylights at the stairwells and clerestory windows in the main entrance lobby. Sidelighting from Architectural Energy Corporation's patented Mini Optical Light Shelf daylighting system occurs on the east, south, and west facades.
Lighting Design Levels:	20–25 fc ambient lighting with 40–45 fc task lighting integrated into the open office furniture system.
Electric Lighting Controls:	Photosensor-controlled dimming ballasts on all perimeter office zones. Occupancy sensors throughout conference rooms, restrooms, break rooms, etc.
Mechanical System:	Rooftop units provide air to an underfloor air distribution system.
Additional Sustainability Measures:	Pilot (Version 1.0) LEED rating scheme used to guide sustainable design decisions. Low-environmental-impact materials used throughout, including low-VOC paints, bamboo wood floors, local concrete and stone, xeriscape (indigenous, low water) landscaping, interior bicycle racks, etc.
	The building was commissioned by a combination of the design-build contractor, lighting controls manufacturer, and Architectural Energy Corporation.
Architect:	Downing Thorpe & James, Boulder, Colorado
General Contractor:	Neenan Company, Fort Collins, Colorado
Mechanical Engineer:	BCER Engineering, Arvada, Colorado
Electrical Engineer:	Merit Electric, Fort Collins, Colorado
Sustainable Design Consultant:	Architectural Energy Corporation, Boulder, Colorado
Summary:	The client and the design team were committed to high levels of architectural design excellence and to high levels of energy efficiency and environmental responsiveness. Aggressive energy efficiency and sustainable design goals were established through predesign energy use/cost characterization and use of the Pilot LEED rating scheme. Master planning of the campus resulted in the Development Center building being oriented on an east-west axis in the center of the site—becoming the "crossroads" for all pedestrian circulation through the site. With this building orientation, the interior spatial organization logically became perimeter open office zones on the south and the north, with a core zone of support

spaces (conference rooms, break rooms, computer laboratories, restrooms, storage, etc.) in the middle. This overall space-planning concept was very conducive to daylighting the majority of the perimeter office space.

An ambient-task-accent electric lighting scheme was adopted, with daylighting and indirect electric lighting providing the ambient lighting requirements (20–25 fc) and furniture-mounted fluorescent lighting providing the task lighting requirements (40–50 fc). Accent lighting is provided throughout the building to highlight specific areas (i.e., break rooms) or wall surfaces (i.e., art).

The perimeter glazing system was organized into "vision" glass (3 ft above finished floor to about 7 ft above finished floor) and "daylight" glass (7 ft above finished floor to ceiling height—10 ft above finished floor). The vision glass has a relatively low visible light transmission (29%) and a low shading coefficient (0.28). The daylighting glass has a relatively high visible light transmission (76%) and a relatively high shading coefficient (0.62). To redirect daylight onto the ceilings of the east, south, and west perimeter office spaces and provide adequate daylight deep into the open office space, Architectural Energy Corporation's patented Mini Optical Light Shelf (MOLS) daylighting system was placed on the interior side of the daylight glazing. MOLS consists of a series of fixed horizontal louvers (slats), of a unique compound geometry, placed in a supporting frame that redirects daylight uniformly across the ceiling surface. The illuminated ceiling surface provides ambient light to the space below. Photosensors determine ambient light levels and raise or lower the indirect electric lighting to maintain the minimum ambient lighting level. The lighting controls were fully commissioned by Architectural Energy Corporation and the controls contractor to ensure they performed as intended (designed). See Figures 6.39 to 6.49.

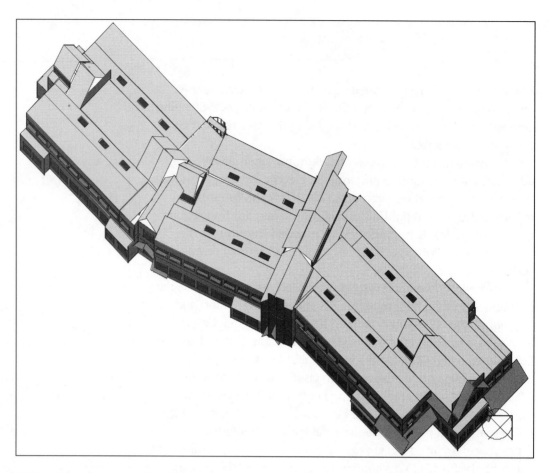

Figure 6.39 Southeast elevation.

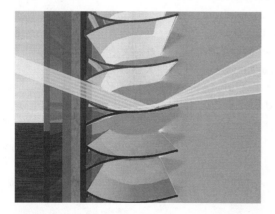

Figure 6.40 Detail section of Mini Optical Light Shelf.

Figure 6.41 Elevation.

Figure 6.42 Fenestration controls.

Figure 6.43 Elevation.

Figure 6.44 Mini Optical Light Shelf illuminating ceiling.

Figure 6.45 Ceiling washed with daylight.

Figure 6.46 High-volume space.

Figure 6.47 Interior showing partitions daylight-washing ceiling tiles.

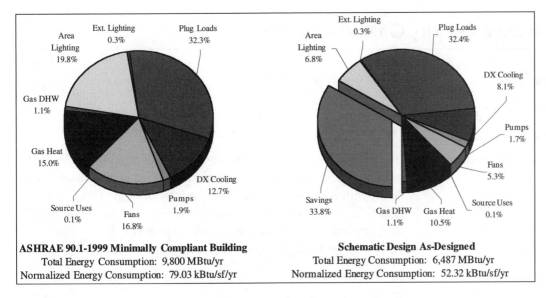

Figure 6.48 Normalized annual energy use comparison by end use.

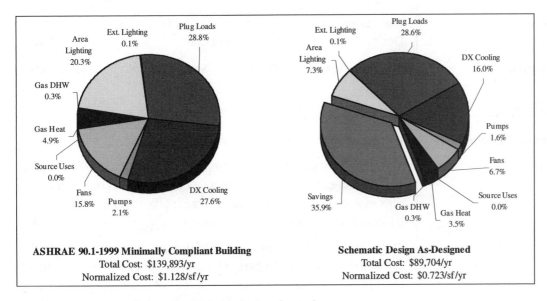

Figure 6.49 Total annual energy cost comparison by end use.

Automotive Industry Office/Warehouse

Building Type: Office/Warehouse

Location: Portland, Oregon

Building Area: 180,000 ft^2

Daylighting Strategies: Daylighting was accomplished through sidelighting strategies in the office space. Window brightness was controlled with light shelves. Roof apertures were introduced in the interior of the building to help balance the daylight coming from the perimeter zones. Significant physical model testing was performed during the design process to optimize and balance daylight performance.

Lighting Design Levels: 30–50 fc in the office areas. Daylight factor of 2% in the office space.

Architect: Group MacKenzie, Robert Thompson, Project Architect, Portland, Oregon

Engineers: *Mechanical/Electrical:* Michael Kinne and Dave Nichols, System Design Consultants, Portland, Oregon

Consultants: *Daylighting:* Lighting Design Lab, Seattle, Washington (Joel Loveland)

Electric Lighting Controls: Dimming.

Mechanical System: Hybrid/chiller/boiler/radiant/natural ventilation.

Summary: This office facility in Portland, Oregon, is a central training and parts distribution center for an automotive company. This building complex essentially comprises two buildings: office and maintenance training building and warehouse building.

Office Area: This building area lies to the northeast of the building compound. It includes a perimeter of largely open-plan office space facing the east and west encircling a core of restrooms, storage areas, and conference rooms. There is also an entry area of display and meeting rooms to the north of the open office bay. The open-plan office areas are illuminated with generous east- or west-oriented sidelight windows, which are partially shaded with deep exterior overhangs and interior light shelves. The open office bay is quite deep from east to west away from the window walls. The perimeter daylight therefore needed to be balanced with light deeper in the space. The architects chose to balance the perimeter with daylight from the skylights at the core, which wash the interior "core" walls.

Training Area: This building area lies to the northeast of the building compound. It includes a large auto maintenance training area primarily illuminated by four large skylights, a classroom at the northern perimeter, and a scattering of storage and small office spaces to the east and south, where they are adjacent to the warehouse space.

Lunch Break Area: This area connects the office wing to the training wing. It is composed of a large lunchroom or cafeteria, a fitness room, and several storage areas and restrooms. The space is quite narrow from the north-facing exterior window wall. It has generous diffuse daylight at all times of day.

Warehouse Facility: This is an extremely large storage area for automobile parts. It lies to the south of the training, cafeteria, and office wings. It is illuminated with a combination of skylights and electric lights.

See Figures 6.50 to 6.65.

Figure 6.50 Elevation. *(Courtesy of Joel Loveland.)*

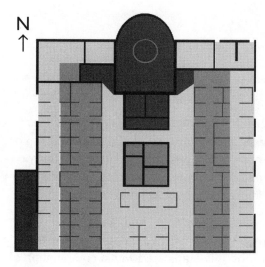

Figure 6.51 Plan. *(Courtesy of Joel Loveland.)*

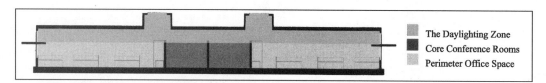

The Daylighting Zone
Core Conference Rooms
Perimeter Office Space

Figure 6.52 Section. *(Courtesy of Joel Loveland.)*

Daylighting Diagram

Figure 6.53 Section. *(Courtesy of Joel Loveland.)*

Figure 6.54 Interior of a daylight model during an overcast test. *(Courtesy of Joel Loveland.)*

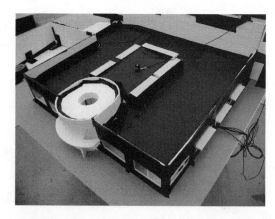

Figure 6.55 Physical model. *(Courtesy of Joel Loveland.)*

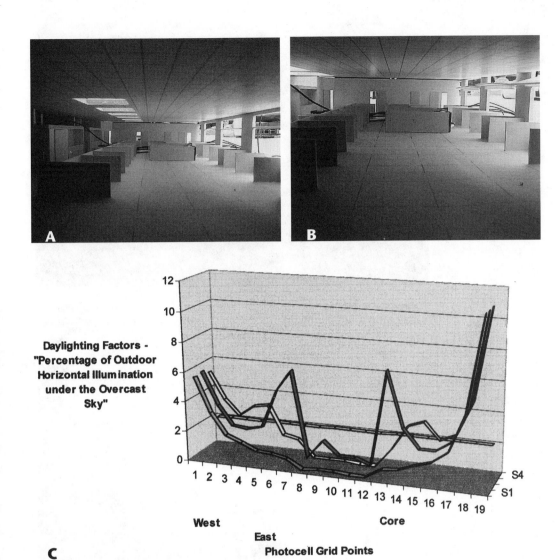

Daylighting Factors -
"Percentage of Outdoor
Horizontal Illumination
under the Overcast
Sky"

West   Core
East
Photocell Grid Points

C

Figure 6.56 Skylight comparison test with daylight factor results: (A) with skylights, (B) without sky-lights, (C) daylight factor under overcast skies. *(Courtesy of Joel Loveland.)*

Figure 6.57 Physical model image of the cho-sen strategy. *(Courtesy of Joel Loveland.)*

Figure 6.58 Interior showing light shelves to the left and toplighting to balance the space on the right. *(Courtesy of Joel Loveland.)*

Figure 6.59 Exterior fenestration controls. *(Courtesy of Joel Loveland.)*

Figure 6.60 Interior with lights on. *(Courtesy of Joel Loveland.)*

Figure 6.61 Interior with lights off. *(Courtesy of Joel Loveland.)*

Figure 6.62 Conference/training space. *(Courtesy of Joel Loveland.)*

Figure 6.63 Exterior control. *(Courtesy of Joel Loveland.)*

Figure 6.64 Physical model. *(Courtesy of Joel Loveland.)*

Figure 6.65 Interior of model. *(Courtesy of Joel Loveland.)*

Johnson Center

Building Type:	Commercial Office
Location:	Racine, Wisconsin
Building Area:	180,000 ft^2
Daylighting Strategies:	Massing, light shelves, spectrally selective glazing, manual and automatic rolling shades, perimeter-zoned fixtures tied to controls.
Electric Lighting Controls:	PEMS (Personal Environment Management System). Includes airflow, temperature, and lighting controls at each individual work-station or meeting area.
Mechanical System:	High-efficiency gas boiler, institutional-grade package units, zone control and underfloor air delivery with variable air volume (VAV) boxes at perimeter.
Additional Sustainability Measures:	William McDonough & Partners and the Johnson Building Design Team sought to create a building that celebrated the abundance of nature and maintained a mindful perspective toward energy and other resources. An integrated design process brought together the construction manager, architects, engineers, and owners' represen-tatives early in the process for team-based decision making. The courtyard has a sod roof and the building has space on a roof set aside for future photovoltaic (PV) panels. Recovered wood is used, as are low-VOC finishes. LEED registered—certification anticipated.
Design Architect:	William McDonough + Partners, Charlottesville, Virginia
Architect of Record:	Epstein Uhen Architects, Milwaukee, Wisconsin
M.E.P. Engineers:	Ring & DuChateau, Milwaukee, Wisconsin
Consultants:	*Daylighting:* Loisos + Ubbelohde, Oakland, California
	Lighting Design: Ring & DuChateau, Milwaukee, Wisconsin
	Ann Kale Associates, New York, New York
Summary:	*Massing, Glazing, and Borrowed Light:* The lower south wing allows light into the courtyard year-round; the south face of the north wing reflects light into the courtyard. Relatively narrow floor plates (77 ft/53 ft) allow daylight deeper into the interior. High floor-to-floor height (14 ft) and clear ceiling heights (10 ft, 10 in. on typical floors) provide better light, air, and space quality. A primary design goal was that everyone should have access to daylight with a view. The glass has an excellent "shading coefficient" that keeps the inside space from overheating. Clear-glass "borrowed lights" at the perimeter offices provide

light and views for workers in the center section. The connection heightens awareness of daylight color and quality throughout the day. Perimeter office workers are likewise encouraged to share the light and views by keeping interior privacy shades open if possible.

Light Shelves and Interior Shading: Among the most unique features of the building are the light shelves, which extend 18 in. from the building above the larger view window. The top surface of the shelf is white and reflects light through the upper window (clerestory) onto the ceiling, reducing the need for electric lighting during the day. The shelf also shades the glass to reduce heat gain. Direct-beam daylight into the interior spaces is minimized. Light shelves reduce glare from views of the sky.

Racine has many overcast days and the building is designed with relatively clear glass to maintain a bright interior under such conditions. In the design of the building, the architects intended for all shades to be raised at the end of the day and lowered only if glare is a problem. Individual rolling shades with some transparency are provided. The color and weave of the shades were selected for the best color rendition and visual comfort. An automated shade deployment system exists for open office areas and is activated by photocells on the roof, but most locations are individually controlled.

Daylight Controls: Rows of light fixtures parallel to the exterior wall are controlled together and are tied to sensors, which turn lights off when daylight is providing sufficient illumination.

See Figures 6.66 to 6.80.

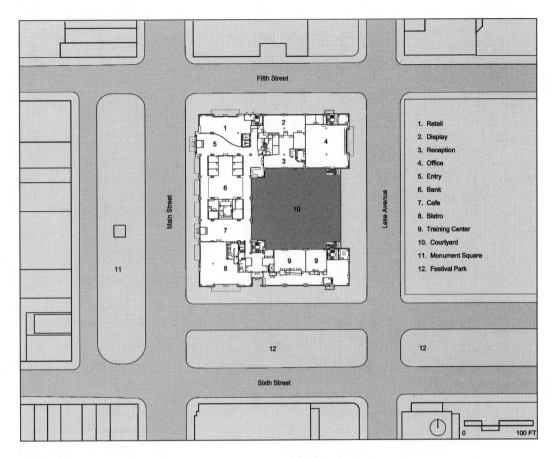

Figure 6.66 Site plan. *(Courtesy of William McDonough + Partners.)*

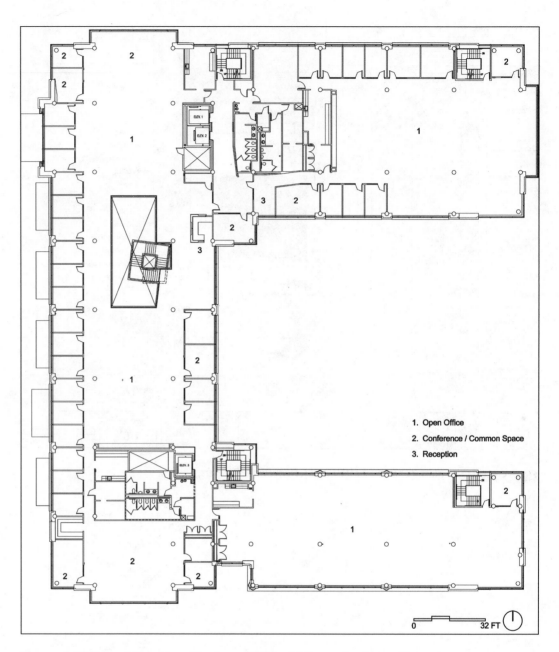

Figure 6.67 Second-floor plan. *(Courtesy of William McDonough + Partners.)*

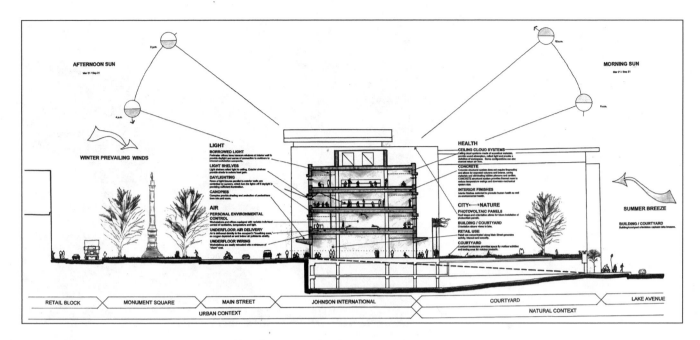

Figure 6.68 Concept section. *(Courtesy of William McDonough + Partners.)*

Figure 6.69 View of northwest corner of courtyard from training room (construction photo). *(Courtesy of William McDonough + Partners.)*

Figure 6.70 View of project with Lake Michigan in background. *(Courtesy of William McDonough + Partners.)*

Figure 6.71 Detail of corner showing transparency of glass. *(Courtesy of William McDonough + Partners.)*

Figure 6.72 Detail of light shelf. *(Courtesy of William McDonough + Partners.)*

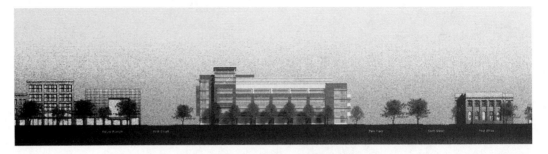

Figure 6.73 Main street elevation. *(Courtesy of Epstein Uhen Architects.)*

Figure 6.74 Computer rendering. *(Courtesy of Epstein Uhen Architects.)*

Figure 6.75 Elevation.

Figure 6.76 Interior of south-facing office at midday in late April (note effectiveness of 18-in. light shelf.) *(Courtesy of William McDonough + Partners.)*

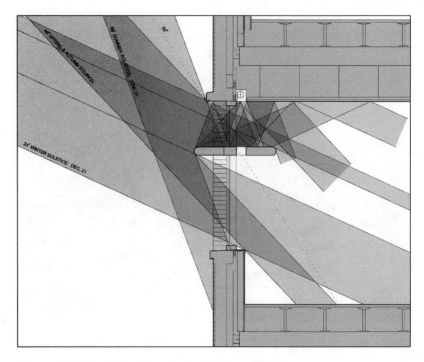

Figure 6.77 Light shelf/sun angle detail.

Figure 6.78 Detail of tower. *(Courtesy of William McDonough + Partners.)*

Figure 6.79 Entry on the main street. *(Courtesy of William McDonough + Partners.)*

Figure 6.80 View of courtyard showing white light shelves to optimize reflection. *(Courtesy of William McDonough + Partners.)*

INDUSTRIAL

REMO, Inc.

Building Type:	Manufacturing and Office
Location:	Valencia, California
Building Area:	214,000 ft^2 (137,000 ft^2 warehouse, 58,000 ft^2 manufacturing, 19,000 ft^2 office)
Daylighting Strategies:	Skylights.
Electric Lighting Controls:	Stepped photocontrols.
Mechanical System:	Indirect/direct evaporating cooling, packaged direct expansion (DX) units.
Additional Sustainability Measures:	Lighting controls were commissioned.
Architect:	Hill Pinckert Architects, Irvine, California
Consultants:	Computer Modeling—Ramin Faramarzi
Summary:	REMO, Inc., is one of the world's largest manufacturers of drums and percussion instruments. The company decided to move its operations and chose a site with an existing set of speculative building plans, which showed 2% of the roof area devoted to skylights. Detailed DOE2 simulations were performed to optimize the daylight performance, and the company decided to increase the skylighting area to 3%, to add photocontrols, and to invest in a direct/indirect evaporative cooling system. One of the objectives for the new building was to enhance the working environment for employees. Company officials hoped that the new building would be a morale booster and that they would keep as many of their existing employees as possible in spite of the move. The manufacture of drums is very labor-intensive, and REMO did not want to lose its investment in its employees. Management also hoped to reduce operating costs in the new location.

Skylighting became a way to address both objectives. The bright, well-lit environment of the new plant is a very pleasant place to work, a dramatic improvement over the previous facilities. REMO has found that a large percentage of its original employees are still with the company after the transition to the new facility.

Engineering analysis during design showed that an optimized skylighting system with daylighting controls would save about $36,000 per year in building operating costs. The most cost-effective design devoted 3% of the gross roof area to skylights and used a slightly more expensive type of skylight dome with a high visible light transmission and a low shading coefficient. The additional costs for photocontrols, the skylight upgrade, and

1% skylight area increase amounted to $54,000 (27¢/ft^2). Painting the interior walls white, which also dramatically increased light levels, cost an additional $4,500 (2.25¢/ft^2).

The building uses 250-W metal halide lamps on a modified grid 20 ft by 24 ft. in size, resulting in a lighting power density of 0.6 W/ft^2. The photocontrols switch one-third or two-thirds of the lights off in a checkerboard pattern. Lights in some critical areas and half of the lights along the perimeter are always left on during working hours.

Selecting on/off controls for metal halide lamps may be considered by some designers to be unusual for a manufacturing setting, because once the lamps are switched off, it takes up to 20 minutes before they will turn back on again. However, as the skies tend to be either clear or cloudy most of the time, with little in between, the lights typically turn off in the morning and remain off for the rest of the workday. The facility experiences very little cycling of the electric lamps.

The maintenance supervisor has found that the skylights are almost maintenance free. However, because the building is located in a construction zone in a desert climate, a lot of dust tends to accumulate on the roof, so he simply has someone hose off the skylights a few times during the summer.

After occupying the building for about 6 months, the supervisor noticed that the lights seemed to be staying on longer during the day. He discovered that because the manufacture of drum heads generates a lot of dust in the interior of the building, the photosensors were acquiring a layer of dust that reduced their sensitivity. He started dusting the small sensors once a month or so, which significantly increased the yearly energy savings. See Figures 6.81 to 6.89.

Figure 6.81 Front entrance. *(Courtesy Paki Muthig.)*

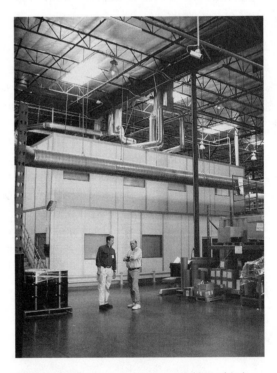

Figure 6.82 Interior. *(Courtesy Paki Muthig.)*

Figure 6.83 Interior fabrication area. *(Courtesy Paki Muthig.)*

Figure 6.84 Skylights and open web trusses. *(Courtesy Paki Muthig.)*

Figure 6.85 Assembly area. *(Courtesy Paki Muthig.)*

Figure 6.86 Photosensor control system to control electric lights. *(Courtesy Paki Muthig.)*

Figure 6.87 Roof showing diffusing skylights. *(Courtesy Paki Muthig.)*

Figure 6.88 Detail of hinged diffusing skylight. *(Courtesy Paki Muthig.)*

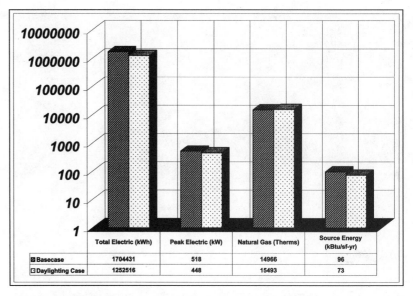

Figure 6.89 Energy summary. Note that the final measures included skylights in the manufacturing area and automatic photosensor controls. *(Courtesy Paki Muthig.)*

INSTITUTIONAL

Younkin Success Center, Ohio State University

Building Type:	Holistic Learning Center
Location:	Columbus, Ohio
Building Area:	72,000 ft²
Daylighting Strategies:	Energy and daylighting analysis was a key component of the design process. Implementing the DOE2 hourly simulation program and the results of a daylighting study model using different skylight configurations, the annual energy consumption of the building was calculated for 32 alternative versions of the building and compared to a base case energy consumption meeting ASHRAE 90.1 and the Ohio State Building Code. The DOE2 analysis showed that an energy-efficient version of the Younkin Success Center could be economically constructed and save 40% of the annual energy cost, consuming 46% fewer BTUs at the building site compared to the base case building.

Key recommendations of the DOE2.1 Energy and Daylighting Analysis are as follows: |
| **Lighting:** | *Daylighting:* The use of daylighting controls in conjunction with dimmable ballasts has a big impact on annual energy consumption. Based on the model studies, it was determined that 16,600 ft² of the building will receive appreciable daylighting. Of this total, 6,600 ft² is lit by the atrium.

Use of Shading Devices: Exterior louvers have only a modest effect on energy consumption, but were recommended for their positive impact on visual comfort and daylight benefits as demonstrated in the model studies.

Electric Lighting: Lighting levels of 1.0 W/ft² in classroom and office space have a big impact on annual energy consumption. |
Glazing:	*Glass Selection:* The use of superwindows (e.g., windows with very low *U*-values and moderate shading coefficients and visible transmittance, such as Visionwall™) saves heating energy and permits the elimination of perimeter radiant systems. A combination of clear glass (behind louvers) and tinted glass allows daylight to penetrate and reduces glare, particularly on the west facade.
Atrium Roof:	*Geometry:* The use of a south-facing sawtooth roof outperformed both the base case configuration and other alternatives. It is interesting to note the south-facing version of roof 2 also outperformed a north-facing version (without louvers) of the same geometry.
Building Envelope:	*Air Retarder:* The use of an air-retarding membrane in the wall construction saves energy and improves building durability.

Lighting Design Levels: 30–40 fc ambient at desk level.

Electric Lighting Controls: Dimming photocontrols and occupancy sensors.

Mechanical System: Superefficient screw-type chillers, an advanced control strategy, variable-speed hot-water circulating pumps and two-speed cooling tower fans, and higher-efficiency modular boilers.

Additional Sustainability Measures: Low-VOC paints specified and material selection.

Architect: Joint venture of Susan Maxman & Partners, Philadelphia, Pennsylvania, and Philip Markwood Associates, Columbus, Ohio

Engineers: Korda/Nemeth Engineering, Columbus, Ohio

Consultants: *Daylighting:* Don Prowler & Associates, Philadelphia, Pennsylvania

Lighting Design: Clanton & Associates, Boulder, Colorado

Energy Simulations: Stephen Winters Associates, Norwalk, Connecticut

Summary: In an effort to ensure the academic success of its students, Ohio State University developed a new concept for a holistic learning center. The Success Center creates an environment in which the integration of varied disciplines leads to a greater understanding of how students learn, while providing resources for students who need additional help.

The joint venture of Susan Maxman & Partners and Philip Markwood Associates programmed and designed the 72,000-ft² facility, conceptualizing this dynamic idea and translating it into the built environment. Central to the building's design is a glass facade to allow the activities inside to be showcased from the street and an interior atrium to stimulate interaction among the various disciplines.

This facility defines the interactive learning center of the future—flexible and dynamic in nature; nurturing yet high-tech and adaptable. Energy efficiency was a key component of the design of this facility. DOE2, a Department of Energy computer simulation program, was used to determine the long-term benefits of the energy-efficient design strategies. These findings encouraged the university to agree to the incorporation of a very energy efficient curtain wall system on the west facade. By utilizing this system, perimeter heating could be eliminated, reducing energy consumption. The central skylit area was modeled to determine the best design for the skylights to optimize daylighting without glare or heat buildup. Consequently, the atrium is a very pleasant space that is well used. See Figures 6.90 to 6.102.

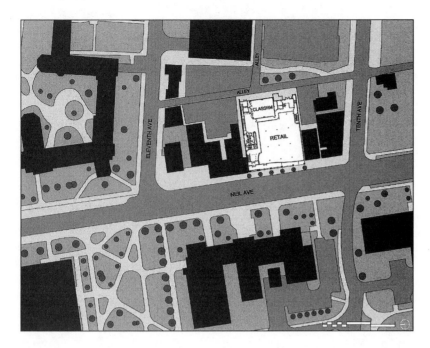

Figure 6.90 Site plan. *(Courtesy of Susan Maxman + Partners, Architects.)*

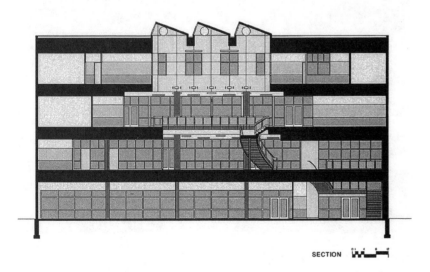

Figure 6.91 Section. *(Courtesy of Susan Maxman + Partners, Architects.)*

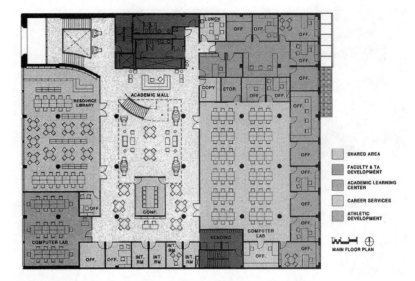

Figure 6.92 Main floor plan. *(Courtesy of Susan Maxman + Partners, Architects.)*

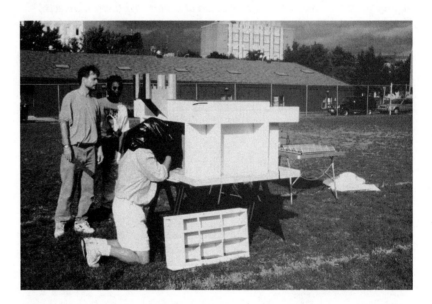

Figure 6.93 Physical model test. *(Courtesy of Susan Maxman + Partners, Architects.)*

Figure 6.94 Model detail showing aperture option. *(Courtesy of Donald Prowler.)*

Figure 6.95 Model interior. *(Courtesy of Donald Prowler.)*

Figure 6.96 Elevation at dusk. *(Courtesy of Barry Halkin.)*

Figure 6.97 Elevation/entrance. *(Courtesy of Barry Halkin.)*

Figure 6.98 Looking up toward the sawtooth fenestration. *(Courtesy of Susan Maxman + Partners, Architects.)*

Figure 6.99 Interior showing roof aperture over the open volume space. *(Courtesy of Barry Halkin.)*

Figure 6.100 Circulation. *(Courtesy of Barry Halkin.)*

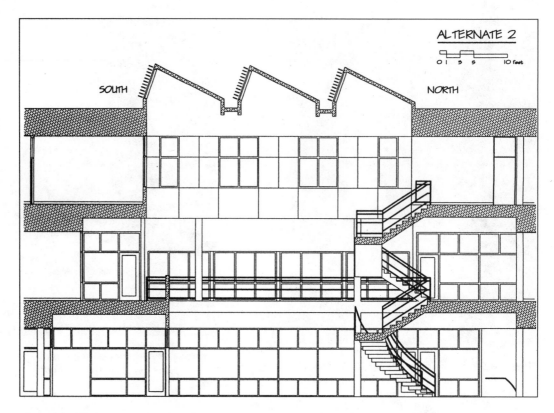

Figure 6.101 Section of open volume space. *(Courtesy of Susan Maxman + Partners, Architects.)*

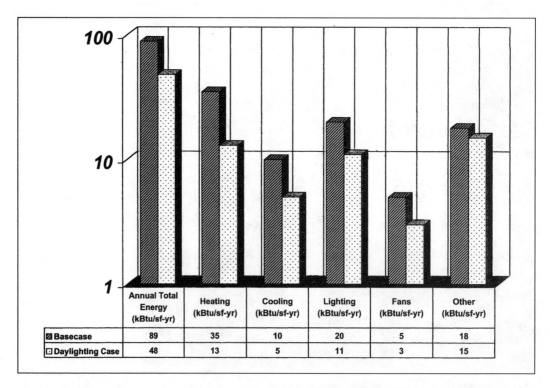

	Annual Total Energy (kBtu/sf-yr)	Heating (kBtu/sf-yr)	Cooling (kBtu/sf-yr)	Lighting (kBtu/sf-yr)	Fans (kBtu/sf-yr)	Other (kBtu/sf-yr)
▨ Basecase	89	35	10	20	5	18
▫ Daylighting Case	48	13	5	11	3	15

Figure 6.102 Energy summary. Note that the final measures included perimeter/atrium daylighting, high-performance glazing, exterior fenestration controls, efficient lighting, low-e skylight glazing, variable-speed circulating pumps, two-speed cooling tower fans, efficient boilers, and DHW.

Evergreen State College

Building Type:	Art Studio Addition, Institutional
Location:	Olympia, Washington
Building Area:	7,200 new ft^2 (rooftop addition on existing 120-ft-by-60-ft structure)
Daylighting Strategies:	Skylights were configured to take advantage of overcast sky conditions by orienting them upward toward the zenith (brightest portion) of the overcast sky. Translucent skylight panels were used to diffuse direct sunrays into softer, more visually comfortable light. Skylights were placed at the perimeter of the studios to "wash" the vertical wall surfaces with light to create ideal conditions for visual art production.
Lighting Design Levels:	The minimum design illumination level is a daylight factor of 4 (4% of outdoor illumination indoors)
Architect:	Miller Hull Partnership
Engineers:	*Electrical:* Atkinson Associates
	Structural: H. K. Kim Engineers
	Mechanical: D. W. Thomson
Consultants:	*Daylighting:* Joel Loveland (Daylighting/Lighting/Computer Modeling/Commissioning)
Summary:	The architects at Evergreen State programmed lighting as a fundamental architectural consideration, and daylighting as the primary source of illumination.

The architects at Evergreen State programmed lighting as a fundamental architectural consideration, and daylighting as the primary source of illumination.

Daylighting consultants were brought into the project for three reasons: (1) a concern by the students that the building addition require as little operating energy as possible within the construction budget; (2) an interest in having the building use local passive sources of energy for heating, cooling (sun shading), and lighting (daylight); (3) emphasis on the building being a healthy, productive, and yet relaxing environment.

There are three spaces in the addition, including graduate painting and drawing studios, two small classrooms, and circulation. The painting studio spaces were the focus of the lighting efforts and formed the majority of the programmed space. The painting studios, as programmed by the client, required a rhythm of light that emphasized the daylight illumination of the painting/work spaces and the electrical illumination of model areas and a minimum of 40 fc of ambient illumination or a daylight factor of 4 (4% of the exterior illumination).

This facility was designed to accommodate 100 students working in two-dimensional media. The art building provides a critique and gathering/exhibition space, four art studios, painting storage, a shared faculty office, and custodial areas. The principal design objective for the painting studios was to introduce natural light, using skylights. The Miller Hull design team performed a series of daylighting studies at the University of Washington Lighting Lab using large-scale models.

The configuration selected has continuous wall-washing translucent skylights along two parallel side walls in each multipurpose studio and critique space. In the main studio, a central skylight distributes light over a still-life podium. The project is an addition to the existing Lab Annex Building, which houses ceramic arts and metal shops.

Because of the requirement for daylight, the project required the integration of the lighting systems with the form of the building. The architectural form, shaped by daylighting considerations, became the primary light fixture. The surfaces in the work/painting areas of the studio, illuminated by daylight, also served as the indirect source of electrical illumination. Skylights were configured to take advantage of overcast sky conditions by "reaching" upward toward the zenith (brightest portion) of the overcast sky. Translucent skylight panels were used to diffuse direct sunrays into softer, more visually comfortable light. Skylights were placed at the perimeter of the studios to "wash" the vertical wall surfaces with light to create ideal conditions for visual art production. The model stand area was illuminated with intermediate-zone daylight and dimmed direct fluorescent luminaires. The integration of carefully designed north- and south-oriented daylight monitors in conjunction with recessed industrial strip fluorescent luminaires, positioned to indirectly illuminate the daylight monitors, forms a lighting design with a minimal energy use while providing a high level of occupant comfort and visual interest.

The available daylight reduces the need for electric illumination to less than 25% of the calculated lighting power density of 1.7 W/ft^2. The integration of the daylighting and electric lighting concepts with the building form simplified the lighting design and reduced its initial cost. To describe the initial cost of the lighting systems as \$2.50/ft^2 is both architecturally misleading and indicative of how effective a "low-cost" lighting design can be when integrated as an architectural concept. Maintenance costs are low due to the rainy weather (window washing) and accessible and commonly available electric lighting components. See Figures 6.103 to 6.111.

Figure 6.103 Physical model during test. *(Courtesy of James Fanning and Joel Loveland.)*

Figure 6.104 Physical model with light sensors. *(Courtesy of James Fanning and Joel Loveland.)*

Figure 6.105 Elevation. *(Courtesy of James Fanning and Joel Loveland.)*

Figure 6.106 Elevation. *(Courtesy of James Fanning and Joel Loveland.)*

Figure 6.107 Interior wall wash. *(Courtesy of James Fanning and Joel Loveland.)*

Figure 6.108 Studio shape. *(Courtesy of James Fanning and Joel Loveland.)*

Figure 6.109 Interior aperture. *(Courtesy of James Fanning and Joel Loveland.)*

Figure 6.110 Open web truss and fenestration. *(Courtesy of James Fanning and Joel Loveland.)*

Figure 6.111 Elevation at dusk. *(Courtesy of James Fanning and Joel Loveland.)*

Mary Ann Cofrin Hall, University of Wisconsin

Building Type:	General Collegiate Classroom
Location:	Green Bay, Wisconsin
Building Area:	120,000 ft^2

Daylighting Strategies: Daylighting strategies were assigned by space function. Offices and hallways were primarily lit using sidelighting strategies. Classrooms and labs were primarily lit using toplighting strategies. Sidelighting strategies included high clerestories and punched view windows with miniblinds installed to provide daylight control. Toplighting strategies included large linear monitors in the ceiling with suspended arched perforated metal diffusers and Soundtex fabric adhered to the top surface. In addition, electrically operated roller blinds were installed to provide blackout control in the classrooms.

Lighting Design Levels: The lighting target for all classrooms and offices is 35 fc at desk level (30 in. AFF).

Electric Lighting Controls: Four photocells were used to control over 20 daylit classrooms and open office spaces. Whenever a photocell exceeds a preset threshold, it switches the lighting in all rooms linked (by software) to that photocell to a new scene. As the photocell sees more light, the room's electric lights dim with a 30-second dim rate (slowly) from one scene to the next lower scene. Since the photocells are mounted toward the interior of the building, they receive more shade (from the building) than many individual roof monitors do. As a result, rooms on the perimeter of the building are exposed to more light than the photocells and may experience higher light levels than the 35 fc on the interior. The rooms closer to the interior of the structure correspond more closely to the photocell. Since certain classrooms have higher lighting levels than the design requires, some energy efficiency is sacrificed by using only four photocells.

The lighting controls are also tied in to the audio/visual (A/V) presentation modes. Several A/V scenes are disassociated from the photocell activity (to keep lights off rather than photocell controlled during video presentations).

Other controls are also operational. Occupancy sensors turn off lights in rooms where no motion is sensed after 15 minutes or more. A time schedule turns lights on in the morning at 6:00 A.M. and off at midnight. An astronomical clock is set with Green Bay coordinates to turn lights off in daylit corridors 2 hours after sunrise and on again 2 hours before sunset. Wall station buttons (TMOs—timed manual overrides) in all scheduled corridor spaces are available to turn the lights on for 2 hours outside of the schedule as required by occupants.

Mechanical System: In addition to standard HVAC equipment, the design integrated a solar wall and building-integrated photovoltaic technologies into the building systems. A solar wall is an unglazed perforated metal solar collector that preheats ventilation air as it is supplied to the building's air-handling units.

The building also integrated two building-integrated photo-voltaic (BIPV) sections with separate photovoltaic (PV) technologies. One uses a commercially available standing seam metal roofing product. The other section incorporates a thin-film BIPV vision glass product.

Additional Sustainability Measures:

High levels of energy conservation and efficiency in all building elements—wall and ceiling insulation, glazing, electric lighting, mechanical systems, controls, etc. Aggressive daylighting of all classrooms, faculty offices, and circulation and support spaces—daylighting provides 85% of the lighting requirements during a typical summer day and 50% during the typical winter day. Building-integrated photovoltaic system to supply electric power to the building or utility electrical grid. Solar wall for preheating ventilation (makeup) air to reduce heating energy requirements. Heat recovery on exhaust air to preheat ventilated makeup air. High-performance glazings used throughout to reduce heat loss, improve comfort, increase daylight transmission, and control summer solar heat gain. Material selection for reliability, durability, and new low-cycle cost. All energy (HVAC and lighting) system selection for comfort, reliability, durability, and low-life-cycle cost.

Architect:

Design Architect: Hellmuth, Obata & Kassabaum, Inc., St. Louis, Missouri

Architect of Record: Sommerville, Inc., Green Bay, Wisconsin

Engineers:

Sommerville, Inc., Green Bay, Wisconsin

PSJ Engineering, Inc., Milwaukee, Wisconsin

Grace, Graef, Anhalt, Schloemer & Associates, Green Bay, Wisconsin

Consultants:

Daylighting: Architectural Energy Corporation, Boulder, Colorado

Energy Modeling: Architectural Energy Corporation, Boulder, Colorado

Commissioning: Architectural Energy Corporation, Boulder, Colorado

PV Consultant: Solar Design Associates, Harvard, Massachusetts

Public Utility: Wisconsin Public Service Corp., Green Bay, Wisconsin

Mechanical: William Tao and Associates, St. Louis, Missouri

Summary:

The challenge in designing the new classroom building involved responding to the original campus concept that developed a windowless below-grade tunnel system connecting all the campus buildings. This new facility creates a new circulation system for the campus that is daylit and visually connected to the campus green spaces. New connecting tunnels between the buildings are inset into the landscape, with most of the tunnels glazed and open to a newly defined central quadrangle on one side. The first floor of Mary Ann Cofrin Hall contains most of the classrooms and special program offices. The rest of the classrooms are located off the building's lower tunnel level, which opens to the central quadrangle. The design team placed all of the large classrooms so there would be no space above them, enabling them to utilize toplighting, the most effective classroom daylighting strategy.

Because both the architectural program and the preliminary energy modeling identified daylighting as a significant energy conservation opportunity, daylighting strategies had a considerable impact on the building's shape and configuration of spaces. The design was developed to maximize the combined impact of windows, rooftop skylights, and light monitors on the interior spaces. Early in the design phase, Architectural Energy Corporation built two daylighting models, with changeable parts so different strategies could be studied as the building design developed, to test and refine the concepts. One model featured one of the building's large lecture halls with a skylight and integrated daylight deflector. The other model included a circulation corridor with a daylight monitor and adjacent office areas using a clerestory daylighting system.

Daylight supplies most of the building's ambient lighting. To provide even, diffused light in the large lecture halls, skylights channel daylight through light shafts with suspended perforated daylight deflectors that diffuse light and redirect it across the ceiling plane. The result is an illuminated ceiling providing sufficient general lighting without using the electric fixtures. Motorized blackout shade panels are available to support classes that need to use audiovisual equipment. The winter garden is the main public space in the building and is daylit from the top and south wall by a curtain wall. To control visual comfort and solar heat gain, the space was modeled and an integrated solution developed. The vertical and sloped curtain wall uses a standard framing system with different types of glazing to respond to the sun. The typical glass panel is a 1-in. insulated unit with spectrally selective coatings. The units from the floor line to 12 ft above the floor are clear to provide clean views of the courtyard beyond. The next 8 ft of glass have ceramic frit on the outside light that filters the light and reduces heat gain. The upper 8 ft of glass and sloped roof section incorporate a thin-film photovoltaic. The translucent photovoltaic was laser-etched onto the outer glass light that acts to diffuse the sunlight and provide power to the building. All major circulation spaces are daylit, ensuring that users rarely lose sight of the outside. The second-floor faculty offices are daylit from clerestory windows bringing borrowed light from the main circulation corridor into each office. To maintain classroom lighting levels, the design incorporates a combination of daylighting and electric lighting with dimmable electronic ballasts. Photocells measure daylight from the daylight sources. On a bright day, the clerestory windows will enable the system to turn off unnecessary lights. On overcast days or evenings, the system will dim the lights and adjust the fluorescent fixtures to the required light level. See Figures 6.112 to 6.121.

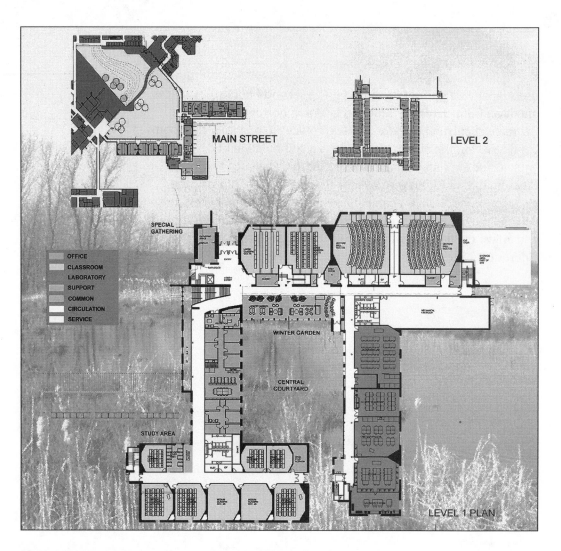

Figure 6.112 The Winter Garden is the heart of Mary Ann Cofrin Hall. Frit, special transparent coatings, and PV are used to diffuse light and control the sun. Photosensors control the electric lights. *(Courtesy of Image Studios and HOK.)*

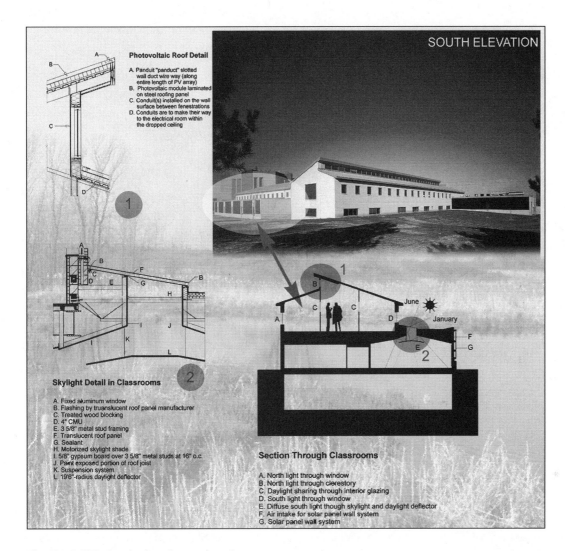

Photovoltaic Roof Detail

A. Panduit "panduct" slotted wall duct wire way (along entire length of PV array)
B. Photovoltaic module laminated on steel roofing panel
C. Conduit(s) installed on the wall surface between fenestrations
D. Conduits are to make their way to the electrical room within the dropped ceiling

SOUTH ELEVATION

Skylight Detail in Classrooms

A. Fixed aluminum window
B. Flashing by truanslucent roof panel manufacturer
C. Treated wood blocking
D. 4" CMU
E. 3 5/8" metal stud framing
F. Translucent roof panel
G. Sealant
H. Motorized skylight shade
I. 5/8" gypsum board over 3 5/8" metal studs at 16" o.c.
J. Paint exposed portion of roof joist
K. Suspension system
L. 19'6"-radius daylight deflector

Section Through Classrooms

A. North light through window
B. North light through clerestory
C. Daylight sharing through interior glazing
D. South light through window
E. Diffuse south light though skylight and daylight deflector
F. Air intake for solar panel wall system
G. Solar panel wall system

Figure 6.113 South elevation and sections.

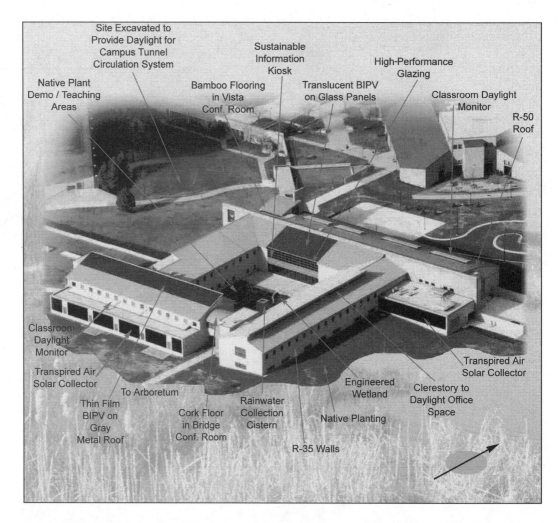

Figure 6.114 Aerial photograph pointing out the green features of Mary Ann Cofrin Hall. *(Courtesy of Wisconsin Public Power.)*

Figure 6.115 West facade from the new quadrangle. *(Courtesy of Bob Freund.)*

Figure 6.117 Windows along the main street allow the circulation space to be daylit and views to the new quadrangle. *(Courtesy of Image Studios.)*

Figure 6.116 Details showing how the interior commons spaces are daylit and BIPV above. *(Courtesy of Bob Freund.)*

Figure 6.118 Typical classroom with toplighting and diffusing screen. Photosensors control the electric lights, and the daylighting glazing can be blocked for special A/V events with a motorized shade. *(Courtesy of Image Studios.)*

Figure 6.119 One of the daylighting models used to study the circulation corridor daylit with a daylight monitor, and adjacent office areas using a clerestory daylighting system. *(Courtesy of Architectural Energy Corporation.)*

Figure 6.120 Elevation/main entrance. *(Courtesy of Jason Ander.)*

Figure 6.121 Elevation showing top-floor clerestories. *(Courtesy of Jason Ander.)*

Multi-Agency Library, College of the Desert

Building Type:	Library
Location:	Palm Desert, California
Building Area:	47,440 ft^2
Daylighting Strategies:	The architecture of the building takes advantage of ample desert light through the use of north-facing skylights and storefronts. Another strategy for controlling the building's intake of light was through the extensive use of clerestories, which stream along the rims of raised roofs, well equipped with awnings and diffusers to control direct-beam sunlight. The design challenge was to achieve a balance in this extreme desert climate of lighting the building primarily with natural sunlight while minimizing heat gain. The concept involved filling in areas of daylight with fixtures so that the interior would give the feeling of the lights being on, even when little power was being added.
Lighting Design Levels:	30–50 fc.
Electric Lighting Controls:	On/off daylighting controls and continuous dimming in reading areas.
Mechanical System:	The mechanical system consists of a chilled-water, variable-air-volume system with hot-water reheat. A natural-gas-fired hot-water boiler and air-cooled rotary chiller provide hot and chilled water to the air handlers. Additionally, the community hall is served by a separate packaged rooftop heat pump unit.
Additional Sustainability Measures:	High-performance glass, extensive fenestration controls, high-efficiency motors.
Architect:	IBI Group/L. Paul Zajfen, Irvine, California
Engineers:	*Civil:* Holt Group, Palm Springs, California
	Structural: Brandow & Johnston, Santa Ana Heights, California
	Mechanical/Electrical: Syska & Hennessy, Los Angeles, California
Consultants:	*Landscaping:* Ronald Gregory Associates, Palm Desert, California
	Acoustical: McKay Conant Brook, Inc., Westlake Village, California
	Cost: Adamson & Adamson, Santa Monica, California
	Lighting: Francis Krahe and Associates, Inc., Laguna Beach, California
	Energy Simulation: Energy Simulation Specialists, Inc., Tempe, Arizona
	Daylighting: ENSAR Group, Boulder, Colorado, and Gregg D. Ander FAIA, Los Angeles, California
Summary:	The predominant challenge in designing the library was to preserve the refined set of circumstances of the community and library and integrate them into a functional plan, while still being able to adapt

the architecture to the inherent desert climate. Sunlight and temperature became two dominant factors that helped sculpt the architectural massing of the building into a complex of volumes consisting of high-vaulted clerestoried public areas and small-scale intimate spaces with skylights.

The concept of lighting the building primarily with natural light was realized through efficient use of energy management systems, daylight controls, and occupancy sensors, well integrated into the architecture of the building. The development of such a design package, which consisted of on/off daylighting controls and continuous dimming in reading areas, significantly contributed to a comprehensive reduction in energy use and costs. See Figures 6.122 to 6.138.

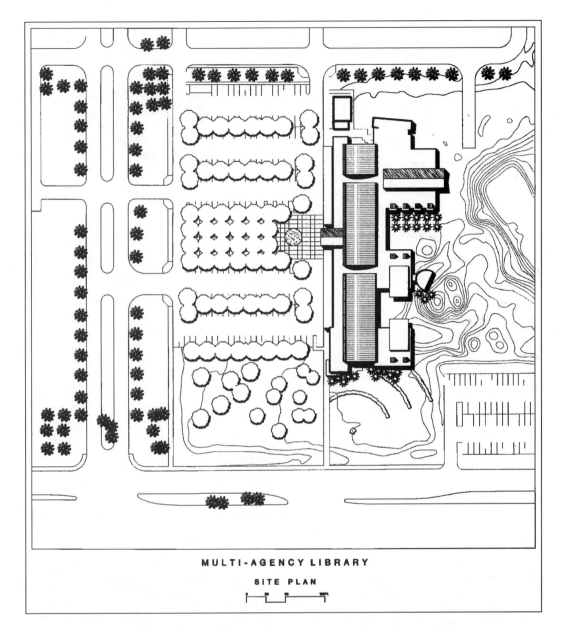

MULTI-AGENCY LIBRARY

SITE PLAN

Figure 6.122 Site plan. The library is located in a manner to form a gateway to the campus while at the same time maintaining high visibility to the public. *(Courtesy IBI Group.)*

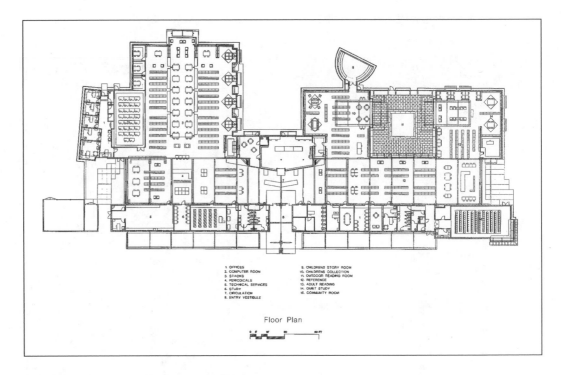

Figure 6.123 Floor plan. *(Courtesy IBI Group.)*

Figure 6.124 Courtyard rendering.

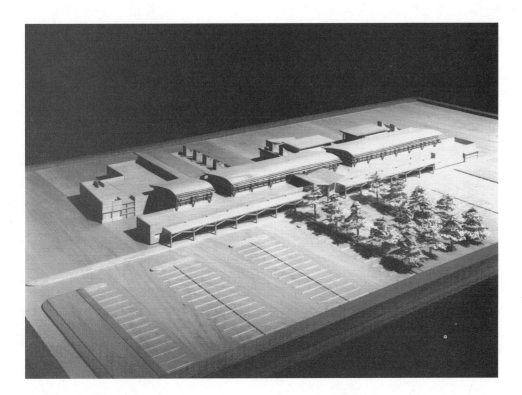

Figure 6.125 Model.

Figure 6.126 The library is a warm, inviting beacon at dusk. The clerestoried, high-vaulted space spans the length of the library and connects the two halves. *(Courtesy of J. Scott Smith.)*

Figure 6.127 Exterior showing fenestration controls.

Figure 6.128 Exterior clerestory with controls.

Figure 6.129 Courtyard sun control.

Figure 6.130 Interior study area. *(Courtesy of Paki Muthig.)*

Figure 6.131 Book checkout. *(Courtesy of Paki Muthig.)*

Figure 6.132 Interior showing sloped ceiling treatment. *(Courtesy of Paki Muthig.)*

Figure 6.133 Book stacks. *(Courtesy of Paki Muthig.)*

Figure 6.134 Circulation area.

Figure 6.135 Book stacks. *(Courtesy of Paki Muthig.)*

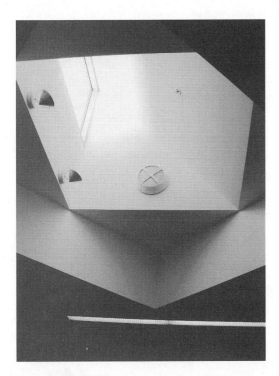

Figure 6.136 Detail of toplighting strategy.
(Courtesy of Paki Muthig.)

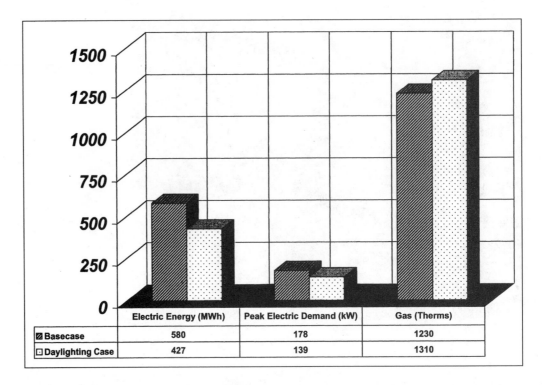

	Electric Energy (MWh)	Peak Electric Demand (kW)	Gas (Therms)
Basecase	580	178	1230
Daylighting Case	427	139	1310

Figure 6.137 Energy performance. Note that the final measures included daylighting controls, high-performance glazing with low-e coating, fenestration controls, and high-efficiency motors for fans and circulation pumps.

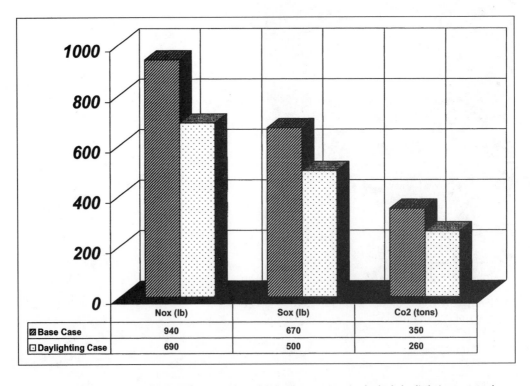

	Nox (lb)	Sox (lb)	Co2 (tons)
Base Case	940	670	350
Daylighting Case	690	500	260

Figure 6.138 Pollution avoidance. Note that the final measures included daylighting controls, high-performance glazing with low-e coating, fenestration controls, and high-efficiency motors for fans and circulation pumps.

Newport Coast Elementary School

Building Type:	School (K–6)
Location:	Newport Coast, California
Building Area:	41,202 ft^2
Daylighting Strategies:	Exterior glazing was optimized and enhanced with interior and exterior light shelves. The heights and slopes of the ceilings were developed using physical daylighting models. Whenever possible, two walls of exterior windows were provided to evenly distribute daylight. Where two walls of glass were not possible, additional clerestory glazing was provided.
Lighting Design Levels:	30–50 fc.
Electric Lighting Controls:	Dimming was provided for main pendant-mounted indirect/direct light fixtures. Supplemental lighting was also provided around the classroom on separate circuits.
Mechanical System:	Individual electric heat pump units in each classroom with remote condensing units.
Additional Sustainability Measures:	Sustainable materials were specified and the building was commissioned.
Architect:	Perkins & Will Architects, Pasadena, California
	Team: Robert Lavey, Principal in Charge; Gaylaird Christopher, Principal; Ryan Hollien; John Dale; Vince Coffeen; Courtney McLeod
Engineers:	TMAD Engineers, Inc., Ontario, California
Consultants:	*Computer Simulations:* Marlin Addison, Tempe, Arizona
	Lighting: Clanton & Associates, Boulder, Colorado
	Daylighting: Deborah Weintraub, Tony Pierce; Kelly Andereck; Gregg D. Ander, Los Angeles, California
	Commissioning: ASW Engineers
Summary:	Recognizing the increasing responsibility architects have to design facilities that reduce the impact structures have on the natural landscape and resources, the project team accepted the challenge of integrating basic concepts of sustainable design to create the best environments for learning in this new school. It was the project team's primary goal not only to identify the means toward energy efficiency and sustainability, but also to express the educational benefits of incorporating energy-conserving features into the design.

This school is the first to be built within the Newport-Mesa Unified School District in 20 years. It was adopted by the Design and Engineering Services Division of Southern California Edison (SCE) as |

a showcase project for the *School of the Future.* Working with the architect from the outset of the project, SCE facilitated an integrated design approach for all building systems to optimize energy usage and improve the overall environmental performance of the school. Detailed energy modeling, natural ventilation studies, physical daylighting modeling, and energy-efficient lighting designs were conducted on the classroom spaces.

Teachers were interested in having greater control of their classrooms in terms of temperature, outside air, mechanical ventilation, electric lighting, daylighting, furniture arrangement, and technology. The opinions gathered in these focus groups were quite similar to those opinions gathered in a much larger national survey of teachers and principals conducted in 1998.

Sophisticated studies were performed to identify areas of the school in which energy efficiency could be achieved. Physical daylight modeling allowed the design team to find a solution that would render the need for window treatments largely unnecessary and reduce the amount of electric lighting required during peak daylighting hours. Even and controlled distribution of natural light has proven to increase student performance by as much as 20% compared to classrooms that rely solely on electric lighting. Natural ventilation options were determined through the use of computational fluid dynamic models. Although air-conditioning was included in the design, highly energy-efficient compact units were specified for use during times of extreme heat.

Energy modeling showed that the single largest energy and cost savings occurred when a dimming system was used with daylighting for classroom lighting. The modeling process concluded that a 43% annual utility savings could be achieved over a minimum Title 24 building by including the use of indirect/direct pendant fixtures, occupancy sensors, multiple light switching, and strategic task lighting.

The integration of energy-efficient technology, recycled "green" materials, and design concepts that will save the district long-term energy costs was just the beginning. The project would not be complete until these features could function as teaching tools, expressing to students how an environmentally friendly building contributes to saving the earth's resources and reduces pollution and waste. Each energy efficiency and sustainability feature included in the design—light shelves and clerestory windows to improve natural daylighting, solar water heating, reclaimed water systems for irrigation and water-saving faucets/fixtures, drought-tolerant landscape—is readily visible and included in the course curriculum. Each component reinforces the concept that buildings are a valuable tool for learning. See Figures 6.139 to 6.153.

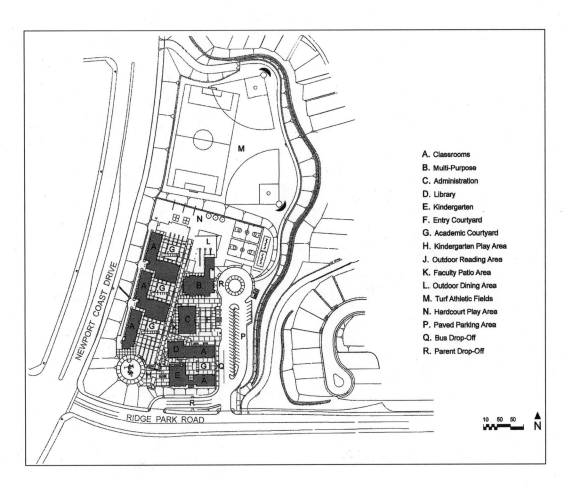

A. Classrooms
B. Multi-Purpose
C. Administration
D. Library
E. Kindergarten
F. Entry Courtyard
G. Academic Courtyard
H. Kindergarten Play Area
J. Outdoor Reading Area
K. Faculty Patio Area
L. Outdoor Dining Area
M. Turf Athletic Fields
N. Hardcourt Play Area
P. Paved Parking Area
Q. Bus Drop-Off
R. Parent Drop-Off

Figure 6.139 Site plan.

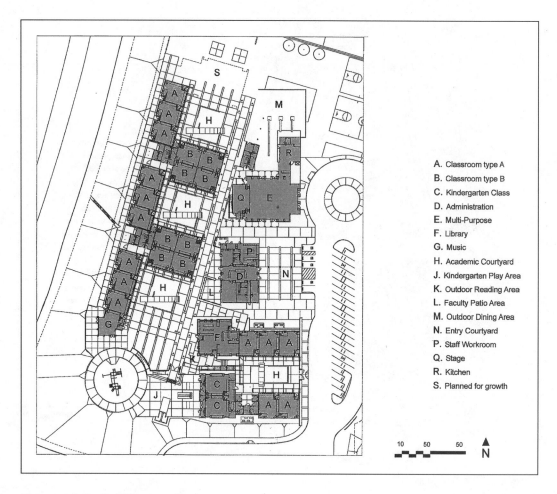

Figure 6.140 Floor plan.

A. Classroom type A
B. Classroom type B
C. Kindergarten Class
D. Administration
E. Multi-Purpose
F. Library
G. Music
H. Academic Courtyard
J. Kindergarten Play Area
K. Outdoor Reading Area
L. Faculty Patio Area
M. Outdoor Dining Area
N. Entry Courtyard
P. Staff Workroom
Q. Stage
R. Kitchen
S. Planned for growth

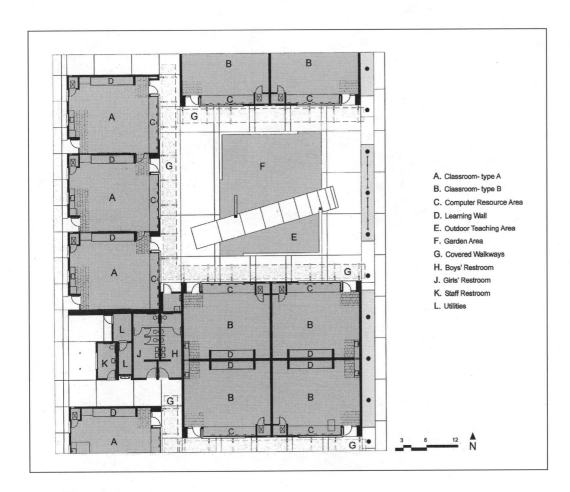

Figure 6.141 Detailed plan.

A. Classroom- type A
B. Classroom- type B
C. Computer Resource Area
D. Learning Wall
E. Outdoor Teaching Area
F. Garden Area
G. Covered Walkways
H. Boys' Restroom
J. Girls' Restroom
K. Staff Restroom
L. Utilities

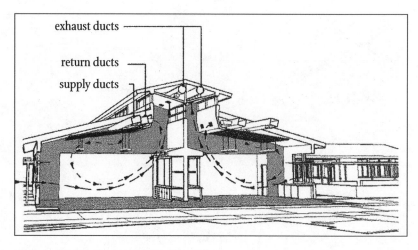

Figure 6.142 Classroom cluster: airflow.

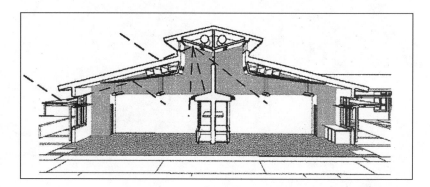

Figure 6.143 Classroom cluster: daylighting.

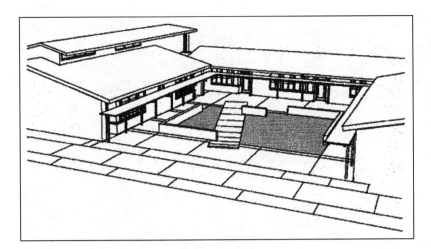

Figure 6.144 Courtyard between classrooms.

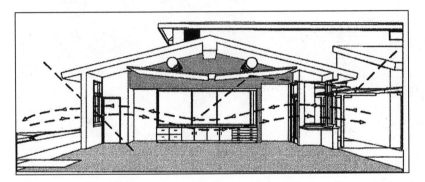

Figure 6.145 Section of linear classroom showing daylighting and airflow.

Figure 6.146 Elevation showing clerestories and shading devices/light shelves at the lower windows.

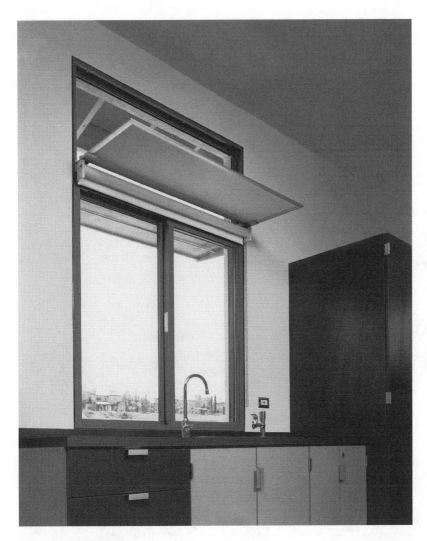

Figure 6.147 Interior light shelf.

Figure 6.148 Interior showing clerestories and electric lights.

Figure 6.149 Multipurpose room.

Figure 6.150 Courtyard with solar thermal panels.

Figure 6.151 Interior upper clerestory.

Figure 6.152 Exterior light shelves.

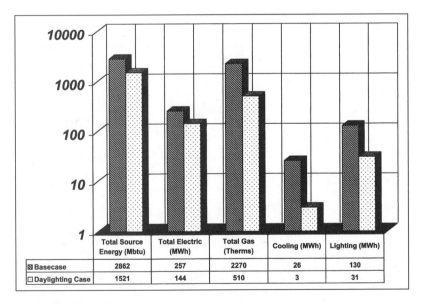

	Total Source Energy (Mbtu)	Total Electric (MWh)	Total Gas (Therms)	Cooling (MWh)	Lighting (MWh)
▨ Basecase	2862	257	2270	26	130
☐ Daylighting Case	1521	144	510	3	31

Figure 6.153 Energy performance. Note that the final measures included daylighting with dimming controls, increased insulation, operable windows, interior and exterior fenestration controls, and high-efficiency heat pumps.

Daylighting Feasibility Worksheets and Data*

WORKSHEET 1

(Note: See [Trial Design Worksheet, pages 56–57] for more information and an example of the use of the form.)

STEP 1: CHOOSE REPRESENTATIVE LOCATION

The map shows zones of roughly equal daylight availability. Each has a representative city. Choose the zone that contains your own location. Note: For Zone 2, data is provided for both Madison, WI and Washington, DC. Choose the location whose climate, especially for cooling, is most similar to that of your location.

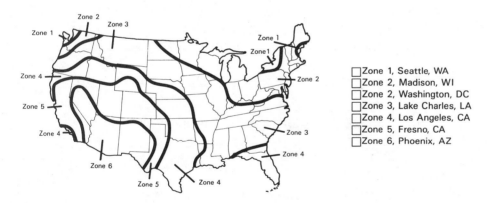

☐ Zone 1, Seattle, WA
☐ Zone 2, Madison, WI
☐ Zone 2, Washington, DC
☐ Zone 3, Lake Charles, LA
☐ Zone 4, Los Angeles, CA
☐ Zone 5, Fresno, CA
☐ Zone 6, Phoenix, AZ

STEP 2: FIND BASIC BUILDING INFORMATION

Occupancy

|_____|
(office, retail, etc.)

Desired Average Illuminance (default: 50 fc) |_____| fc

Gross Floor Area |_____| sf
(with daylighting)

---

*Excerpted with permission from the *American Architectural Manufacturers Association Skylight Handbook—Design Guidelines* (SHDG-1-88) with PC disk. Available: $100.00 (book only $52.00). Write to AAMA, 1827 Walden Office Square, Suite 550, Schaumburg, IL 60173. Call (847) 303-5664. E-mail: aamanet.org.

Lighting Power Density (default: 1.5) [   ] W/sf

Daylighting Control System: (Continuous Dimming) ☐   1-Step ☐   2-Step ☐

(Note: Ceiling height does not enter into this calculation. It is assumed that skylight spacing is less than or equal to 1.5 times ceiling height. . . .)

STEP 3: SELECT TRIAL SKYLIGHT

If possible, list the following details for a trial skylight. If not, enter the default values and skip to end of Step 4.

Area of typical skylight opening (individual unit) [   ] sf
(default: 16)

Visible transmittance, VT = [   ]
(default: 50)

Shading coefficient, SC = [   ]
(default: 44)

STEP 4: DETERMINE TRIAL WELL FACTOR (WF)

If possible, perform this analysis with a trial light well design. If not, use [the following] default well factor. . . . Sketch trial design below: List the well dimensions:

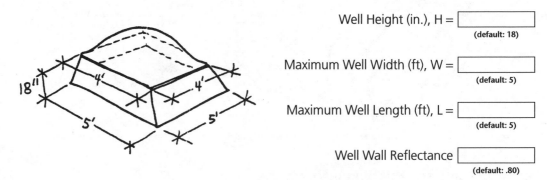

Well Height (in.), H = [   ]
(default: 18)

Maximum Well Width (ft), W = [   ]
(default: 5)

Maximum Well Length (ft), L = [   ]
(default: 5)

Well Wall Reflectance [   ]
(default: .80)

Calculate Well Index, using well dimensions listed above:

$$\text{Well Index} = \frac{H \times (L + W)}{24 \times W \times L} = \frac{\boxed{} \times \boxed{} + \boxed{}}{\times \boxed{} \times \boxed{}} = \boxed{0.30}$$
(default: .3)

Use the graph to find Well Factor, using values listed above. Start at Well Index. Draw up to appropriate wall reflectance curve, and across to find Well Factor; enter result below.

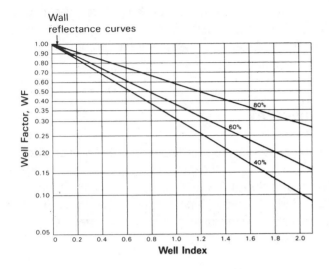

Well Factor, WF = [   ]
(default: .90)

STEP 5: DETERMINE SKYLIGHT EFFICACY (SE)

Use values listed above in Steps 3 and 4 to calculate SE. . . .

$$\text{Skylight Efficacy} = \frac{WF \times VT}{SC} = \frac{\boxed{} \times \boxed{}}{\boxed{}} = \boxed{1.02}$$

(default: 1.02)

WORKSHEET 2

Note: Use [page 206] of this form (Steps 6–9) for first cut estimates of skylight area; use [page 207] (Steps 10–12) for subsequent analysis, when actual skylight sizes are known. See [Skylight Area Worksheet, pages 60–63] for more information and an example of the use of this form. Some "Step" numbers refer to Form 1 information.

STEP 6: FIND TRIAL EFFECTIVE APERTURE (EA)

Choose the graph from [pages 61–63 that] corresponds to your Representative Location (Step 1) and to your Desired Average Illuminance (Step 2). Enter the graph at the LPD for your design (Step 2). Draw up to the dashed line curve that is closest to your SE (Step 5); mark the intersection points (you may interpolate between dashed curves). Repeat this step for the solid line curves. Draw horizontal lines from these points to find minimum and maximum Effective Apertures (EA). Enter these numbers in Step 7 below.

STEP 7: DETERMINE TRIAL SKYLIGHT-TO-FLOOR RATIO (SFR)

Minimum EA = ☐   Maximum EA = ☐

$$SFR = \frac{Max\ EA}{VT \times WF} = \frac{\boxed{}}{\boxed{} \times \boxed{}}$$

$$SFR = \frac{Max\ EA}{VT \times WF} = \frac{\boxed{}}{\boxed{} \times \boxed{}}$$

(Step 3) (Step 4)   **(Step 3) (Step 4)**

Minimum SFR = ☐   Maximum SFR = ☐

STEP 8: DETERMINE TRIAL SKYLIGHT AREA

Minimum Total Skylight Area:

Min. Area = Min. SFR × Gross Area = ☐ × ☐
            (Step 7)   **(Step 2)**   sf

Minimum Area = ☐ sf

Maximum Total Skylight Area:

Max. Area = Max. SFR × Gross Area = ☐ × ☐
            (Step 7)   **(Step 2)**   sf

Maximum Area = ☐ sf

STEP 9: DETERMINE TRIAL NUMBER OF SKYLIGHTS

Minimum Number of Skylights:
Min. Nmbr = Min. Area ÷ Unit Area = ☐ ÷ ☐
            (Step 8)   (Step 3)   sf

Minimum Number = ☐
                  (round up)

Maximum Number of Skylights:
Max. Nmbr = Max. Area ÷ Unit Area = ☐ ÷ ☐
            (Step 8)   (Step 3)   sf

Maximum Number = ☐
                  (round up)

Note: The following three steps are used to calculate Effective Aperture (EA) when the number of skylights, the well factor, and the visible transmittance of the skylight are known. . . .

STEP 10: DETERMINE TOTAL SKYLIGHT AREA

Number of Skylights × Unit Area = ☐ × ☐ × ☐ Total Skylight Area
        (#)   (sf each)   #   sf each   sf
                          (Step 3)

STEP 11: DETERMINE SKYLIGHT-TO-FLOOR RATIO (SFR)

Total Skylight Area ÷ Gross Floor Area = ☐ ÷ ☐ = ☐ Skylight-to-Floor Ratio (SFR)
     (Step 10)   (Step 2)   sf   sf

STEP 12: DETERMINE EFFECTIVE APERTURE (EA)

☐ × ☐ × ☐ = ☐ Effective Aperture
SFR   VT   WF   EA

(Step 11) (Step 3) (Step 4)

WORKSHEET 4

Note: See [Lighting Savings Worksheet, pages 68–70] for more information and an example of the use of this form. Some "Step" numbers refer to previous Form information.

STEP 13: FINDING FULL-LOAD LIGHTING HOURS

The default value corresponds to typical office working hours, as shown in the schedule in [the previous section]. If that schedule differs greatly from the schedule in your building, refer to [Appendix E] for the procedure for finding your full-load operating hours. Otherwise, use the default value.

Full-load lighting hours = ☐ hrs.
(default: 2600)

STEP 14: FIND FRACTION OF LIGHTING ENERGY SAVED

Use the graph from [the Lighting Energy Savings Graphs, pages 69–70] corresponding to your Representative Location (Step 1) and your Desired Average Illuminance (Step 2). Enter graph at the EA value (Step 12) corresponding to your skylight design. Draw a line up to the curve for your Daylighting Control System (Step 2), then across to the fraction of lighting energy saved. Enter the fraction below.

EA = 0.022 (Step 12)
Fraction of Lighting Energy Saved ☐

STEP 15: CALCULATE LIGHTING ENERGY SAVED

$$\frac{\text{LPD (Step2)}}{1000} \times \text{Gross Floor Area} \times \text{Full Load Hours} \times \text{Fraction Saved} = \text{Lighting Energy Saved (kWh)}$$

(Step 2)   (Step 13)   (Step 14)

$$\frac{\boxed{}}{1000} \times \boxed{} \times \boxed{} \times \boxed{} = \boxed{} \text{ kWh/yr}$$

STEP 16: CALCULATE LIGHTING COST SAVED

. . . If actual electricity costs are not known, [contact your local utility for a current rate schedule].

$$\text{Lighting Energy Saved} \times \text{Average Electricity Cost} = \boxed{} \times \boxed{} = \boxed{}$$

(Step 15)   ($/kWh)   kWh/yr $/kWh $/yr

WORKSHEET 5

Note: See [Cooling Calculation Worksheet, page 72] for more information and an example of the use of this form. Some "Step" numbers refer to previous Form information.

STEP 17: NOTE REPRESENTATIVE CITY

This calculation makes use of the same representative cities selected in Step 1. Check off your selection again here, for reference:

☐ Seattle, WA
☐ Madison, WI
☐ Washington, DC
☐ Lake Charles, LA
☐ Los Angeles, CA
☐ Fresno, CA
☐ Phoenix, AZ

STEP 18: FIND COEFFICIENTS FOR REPRESENTATIVE COOLING CITY

	B1	B2
Seattle, WA	0.19	11.5
Madison, WI	0.31	16.6
Washington, DC	0.42	21.1
Lake Charles, LA	0.66	30.8
Los Angeles, CA	0.53	28.1
Fresno, CA	0.51	36.9
Phoenix, AZ	0.68	47.3

STEP 19: CALCULATE COOLING ENERGY AND COST EFFECTS

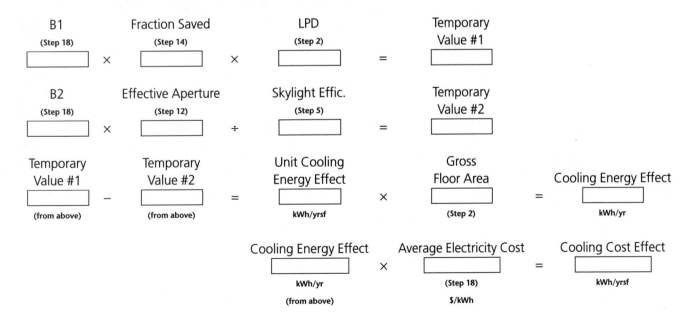

Standard Commissioning Procedure for Daylighting Controls*

BUILDING NAME: _____ APPLICATION #: _____

BUILDING ADDRESS: _____

_____

NAME & FIRM OF PERSON(S) DOING TEST: _____

DATE(S) OF TEST: _____

General Notes:

1. This is a generic test procedure for daylighting control systems. If the complexity, configuration, or other aspects of a specific project require substitute tests or additional tests, explain on the comments sheets, and attach the additional test procedures and field data. Use additional copies of this procedure as required for the total number of zones to be commissioned.
2. In all test sections, circle or otherwise highlight any responses that indicate deficiencies (i.e., responses that don't meet the criteria for acceptance). Acceptance requires correction and retest of all deficiencies, as defined in each test section under "Criteria for Acceptance" or "Acceptance." Attach all retest data sheets. Complete the Deficiency Report Form for all deficiencies.
3. This Commissioning Procedure does not address fire and life safety or basic equipment safety controls.
4. To ensure that this Commissioning Procedure will not damage any equipment or affect any equipment warranties, have the equipment manufacturer's representative review any interventive test procedures prior to execution.

OPERATOR INTERVIEW (Existing Buildings Only):

Determine from a discussion with the building operator whether the daylighting controls are operating properly to the best of their knowledge. Note any known problems, and possible solutions.

_____

_____

_____

_____

LIGHTING ZONE SCHEDULE:

For the purposes of this commissioning procedure, a lighting zone is defined as a group of luminaires that are controlled by a single daylighting/lumen maintenance signal output.

---

*Published with permission from the Seattle Lighting Laboratory.

Sampling: If there are more than eight lighting zones in the building, you may select a sample for the following performance tests. The sample should include at least 10% of the total number of zones, or eight zones, whichever is greater. Zones should be selected from different areas of each floor, and from different floors. Also, if banks of luminaires in spaces are controlled by separate sensors/controllers, include at least one space with two such zones, and test both zones. Note in the table below which zones are selected for the sample.

Criteria for Acceptance: Lighting zoning must be in accordance with submittals as approved by Designer.

ZONE #	SAMPLE ZONE? (✓)	DESCRIPTION OF LOCATION	CIRCUIT # (if available)

COMMENTS ON ZONING (add more sheets if needed):

Zone #   *Comment*

DAYLIGHTING CONTROL SYSTEM, INSTALLED CHARACTERISTICS (from field inspection):

Criteria for Acceptance: Installed characteristics must be in accordance with submittals as approved by designer, or as noted otherwise. "No" answers to questions marked with an "✳" shall also be considered deficiencies.

DESCRIPTION	RESPONSE (Note: If different lighting zones have different responses to these questions, respond specifically to each group of zones and define which zones lie within each group. Add sheets as necessary.)
1. Does system include lumen maintenance** control? If so, describe scope & intent.	
2. Luminaire control (dimming or switching)?	
3. If luminaire control is dimming, what is setpoint for minimum % of full light output? Acceptance: <30% of full light output.	
4. Design illuminance setpoint (foot-candles at work plane**). Acceptance: per design or <100 fc, whichever is less.	
5. Define work plane for this application (e.g. desk level, 10 feet from windows).	
6. Is there at least one lighting control zone per each perimeter exposure on each floor? ✳	
7. Were controls calibrated as part of system start-up? (If not, do not proceed with this procedure until calibration is complete.) ✳	
8. Was calibration done with finishings and furniture in place, and after approximately 100 hours of lamp burn-in? ✳	
9. Daylighting control type (closed-loop integral** or open-loop proportional**; or describe other control sequence)? Acceptance: Open-loop control may not be used for applications that include lumen maintenance.	
10. Describe any special system features (e.g. light shelves, skylights, fins, sloped ceilings, special glazings, tracking mirrors, automatic window aperture controls, etc.).	
11. Have occupants been explained the intent and operation of the control system? ✳	
12. Describe any other ways in which the installed system differs from the design intent &/or approved submittals.	

**See glossary on last page of test.

COMMENTS ON INSTALLED CHARACTERISTICS (add more sheets if needed):

Item #   *Comment*

_____   _____
_____   _____
_____   _____
_____   _____

NAMEPLATE DATA (from equipment nameplates, as recorded in field):

Criteria for Acceptance: Nameplate data must be in accordance with submittals as approved by Designer.

DESCRIPTION	MANUFACTURER	MODEL #	COMMENTS
Photosensor			
Lighting Controller			
Controlled Ballasts			
EMS Interface			
Other:			
Other:			

INSTALLATION VERIFICATION:

Instructions: Under each zone write "Y" for yes, "N" for no, "NA" for not applicable, or a number to refer to any needed comments. Explain any "N" answers in the comment section. If other information is requested, write the appropriate values.

Criteria for Acceptance: All items require answers of "Y" (or "NA", where relevant) except where other criteria are noted. If there is failure in any of the following tests for more than 20% of the sampled zones (or two zones, whichever is more), then the entire daylighting control installation shall be considered to be not in conformance. In this case, the installing contractor is responsible to test all zones prior to calling for a retest under this procedure.

DESCRIPTION	ZONE #							
1. Lighting zone generally correlates with area of daylight availability.								
2. There is separate control of luminaires close to and far from the windows.								
3. Photosensor is mounted in proper location, per manufacturer's directions & in a position to accurately control work plane illuminance.								
4. Photosensor is protected from direct sunlight.								
5. If indirect lighting** is used, photosensor is mounted at lower plane of fixture, facing down.								
6. Are interior finishes and work space location consistent with efficient use of daylighting?								
7. Are skylights & other toplighting glazing clean?								
8. Do all lamps in lighting zone dim to approximately the same level?								
9. If lamp switching is used, do controls include deadband & time delay?								
10. Describe in comments anything that interferes with design intent of system.[1]								
11.								
12.								

Notes To Table:
[1]For example, storage or dirt on light shelves, dark interior surfaces, blinds that are closed all the time, exterior obstructions, glare, solar gain problems, objectionable changes in light level, etc.

COMMENTS ON INSTALLATION VERIFICATION CHECKLIST ITEMS (add more sheets if needed):

Item #   *Zone #*   *Comment*

_____   _____   _____

_____   _____   _____

_____   _____   _____

_____   _____   _____

_____   _____   _____

_____   _____   _____

_____   _____   _____

_____   _____   _____

FUNCTIONAL PERFORMANCE VERIFICATION:

Daylighting and Lumen Maintenance Control Tests: Perform the following tests by monitoring and/or observing each lighting zone under actual operation. If the actual control sequence differs from that implied by the tests, attach a description of the control sequence, the tests that were done to verify the sequence, and your conclusions. Use of current data loggers over a period of several days to document operation is recommended, though visual observation is acceptable. Annotate any logger data and graphs so that it is clear what the data are proving, and attach these to this form. Attach sketch (or marked-up floor plan) showing location of illuminance test points. Trend logs of EMS outputs or schedule printouts *are not acceptable* as proof of operation.

Test Conditions: Do daytime tests on a bright day, preferably between 10 A.M. and 2 P.M. There should be no direct sun shining on the work plane at the time of testing.

Criteria for Acceptance: Footcandle reading during nighttime test should be within ±20% of design illuminance. (Use 50 to 100 footcandles for office occupancies if no design values are available.) For daytime test 1, circuit amps must be at least 25% lower than nighttime test values. Footcandle values for both daytime tests may not exceed design illuminance by more than 20% unless amp readings indicate circuit is fully dimmed. If there is failure in any of the following tests for more than 20% of the sampled zones (or two zones, whichever is more), then the entire daylighting control installation shall be considered to be not in conformance. In this case, the installing contractor is responsible to test all zones prior to calling for a retest under this procedure.

DESCRIPTION	ZONE #							
1. Nighttime test: record footcandles at work plane. Record lighting circuit amps.	fc	fc	fc	fc	fc	fc	fc	fc
	amps	amps	amps	amps	amps	amps	amps	amps
2. Daytime test 1: record work plane fc & lighting circuit amps with blinds open.	fc	fc	fc	fc	fc	fc	fc	fc
	amps	amps	amps	amps	amps	amps	amps	amps
3. Daytime test 2: record work plane fc & lighting circuit amps w/blinds ½ closed. (This test is not required for closed-loop control zones.)	fc	fc	fc	fc	fc	fc	fc	fc
	amps	amps	amps	amps	amps	amps	amps	amps
4. Observe zone during daytime under normal operation, three times in a 12 hour period, at least 3 hours apart and for at least 5 minutes each time. Verify that there is no unusual ballast hum, light-level hunting, or other problems.								

COMMENTS ON FUNCTIONAL PERFORMANCE VERIFICATION ITEMS (add more sheets as needed):

Item #	*Zone #*	*Comment*
_____	_____	_____
_____	_____	_____
_____	_____	_____
_____	_____	_____
_____	_____	_____

_____   _____   _____
_____   _____   _____
_____   _____   _____
_____   _____   _____
_____   _____   _____

I certify that the data and test results as recorded herein are accurate.

_____   _____

Signature, Commissioning Agent   Date

_____   _____

Firm Name   (Area Code) Phone Number

GLOSSARY OF TERMS:

Closed-Loop Integral Control: A closed-loop integral controller continuously adjusts the output of the electric lights so that the photosensor output is maintained at the setpoint level. As the photosensor detects an increase in light in the space due to daylight, the controller reduces the electric light level to restore the photosensor signal to the setpoint level. This algorithm only works if the photosensor can "see" the electric light it controls.

Indirect Lighting: A lighting design in which the fixtures direct the lighting upward to reflect against the ceiling. The luminaires are not directly visible from the space below.

Lamp Switching: Use of photoelectric control switches to switch off, rather than dim, lights in daylight perimeter zones. These switches should incorporate a "deadband" so that the lights don't cycle between levels if the ambient light level is near the sensor trip level. Some switches also allow the user to adjust a time delay constant that reduces the likelihood of cycling.

Lumen Maintenance: A control strategy that uses a photocell to detect the actual illuminance in the space, and adjusts the light level accordingly, so that the design illuminance is maintained at setpoint at all times, not just at the end of the maintenance cycle.

Open-Loop Proportional Control: With an open-loop proportional controller, the photosensor is mounted so that it does not detect the light that is controlled. The photosensor detects only the independent stimulus of daylight.

Work Plane: The level (plane) and general location to which the daylight zone illuminance setpoint applies. In office occupancies, this is usually at desk level, and about 10 to 15 feet from the perimeter windows. In retail applications the work plane may be vertical, extending from about 3 feet to 6 feet above the floor.

Weather Data

TEMPERATURE RANGE - ATLANTA

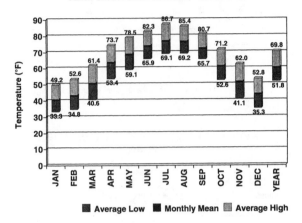

AVERAGE DAILY EXTERIOR ILLUMINANCE
ATLANTA

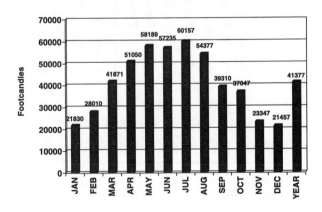

AVERAGE SKY COVER - ATLANTA

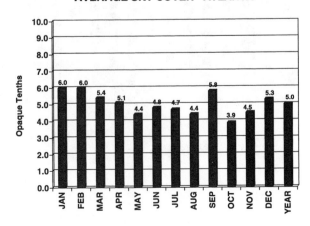

TEMPERATURE RANGE - CHICAGO

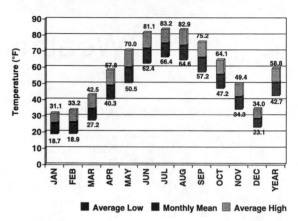

■ Average Low   ■ Monthly Mean   ▨ Average High

AVERAGE DAILY EXTERIOR ILLUMINANCE CHICAGO

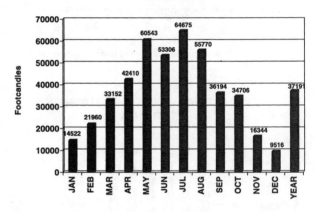

AVERAGE SKY COVER - CHICAGO

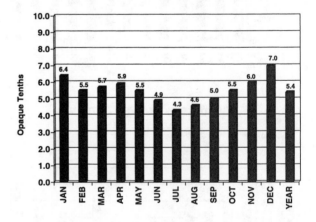

TEMPERATURE RANGE - DENVER

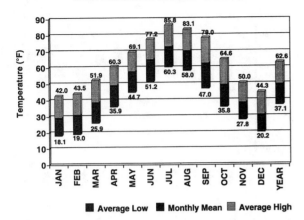

AVERAGE DAILY EXTERIOR ILLUMINANCE DENVER

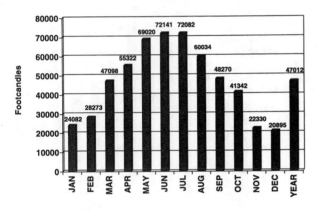

AVERAGE SKY COVER - DENVER

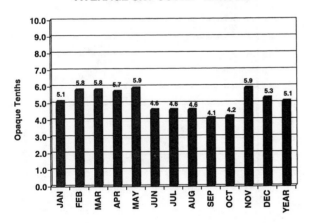

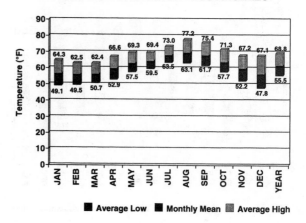

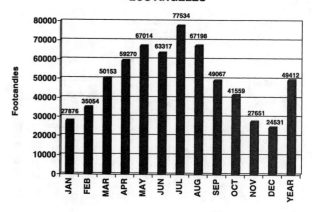

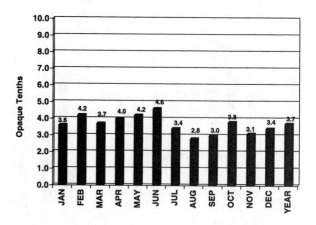

TEMPERATURE RANGE - NEW YORK

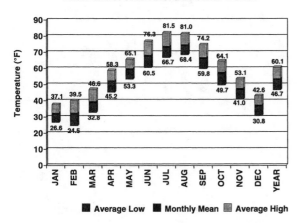

■ Average Low   ■ Monthly Mean   ■ Average High

AVERAGE DAILY EXTERIOR ILLUMINANCE
NEW YORK

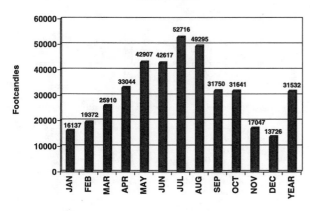

AVERAGE SKY COVER - NEW YORK

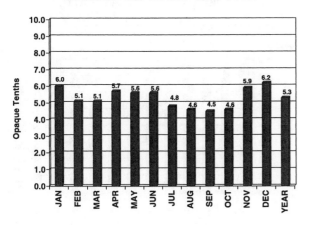

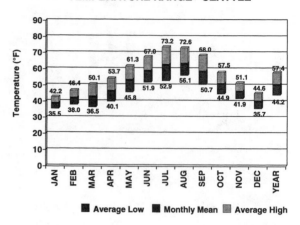

TEMPERATURE RANGE - SEATTLE

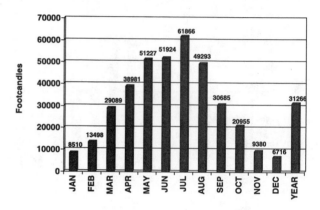

AVERAGE DAILY EXTERIOR ILLUMINANCE SEATTLE

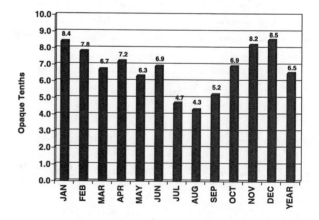

AVERAGE SKY COVER - SEATTLE

Glazing Material Properties

Typical Visible Transmittance Values

MONOLITHIC GLASS CLEAR AND TINTED				
GLASS	**THICKNESS**		**TRANSMITTANCE**	
	in.	mm	**Average Daylight (%)**	**Total Solar (%)**
Sheet	SS	2.5	90	85
	DS 3	3	89	80
	3/16	5	89	78
	1/8	3	89	80
Clear	3/16	5	88	78
	1/4	6	87	75
	5/16	8	86	70
	3/8	10	84	67
	1/2	12	82	61
Clear heavy-duty	5/8	15	80	56
	3/4	19	78	51
	7/8	22	75	48
	1/8	3	83	63
Blue-green	3/16	5	79	55
	1/4	6	75	47
	1/8	3	61	63
	3/16	5	51	53
Gray	1/4	6	44	46
	5/16	8	35	38
	3/8	10	28	21
	1/2	12	19	22
INSULATING GLASS				
(Inboard light clear)				
Clear	1/8	3	80	69
	3/16	5	79	62
	1/4	6	77	59
	1/8	3	75	52
Blue-green	3/16	5	70	43
	1/4	6	66	36
	1/8	3	55	52
Gray	3/16	5	45	42
	1/4	6	39	35
	1/8	3	61	54
Bronze	3/16	5	53	43
	1/4	6	46	38

Note: Check manufacturers' literature for specific values.

Alternative to Lighting Savings Graphs*

The procedure outlined in this appendix provides an alternative to the procedure for determining Lighting Energy Saved found on pages 68–70. It allows one to more accurately determine lighting energy savings for situations that differ significantly from those assumed in the analysis which underlies the worksheets. This procedure should be used where:

1) The Desired Average Illuminance (Step 2) is much greater than 70 footcandles, or much less than 30 footcandles, or
2) The operating schedule for the building is not similar to the default schedule shown on pages 68–70 (Step 13), which is a typical 8–5 office schedule. Examples of dissimilar schedules would be elementary schools and retail stores.

It may also be used when:

3) You wish to develop a detailed profile of average daylighting illuminances.

This procedure is based on simulation data that gives the monthly average illuminance for each hour of the day in the skylighted space for a given Effective Skylight Area (EA). This data is shown for six representative daylighting climates, using an EA of 0.01. The representative climates are:

Seattle
Madison/Washington
Lake Charles
Los Angeles
Fresno
Phoenix

There is a separate data table for each of the locations (Figures E.6 to E.11), plus blank calculation tables which are filled in during the procedure (Figure E.12).

The illuminance in a space is very nearly proportional to the EA. For example, for an EA = .02, the illuminance in Figure E.1 would be double the values shown for each hour.

---

*Excerpted with permission from the *American Architectural Manufacturers Association Skylight Handbook—Design Guidelines* (SHDG-1-88) with PC disk. Available: $100.00 (book only $52.00). Write to AAMA, 1827 Walden Office Square, Suite 550, Schaumburg, IL 60173. Call (847) 303-5664. E-mail: aamanet.org.

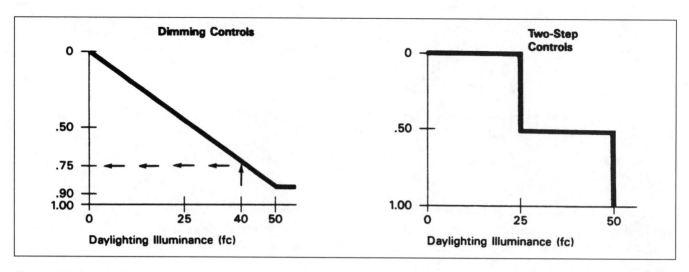

Figure E.1 Sample daylighting control operation.

This fact is the basis for this procedure; in essence, it has you adjust the illuminances for each hour, and project these values through to the hourly and total lighting energy savings. These adjustments are:

- Adjust illuminance levels for your actual EA
- Estimate lighting savings by your control system
- Determine full load lighting power
- Determine lighting energy savings

The details of the calculation follow:

1) Complete Forms 1, 2, & 3 to determine your trial skylight design. Note that the graphs in the analysis method to determine initial EA's for design (Step 6) were based on the typical, 8–5 schedule. If your operating schedule contains less daylighting hours, you should pick a smaller EA for initial design, such as the minimum EA found.
2) Select the data table for your Representative Location (Step 1) from Figures E.6 to E.11. For each value on the data table, multiply by the factor:

$$(\text{Value from table}) \times \frac{EA}{.01} = \text{new value}$$

and enter the result in the same location on a blank data table (Figure E.12). For example, the Washington, DC, value for hour 12 in January is 24 fc (see Figure E.7). If your EA is .02, multiply:

$$24 \text{ fc} \times \frac{.02}{.01} = 48 \text{ fc}$$

This number would be placed in the hour 12 location for January on a blank data table. The calculation would be repeated for each location on the worksheet. This should be labeled "Data Table 2, Average Daylight Illuminances" (see Figure E.2); it shows the monthly average daylight illuminance for each hour of an average day.

3) Based on the indicated illuminances, determine, for each hour of each month, the fraction of lighting energy that would be saved by your lighting control system. The following graphs illustrate how you could determine this for a dimming system and a two-step system. A similar analysis could be readily developed for different kinds of control systems. For example, use the graph below for a dimming system. If the daylighting illuminance were shown in Data Table 2 to be 40 footcandles for hour 10 in June, you would enter the graph at 40 fc, draw a vertical up to the sloped line, and thence horizontally to find the Lighting Fraction Saved to be 0.75. This value would be entered in a new blank data table for hour 10 in June. The procedure would be repeated for all hours. Note that in this example, many hours are at the minimum or maximum lighting savings values, and will not require calculation. The results of these calculations should be labeled "Data Table 3, Fraction of Lighting Energy Saved" (see Figure E.3).

4) Start with a new blank data table, labeled "Data Table 4, Full Load Lighting Power" (see Figure E.4). Determine the full load lighting power for the daylighted space by multiplying the Gross Floor Area times Lighting Power Density (both from Step 2). Determine your building's lighting schedule, as a decimal fraction of full load lighting for each hour of each month. For example, a typical building might require 85% of the lights on at noon, and only 50% of the lights on at 7 P.M. For each hour, multiply the lighting schedule decimal fraction times the full load lighting power times the number of operating days per month; divide by 1000. This will yield the number of kilowatt hours (kWh) used when there is no daylighting.

5) Start with another blank data table, labeled "Data Table 5, Lighting Energy Savings" (see Figure E.5). Determine the lighting energy saved by daylighting, multiplying the numbers in Data Table 3 by their corresponding values in Data Table 4. For example, if the value for hour 3 in December in Table 3 were .40, and the value for the same hour in Table 4 were 15,600, then you would enter the following value for hour 3 in December in Table 5:

$$.40 \times 15{,}600 \, \text{kWh} = 6240 \, \text{kWh}$$

6) Sum all the numbers in all columns and rows in Data Table 5. Carry this number back to Step 15 on Form 4; enter it as the answer, Lighting Energy Saved (kWh). Proceed on to Step 16 and the following forms.

The following pages include a worked example of this calculation (Figures E.2 to E.5). Following that are the source data tables (Figures E.6 to E.11), and a blank data table (Figure E.12).

Data Table No. 2
Title   Average Daylight Illuminances, EA = 0.02

Washington, DC
70 fc set point
1.8 W/sf Skylight SE = 1.0
Dimming system chosen for 1000 sf retail

	1	2	3	4	5	6	7	8	9	10	11	12	13	14	15	16	17	18	19	20	21	22	23	24
Jan.								2	12	24	38	46	48	42	30	16	4							
Feb.								6	20	40	60	72	72	64	48	30	12							
March							2	16	36	62	78	90	92	84	68	44	22	6						
April							2	16	36	60	80	94	102	102	94	76	56	34	14					
May							10	28	56	80	102	116	116	114	108	94	76	46	22	6				
June							12	30	58	88	108	122	130	124	122	112	92	62	32	12				
July							8	26	56	88	110	124	140	144	140	114	86	58	30	10				
Aug.							4	20	46	78	108	126	140	138	124	104	80	48	20	4				
Sept.								10	32	60	80	96	110	106	96	80	56	26	6					
Oct.								2	18	38	60	74	80	78	68	50	28	10						
Nov.								6	20	32	44	52	48	38	24	12								
Dec.								2	12	24	34	40	38	32	22	10								

Figure E.2 Example: Data Table 2.

Data Table No. 3
Title   Fraction Lighting Energy Saved

	1	2	3	4	5	6	7	8	9	10	11	12	13	14	15	16	17	18	19	20	21	22	23	24
Jan.								.03	.15	.31	49	.59	.62	.54	.39	.21	.05							
Feb.								.08	.26	.51	.77	.90	.90	.82	.62	.39	.15							
March							.03	.21	.46	.80	.90	.90	.90	.90	.87	.57	.28	.08						
April							.03	.21	.46	.77	.90	.90	.90	.90	.90	.90	.72	.44	.18					
May							.13	.36	.72	.90	.90	.90	.90	.90	.90	.90	.90	.59	.28	.08				
June							.15	.39	.75	.90	.90	.90	.90	.90	.90	.90	.90	.80	.41	.15				
July							.10	.33	.72	.90	.90	.90	.90	.90	.90	.90	.90	.75	.39	.13				
Aug.							.05	.26	.59	.90	.90	.90	.90	.90	.90	.90	.90	.62	.26	.05				
Sept.								.13	.41	.77	.90	.90	.90	.90	.90	.90	.72	.33	.08					
Oct.								.03	.23	.49	.77	.90	.90	.90	.87	.64	.36	.13						
Nov.								.08	.26	.41	.57	.67	.62	.49	.31	.15								
Dec.								.03	.15	.31	.44	.51	.49	.41	.28	.13								

Figure E.3 Example: Data Table 3.

Open 7 days/week

1.8 W/sf, 1000 sf

Lighting schedule:
70% 10 A.M.–11 A.M.
100% 11 A.M.–7 P.M.
70% 7 P.M.–8 P.M.
50% 8 P.M.–9 P.M.

Data Table No. 4
Title   Full Load Lighting Power (KWH)

Hours of Day

	1	2	3	4	5	6	7	8	9	10	11	12	13	14	15	16	17	18	19	20	21	22	23	24
Jan.											39	56	56	56	56	56	56	56	56	39	28			
Feb.											35	50	50	50	50	50	50	50	50	35	25			
March											39	56	56	56	56	56	56	56	56	39	28			
April											38	54	54	54	54	54	54	54	54	38	27			
May											39	56	56	56	56	56	56	56	56	39	28			
June											38	54	54	54	54	54	54	54	54	38	27			
July											39	56	56	56	56	56	56	56	56	39	28			
Aug.											39	56	56	56	56	56	56	56	56	39	28			
Sept.											38	54	54	54	54	54	54	54	54	38	27			
Oct.											39	56	56	56	56	56	56	56	56	39	28			
Nov.											38	54	54	54	54	54	54	54	54	38	27			
Dec.											39	56	56	56	56	56	56	56	56	39	28			

Figure E.4 Example: Data Table 4.

Data Table No. 5
Title   Lighting Energy Savings (KWH)

Hours of Day

	1	2	3	4	5	6	7	8	9	10	11	12	13	14	15	16	17	18	19	20	21	22	23	24
Jan.											19	33	35	30	22	12	3	0	0	0	0			
Feb.											27	45	45	41	31	18	8	0	0	0	0			
March											35	50	50	50	49	32	16	4	0	0	0			
April											34	49	49	49	49	39	24	10	0	0	0			
May											35	50	50	50	50	50	33	16	4	0	0			
June											34	49	49	49	49	49	43	22	8	0	0			
July											35	50	50	50	50	50	42	22	7	0	0			
Aug.											35	50	50	50	50	50	35	15	3	0	0			
Sept.											34	49	49	49	49	39	18	4	0	0	0			
Oct.											35	50	50	49	36	20	7	0	0	0	0			
Nov.											22	36	33	26	17	8	0	0	0	0	0			
Dec.											17	29	27	23	16	7	0	0	0	0	0			

Total lighting savings = 3128 KWH/yr

Figure E.5 Example: Data Table 5.

Hours of Day

	1	2	3	4	5	6	7	8	9	10	11	12	13	14	15	16	17	18	19	20	21	22	23	24
Jan.										1	10	12	13	12	9	5	1							
Feb.										10	18	21	22	21	17	11	5							
March									9	20	28	34	36	35	29	20	11	5						
April									9	24	31	41	48	51	49	41	32	23	12	3				
May									23	33	44	54	60	62	59	51	41	32	23	12	3			
June								8	22	31	46	58	64	64	63	55	45	34	22	9	3			
July								6	27	38	55	68	76	79	77	68	57	45	29	12	2			
Aug.									14	30	40	52	60	61	58	51	39	27	15	5				
Sept.									2	19	28	38	47	49	45	38	27	15	5					
Oct.										7	19	25	28	29	25	20	13	4						
Nov.										8	13	16	18	14	10	4	1							
Dec.										1	10	11	11	9	7	3								

Figure E.6 Representative daylighting illuminances (fc): Seattle. EA = 0.01.

Hours of Day

	1	2	3	4	5	6	7	8	9	10	11	12	13	14	15	16	17	18	19	20	21	22	23	24
Jan.									1	6	12	19	23	24	21	15	8	2						
Feb.									3	10	20	30	36	36	32	24	15	6						
March								1	8	18	31	39	45	46	42	34	22	11	3					
April							1	8	18	30	40	47	51	51	47	38	28	17	7					
May							5	14	28	40	51	58	58	57	54	47	37	23	11	3				
June							6	15	29	44	54	61	65	62	61	56	46	31	16	6				
July							4	13	28	44	55	62	70	74	70	57	43	29	15	5				
Aug.							2	10	23	39	54	63	70	69	62	52	40	24	10	2				
Sept.							5	16	30	40	48	55	53	48	40	28	13	3						
Oct.								1	9	19	30	37	40	39	34	25	14	5						
Nov.									3	10	16	22	26	24	19	12	6							
Dec.									1	6	12	17	20	19	16	11	5							

Figure E.7 Representative daylighting illuminances (fc): Madison/Washington. EA = 0.01.

Hours of Day

	1	2	3	4	5	6	7	8	9	10	11	12	13	14	15	16	17	18	19	20	21	22	23	24
Jan.								1	8	18	27	33	34	33	28	18	7							
Feb.								4	14	26	36	42	45	42	35	24	12	3						
March								7	18	34	47	55	57	53	45	32	17	5						
April							4	15	33	48	59	63	64	60	50	36	19	7						
May							9	23	39	53	63	69	70	66	58	43	27	13	2					
June						1	10	25	43	57	69	74	74	66	60	49	32	15	3					
July							7	22	40	56	65	66	69	65	58	44	28	13	2					
Aug.							5	17	34	53	62	64	65	61	53	40	24	10	1					
Sept.							3	15	31	47	59	61	63	57	47	35	19	5						
Oct.							1	11	26	42	51	60	58	52	40	23	10	1						
Nov.								5	16	28	37	42	41	36	25	14	4							
Dec.								2	9	19	27	32	34	30	22	12	3							

Figure E.8 Representative daylighting illuminances (fc): Lake Charles. EA = 0.01.

Hours of Day

	1	2	3	4	5	6	7	8	9	10	11	12	13	14	15	16	17	18	19	20	21	22	23	24
Jan.								4	13	24	35	42	42	36	24	13	4							
Feb.								7	18	33	46	52	52	46	36	21	9	1						
March							3	13	28	44	57	65	67	62	51	34	16	4						
April						1	9	22	39	56	67	72	71	68	56	42	22	8						
May						2	13	26	43	59	72	78	79	75	64	48	28	12	1					
June						4	14	27	43	57	67	74	76	74	64	49	30	14	4					
July						2	13	28	47	64	74	82	82	79	69	53	32	15	3					
Aug.						1	9	22	43	60	73	80	81	76	64	47	26	10						
Sept.							5	16	33	50	64	72	74	68	54	35	15	4						
Oct.							3	12	25	39	49	56	57	50	37	19	7							
Nov.							1	8	18	31	42	46	44	37	24	11	2							
Dec.								4	13	23	33	39	39	32	20	9	2							

Figure E.9 Representative daylighting illuminances (fc): Los Angeles. EA = 0.01.

Hours of Day

	1	2	3	4	5	6	7	8	9	10	11	12	13	14	15	16	17	18	19	20	21	22	23	24
Jan.									6	15	23	29	30	26	19	11	3							
Feb.								3	11	22	33	39	39	36	28	18	8	1						
March							1	10	24	41	52	59	60	55	46	32	17	5						
April								9	23	43	59	70	75	75	71	61	47	27	12	1				
May							4	15	33	53	69	79	85	85	81	70	56	36	17	6				
June							6	18	39	59	75	85	91	91	88	79	64	45	23	9				
July							4	15	35	57	75	87	92	95	92	83	67	47	22	8				
Aug.								10	27	50	68	81	88	89	85	75	58	36	16	3				
Sept.								6	19	40	58	71	77	77	71	59	41	20	8					
Oct.							1	11	24	41	51	57	56	49	37	20	8							
Nov.							4	14	25	35	40	38	31	21	11	2								
Dec.								7	14	21	26	27	22	15	8									

Figure E.10 Representative daylighting illuminances (fc): Fresno. EA = 0.01.

Hours of Day

	1	2	3	4	5	6	7	8	9	10	11	12	13	14	15	16	17	18	19	20	21	22	23	24
Jan.								8	19	33	44	48	46	36	23	10	1							
Feb.								2	13	29	47	57	62	60	52	36	18	6						
March								8	26	49	65	74	76	73	62	47	27	10	1					
April							5	19	43	64	79	88	90	86	75	60	39	17	4					
May						1	10	29	55	75	90	97	97	95	86	70	50	24	8					
June						1	11	29	55	75	89	94	96	96	86	71	52	28	10	1				
July							5	22	49	69	84	91	94	95	89	74	53	25	7					
Aug.							4	19	43	65	82	91	94	93	84	68	46	20	5					
Sept.							2	14	36	61	77	86	87	82	70	52	29	10	1					
Oct.								8	24	45	60	68	69	65	54	34	15	2						
Nov.								3	13	29	45	56	57	53	38	21	7							
Dec.								1	8	19	31	41	45	40	29	16	6							

Figure E.11 Representative daylighting illuminances (fc): Phoenix. EA = 0.01.

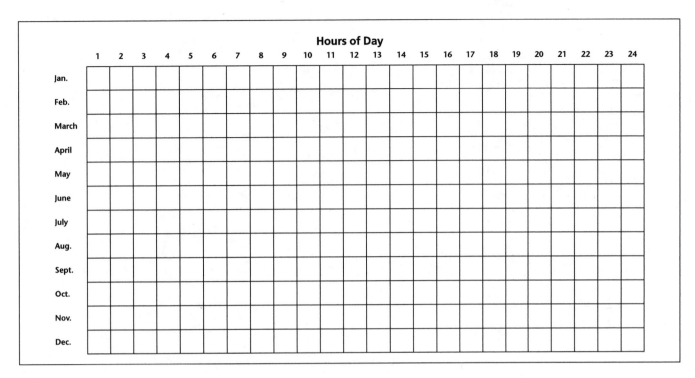

Figure E.12 Blank data table.

Daylight Parametrics

Appendix F describes a daylighting evaluation of a "typical" two-story office building. The purpose of the DOE2-based analysis was to evaluate and demonstrate the savings achievable through the use of automatic on/off daylighting controls in an otherwise standard two-story office building. Both perimeter daylighting and skylights were considered. The performance impacts of the daylight-controlled building were compared with an identical building without daylight controls in six weather locations: Chicago, New York, Atlanta, Denver, Los Angeles, and Seattle.

The base case building was assumed to be a "typical" two-story, 70,000-ft^2 office building with a 61% gross window-to-wall ratio on all orientations. The glass type was assumed to be double pane, light solar bronze (SC = 0.57, VT = 0.47) with shading provided by interior venetian blinds. Interior lighting consisted of fluorescent, two-lamp fixtures with energy-saving magnetic ballasts and energy-saving lamps (76 W/fixture). The installed lighting power density was modeled at 1.5 W/ft^2. Air-conditioning is provided by rooftop unitary equipment (gas packs, SEER 10). A more complete building description is provided in Appendix F.1. The prototype building model is compliant with both Title-24 and ASHRAE 90.1 building energy standards.

Perimeter daylighting (Alternative 1) was modeled assuming a 15-ft perimeter zone and simple on/off daylight controls. Approximately 33% of the total building lighting is controlled by perimeter daylight controls. The benefit of adding skylights (Alternative 2) to provide daylighting to the core zone of the second floor was also investigated. The skylights (SC = 0.78, VT = 0.75) were modeled with a 4% skylight-to-roof area. Approximately 34% of the total building lighting is controlled by horizontal daylight controls. An illuminance setpoint of 50 footcandles was assumed for both the perimeter daylighting and the skylight alternatives.

The incremental first cost of installing perimeter daylight controls was estimated to be $7,530. The incremental first cost for providing skylights and the associated controls on the second floor was estimated to be $20,145. This cost includes lighting control costs of $1,245 and skylight costs of $18,900. A more detailed breakdown of the capital costs is provided in Appendix F.2.

Utility costs were calculated assuming an average national cost of 7.2¢/kWh for electricity and 60.1¢/therm for natural gas. Note that the electric rate schedule used assumes a uniform annual energy charge and has no demand charges. A tax rate of 6% has been added to both the electric and the gas charges.

The annual energy use in Appendix F.3 provides an energy summary for both the daylighting and the skylight alternatives. Each of the six sections (one per weather location) in Tables F.3.1 to F.3.6 are subdivided horizontally into three sections. The upper portion represents the *absolute* results. The middle and lower portions present *incremental* and *cumulative* savings for the current alternative compared with the previously implemented alternative. Therefore, the numbers given for skylights (Alternative 2) represent the incremental savings due to skylights after the perimeter daylighting (Alternative 1) has been implemented. Under the cumulative savings, each row represents savings relative to the base case (nondaylit) building. In both the incremental and the cumulative savings sections, savings reported for perimeter daylighting are relative to the base case. Negative savings represent increased energy use.

The annual cost summary, also in tables in Appendix F.3, presents a utility cost summary and a simple payback analysis for both perimeter daylighting and skylights. Each of the six sections is subdivided into an *absolute* results section and an *incremental* and *cumulative* savings section. Under the incremental savings section, the simple payback for skylights (Alternative 2) assumes the perimeter daylight controls have already been implemented and therefore represents the payback for the skylights alone. Under the cumulative savings section, the simple payback for skylights (Alternative 2) represents the combined payback for both perimeter daylighting and skylights. Negative savings represent increased utility (natural gas) costs.

The light power reduction summary in Appendix F.4 presents representative lighting power reduction results, and Appendix F.5 presents average illuminance in footcandles by month and time of day for each orientation and the second-floor core zone (toplit) (courtesy of ESS, Inc.).

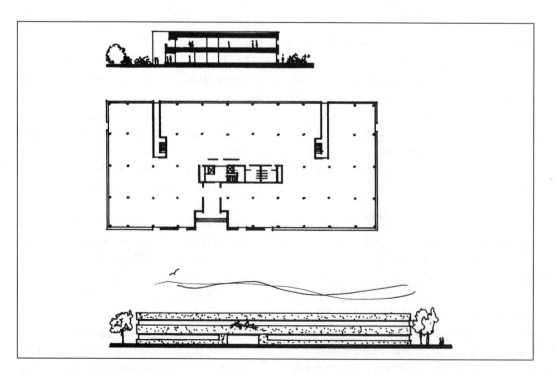

Generic office building.

Appendix F.1 Base Case Building Description

Base Case Building Description Generic Office Building Daylighting Evaluation

Architectural	
Building type	Two-story, office
Conditioned area	66,250 ft^2
Aspect ratio	2.12
Window-to-wall ratio	61%
Wall construction	Metal stud wall with brick facing
Wall *R*-value	7.0
Root construction	Built-up roofing on a metal deck
Root *R*-value	20
Window type	Double pane, solar bronze
Shading coefficient	0.57
Visible transmittance	0.47

HVAC System	
Type	Rooftop package units with gas furnace
Cooling efficiency	10 SEER
Furnace efficiency	80%
Cooling set point	74°F
Heating set point	70°F
Economizing	Yes
Outside air supply	20 ft^3/min/person

Building Operation and Internal Loading		
Occupancy schedule	Monday–Friday:	7 A.M.–7 P.M.
	Saturday:	8 A.M.–12 P.M.
	Sunday and holidays:	Closed
Lighting density	1.5 W/ft^2	
Equipment density	1.5 W/ft^2	
Occupant density	250 ft^2/person	

Appendix F.2   Capital Cost Summary

Capital Cost Summary Generic Office Building Daylighting Evaluation

Perimeter Daylighting		
Controller	8 × $560	$4,480
Transformer	12 × $45	540
Subtotal		5,020
Labor	(50%)	2,510
Total		$7,530
Skylights		
Controller	1 × $560	$560
Transformer	6 × $45	270
Subtotal		830
Labor	(50%)	415
Subtotal		$1,245
Skylights	21 × 250	5,250
Light well	21 × 400	8,400
Labor	21 × 250	5,250
Subtotal		$18,900
Total		$20,145

Appendix F.3   Annual Cost and Energy Use Summary

Atlanta

Case	Measures		Elect. (MWh)	N. Gas (Therms)	Total (MBtu)	Intensity (kBtu/ft²)	Electric ($)	Gas ($)	Total ($)	Intensity ($/ft²)	Capital Cost ($)	Simple Payback (Years)
						Site Energy		Utility Costs				
Absolute Results												
	Base		865	2,540	3,210	48	65,990	160	66,150	1.00	na	na
Alt 1	Base	+ Daylighting	767	3,070	2,920	44	58,530	190	58,720	0.89	7,530	na
Alt 2	Alt 1	+ Skylights	710	3,420	2,770	42	54,210	210	54,420	0.82	27,675	na
Incremental Savings (relative to previously adopted measures; negative entries represent increases)												
Alt 1	Base	+ Daylighting	98	−530	290	4	7,460	−30	7,430	0.11	7,530	1.0
Alt 2	Alt 1	+ Skylights	57	−350	150	2	4,320	−20	4,300	0.06	20,145	4.7
Cumulative Savings (relative to DFE base; negative entries represent increases)												
Alt 1	Base	+ Daylighting	98	−530	290	4	7,460	−30	7,430	0.11	7,530	1.0
Alt 2	Alt 1	+ Skylights	154	−880	440	7	11,780	−50	11,730	0.18	27,675	2.4

Case	Measures		Elect. (MWh)	N. Gas (Therms)	Total (MBtu)	Intensity (kBtu/ft²)	Total (MBtu)	Intensity (kBtu/ft²)	Peak Demand (kW)	Light Elect. (MWh)	Elect. (MWh)	N. Gas (Therms)	Total (MBtu)	Peak Cooling (tons)
				Site Energy			Source Energy				HVAC Energy			
Absolute Results														
	Base		865	2,540	3,210	48	9,116	138	350	306	376	2,540	1,540	133
Alt 1	Base	+ Daylighting	767	3,070	2,920	44	8,168	123	305	237	347	3,070	1,490	117
Alt 2	Alt 1	+ Skylights	710	3,420	2,770	42	7,621	115	297	174	354	3,420	1,550	117
Incremental Savings (relative to previously adopted measures; negative entries represent increases)														
Alt 1	Base	+ Daylighting	98	−530	290	4	948	14	45	69	29	−530	50	16
Alt 2	Alt 1	+ Skylights	57	−350	150	2	547	8	8	64	−7	−350	−60	1
Cumulative Savings (relative to DFE base; negative entries represent increases)														
Alt 1	Base	+ Daylighting	98	−530	290	4	948	14	45	69	29	−530	50	16
Alt 2	Alt 1	+ Skylights	154	−880	440	7	1,495	23	53	132	22	−880	−10	17

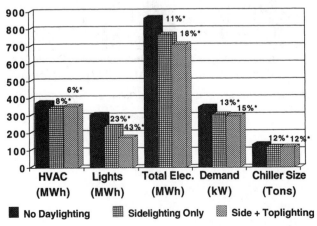

2 - STORY OFFICE BUILDING - ATLANTA

■ No Daylighting   ▦ Sidelighting Only   ▨ Side + Toplighting

* Percentage savings (compared to base case)

Chicago

		Elect. (MWh)	N. Gas (Therms)	Total (MBtu)	Intensity (kBtu/ft²)	Electric ($)	Gas ($)	Total ($)	Intensity ($/ft²)	Capital Cost ($)	Simple Payback (Years)
		Site Energy				**Utility Costs**					
Case	**Measures**										
Absolute Results											
	Base	846	9,640	3,850	58	64,540	600	65,140	0.98	na	na
Alt 1	Base + Daylighting	758	10,660	3,650	55	57,820	690	58,510	0.88	7,530	na
Alt 2	Alt 1 + Skylights	719	11,960	3,650	55	54,900	740	55,640	0.84	27,675	na
Incremental Savings (relative to previously adopted measures; negative entries represent increases)											
Alt 1	Base + Daylighting	88	−1,020	200	3	6,720	−90	6,630	0.10	7,530	1.1
Alt 2	Alt 1 + Skylights	38	−1,300	0	0	2,920	−50	2,870	0.04	20,145	7.0
Cumulative Savings (relative to DFE base; negative entries represent increases)											
Alt 1	Base + Daylighting	88	−1,020	200	3	6,720	−90	6,630	0.10	7,530	1.1
Alt 2	Alt 1 + Skylights	126	−2,320	200	3	9,640	−140	9,500	0.14	27,675	2.9

		Elect. (MWh)	N. Gas (Therms)	Total (MBtu)	Intensity (kBtu/ft²)	Total (MBtu)	Intensity (kBtu/ft²)	Peak Demand (kW)	Light Elect. (MWh)	Elect. (MWh)	N. Gas (Therms)	Total (MBtu)	Peak Cooling (tons)
		Site Energy				**Source Energy**			**HVAC Energy**				
Case	**Measures**												
Absolute Results													
	Base	846	9,640	3,850	58	9,631	145	336	306	357	9,640	2,180	116
Alt 1	Base + Daylighting	758	10,660	3,650	55	8,831	133	298	244	331	10,660	2,200	101
Alt 2	Alt 1 + Skylights	719	11,960	3,650	55	8,569	129	297	187	350	11,960	2,390	103
Incremental Savings (relative to previously adopted measures; negative entries represent increases)													
Alt 1	Base + Daylighting	88	−1,020	200	3	800	12	38	62	26	−1,020	−20	16
Alt 2	Alt 1 + Skylights	38	−1,300	0	0	262	4	1	57	−19	−1,300	−190	−2
Cumulative Savings (relative to DFE base; negative entries represent increases)													
Alt 1	Base + Daylighting	88	−1,020	200	3	800	12	38	62	26	−1,020	−20	16
Alt 2	Alt 1 + Skylights	126	−2,320	200	3	1,062	16	39	119	7	−2,320	−210	14

2 - STORY OFFICE BUILDING - CHICAGO

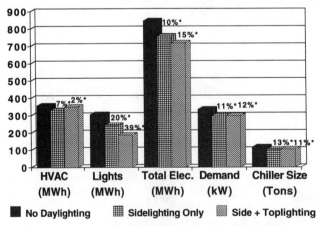

* Percentage savings (compared to base case)

Denver

Case	Measures		Elect. (MWh)	N. Gas (Therms)	Total (MBtu)	Intensity (kBtu/ft²)	Electric ($)	Gas ($)	Total ($)	Intensity ($/ft²)	Capital Cost ($)	Simple Payback (Years)
			Site Energy				**Utility Costs**					
Absolute Results												
	Base		832	6,530	3,490	53	63,500	400	63,900	0.96	na	na
Alt 1	Base	+ Daylighting	748	7,410	3,290	50	57,080	460	57,540	0.87	7,530	na
Alt 2	Alt 1	+ Skylights	696	8,240	3,200	48	53,130	510	53,640	0.81	27,675	na
Incremental Savings (relative to previously adopted measures; negative entries represent increases)												
Alt 1	Base	+ Daylighting	84	−880	200	3	6,420	−60	6,360	0.10	7,530	1.2
Alt 2	Alt 1	+ Skylights	52	−830	90	1	3,950	−50	3,900	0.06	20,145	5.2
Cumulative Savings (relative to DFE base; negative entries represent increases)												
Alt 1	Base	+ Daylighting	84	−880	200	3	6,420	−60	6,360	0.10	7,530	1.2
Alt 2	Alt 1	+ Skylights	136	−1,710	290	4	10,370	−110	10,260	0.15	27,675	2.7

Case	Measures		Elect. (MWh)	N. Gas (Therms)	Total (MBtu)	Intensity (kBtu/ft²)	Total (MBtu)	Intensity (kBtu/ft²)	Peak Demand (kW)	Light Elect. (MWh)	Elect. (MWh)	N. Gas (Therms)	Total (MBtu)	Peak Cooling (tons)
			Site Energy				**Source Energy**				**HVAC Energy**			
Absolute Results														
	Base		832	6,530	3,490	53	9,181	139	336	306	344	6,530	1,830	142
Alt 1	Base	+ Daylighting	748	7,410	3,290	50	8,407	127	295	246	319	7,410	1,830	123
Alt 2	Alt 1	+ Skylights	696	8,240	3,200	48	7,959	120	283	177	337	8,240	1,970	123
Incremental Savings (relative to previously adopted measures; negative entries represent increases)														
Alt 1	Base	+ Daylighting	84	−880	200	3	774	12	41	60	24	−880	0	19
Alt 2	Alt 1	+ Skylights	52	−830	90	1	448	7	12	69	−17	−830	−140	−1
Cumulative Savings (relative to DFE base; negative entries represent increases)														
Alt 1	Base	+ Daylighting	84	−880	200	3	774	12	41	60	24	−880	0	19
Alt 2	Alt 1	+ Skylights	136	−1,710	290	4	1,221	19	53	129	7	−1,710	−140	18

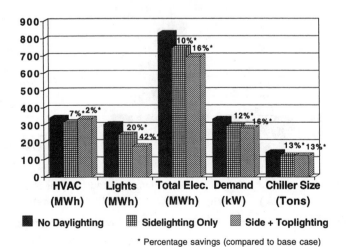

2 - STORY OFFICE BUILDING - DENVER

■ No Daylighting   ▦ Sidelighting Only   ▨ Side + Toplighting

* Percentage savings (compared to base case)

Los Angeles

			Site Energy				Utility Costs					
			Elect. (MWh)	N. Gas (Therms)	Total (MBtu)	Intensity (kBtu/ft²)	Electric ($)	Gas ($)	Total ($)	Intensity ($/ft²)	Capital Cost ($)	Simple Payback (Years)
Case	**Measures**											
Absolute Results												
	Base		788	110	2,700	41	60,160	10	60,170	0.91	na	na
Alt 1	Base	+ Daylighting	689	170	2,370	36	52,570	10	52,580	0.79	7,530	na
Alt 2	Alt 1	+ Skylights	616	190	2,120	32	47,000	10	47,010	0.71	27,675	na
Incremental Savings (relative to previously adopted measures; negative entries represent increases)												
Alt 1	Base	+ Daylighting	100	−60	330	5	7,590	0	7,590	0.11	7,530	1.0
Alt 2	Alt 1	+ Skylights	73	−20	250	4	5,570	0	5,570	0.08	20,145	3.6
Cumulative Savings (relative to DFE base; negative entries represent increases)												
Alt 1	Base	+ Daylighting	100	−60	330	5	7,590	0	7,590	0.11	7,530	1.0
Alt 2	Alt 1	+ Skylights	173	−80	580	9	13,160	0	13,160	0.20	27,675	2.1

			Site Energy				Source Energy			HVAC Energy			
			Elect. (MWh)	N. Gas (Therms)	Total (MBtu)	Intensity (kBtu/ft²)	Total (MBtu)	Intensity (kBtu/ft²)	Peak Demand (kW)	Light Elect. (MWh)	Elect. (MWh)	N. Gas (Therms)	Total (MBtu)	Peak Cooling (tons)
Case	**Measures**												
Absolute Results													
	Base		788	110	2,700	41	8,090	122	311	306	300	110	1,030	116
Alt 1	Base	+ Daylighting	689	170	2,370	36	7,076	107	264	232	274	170	950	90
Alt 2	Alt 1	+ Skylights	616	190	2,120	32	6,331	96	254	159	274	200	960	96
Incremental Savings (relative to previously adopted measures; negative entries represent increases)													
Alt 1	Base	+ Daylighting	100	−60	330	5	1,014	15	47	74	25	−60	80	27
Alt 2	Alt 1	+ Skylights	73	−20	250	4	745	11	10	73	0	−30	−10	−6
Cumulative Savings (relative to DFE base; negative entries represent increases)													
Alt 1	Base	+ Daylighting	100	−60	330	5	1,014	15	47	74	25	−60	80	27
Alt 2	Alt 1	+ Skylights	173	−80	580	9	1,759	27	57	147	26	−90	70	20

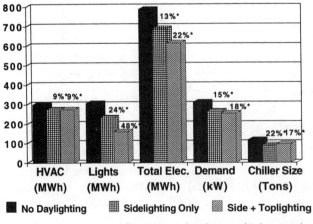

2 - STORY OFFICE BUILDING - LOS ANGELES

■ No Daylighting   ▦ Sidelighting Only   ▨ Side + Toplighting

* Percentage savings (compared to base case)

New York

Case	Measures		Elect. (MWh)	N. Gas (Therms)	Total (MBtu)	Intensity (kBtu/ft²)	Electric ($)	Gas ($)	Total ($)	Intensity ($/ft²)	Capital Cost ($)	Simple Payback (Years)
			Site Energy				**Utility Costs**					
Absolute Results												
	Base		819	6,130	3,410	51	62,470	380	62,850	0.95	na	na
Alt 1	Base	+ Daylighting	737	6,850	3,200	48	56,280	420	56,700	0.86	7,530	na
Alt 2	Alt 1	+ Skylights	699	7,480	3,140	47	53,380	430	53,810	0.81	27,675	na
Incremental Savings (relative to previously adopted measures; negative entries represent increases)												
Alt 1	Base	+ Daylighting	81	−720	210	3	6,190	−40	6,150	0.09	7,530	1.2
Alt 2	Alt 1	+ Skylights	38	−630	60	1	2,900	−10	2,890	0.04	20,145	7.0
Cumulative Savings (relative to DFE base; negative entries represent increases)												
Alt 1	Base	+ Daylighting	81	−720	210	3	6,190	−40	6,150	0.09	7,530	1.2
Alt 2	Alt 1	+ Skylights	119	−1,350	270	4	9,090	−50	9,040	0.14	27,675	3.1

Case	Measures		Elect. (MWh)	N. Gas (Therms)	Total (MBtu)	Intensity (kBtu/ft²)	Total (MBtu)	Intensity (kBtu/ft²)	Peak Demand (kW)	Light Elect. (MWh)	Elect. (MWh)	N. Gas (Therms)	Total (MBtu)	Peak Cooling (tons)
			Site Energy				**Source Energy**				**HVAC Energy**			
Absolute Results														
	Base		819	6,130	3,410	51	9,003	136	324	306	330	6,140	1,740	111
Alt 1	Base	+ Daylighting	737	6,850	3,200	48	8,243	124	297	248	307	6,850	1,730	101
Alt 2	Alt 1	+ Skylights	699	7,480	3,140	47	7,916	120	298	196	321	7,480	1,840	103
Incremental Savings (relative to previously adopted measures; negative entries represent increases)														
Alt 1	Base	+ Daylighting	81	−720	210	3	761	12	27	58	23	−710	10	10
Alt 2	Alt 1	+ Skylights	38	−630	60	1	326	5	−1	52	−14	−630	−110	−2
Cumulative Savings (relative to DFE base; negative entries represent increases)														
Alt 1	Base	+ Daylighting	81	−720	210	3	761	12	27	58	23	−710	10	10
Alt 2	Alt 1	+ Skylights	119	−1,350	270	4	1,087	16	26	110	9	−1,340	−100	8

2 - STORY OFFICE BUILDING - NEW YORK

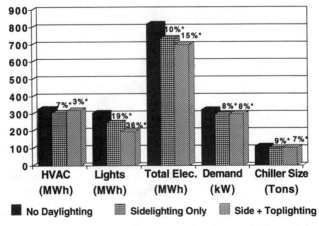

* Percentage savings (compared to base case)

Seattle

Case	Measures		Site Energy				Utility Costs				Capital Cost ($)	Simple Payback (Years)
			Elect. (MWh)	N. Gas (Therms)	Total (MBtu)	Intensity (kBtu/ft²)	Electric ($)	Gas ($)	Total ($)	Intensity ($/ft²)		
Absolute Results												
	Base		757	4,900	3,070	46	57,800	300	58,100	0.88	na	na
Alt 1	Base	+ Daylighting	689	5,680	2,920	44	52,590	350	52,940	0.80	7,530	na
Alt 2	Alt 1	+ Skylights	651	6,210	2,840	43	49,720	380	50,100	0.76	27,675	na
Incremental Savings (relative to previously adopted measures; negative entries represent increases)												
Alt 1	Base	+ Daylighting	68	−780	150	2	5,210	−50	5,160	0.08	7,530	1.5
Alt 2	Alt 1	+ Skylights	38	−530	80	1	2,870	−30	2,840	0.04	20,145	7.1
Cumulative Savings (relative to DFE base; negative entries represent increases)												
Alt 1	Base	+ Daylighting	68	−780	150	2	5,210	−50	5,160	0.08	7,530	1.5
Alt 2	Alt 1	+ Skylights	106	−1,310	230	4	8,080	−80	8,000	0.12	27,675	3.5

Case	Measures		Site Energy				Source Energy		Peak Demand (kW)	Light Elect. (MWh)	HVAC Energy			Peak Cooling (tons)
			Elect. (MWh)	N. Gas (Therms)	Total (MBtu)	Intensity (kBtu/ft²)	Total (MBtu)	Intensity (kBtu/ft²)			Elect. (MWh)	N. Gas (Therms)	Total (MBtu)	
Absolute Results														
	Base		757	4,900	3,070	46	8,252	125	295	306	269	4,900	1,410	81
Alt 1	Base	+ Daylighting	689	5,680	2,920	44	7,630	115	251	252	254	5,680	1,440	70
Alt 2	Alt 1	+ Skylights	651	6,210	2,840	43	7,298	110	239	203	266	6,210	1,530	72
Incremental Savings (relative to previously adopted measures; negative entries represent increases)														
Alt 1	Base	+ Daylighting	68	−780	150	2	622	9	44	54	15	−780	−30	12
Alt 2	Alt 1	+ Skylights	38	−530	80	1	333	5	12	49	−11	−530	−90	−2
Cumulative Savings (relative to DFE base; negative entries represent increases)														
Alt 1	Base	+ Daylighting	68	−780	150	2	622	9	44	54	15	−780	−30	12
Alt 2	Alt 1	+ Skylights	106	−1,310	230	4	954	14	56	103	3	−1,310	−120	9

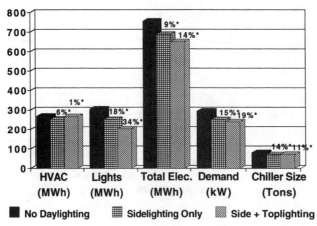

2 - STORY OFFICE BUILDING - SEATTLE

* Percentage savings (compared to base case)

Appendix F.4   Light Power Reduction Summary

Percent Power Reduction: Atlanta

For a typical two-story office building with 15'-0"-deep perimeter zones and a top-lit core zone.

Weather Data:	Atlanta (TMY)	
% Opening:	37.5% WWR (windows)	
	4% of roof area (skylights)	
Overhangs:	2'-3" (horizontal)	
Lighting Control Type:	Stepped (two steps)	
Lighting Set Point:	50 footcandles	
No. of Ref. Points:	One (2'-6" high in the center of zone)	

Glass Type: ¼" solar bronze tinted (single pane) (SC = 0.57; VT = 0.47)

North

Month	1	2	3	4	5	6	7	8	9	10	11	12	13	14	15	16	17	18	19	20	21	22	23	24	Hours
JAN	0	0	0	0	0	0	0	0	23	25	42	52	51	46	57	40	31	5	0	0	0	0	0	0	33
FEB	0	0	0	0	0	0	0	0	22	35	44	57	63	63	63	55	39	19	0	0	0	0	0	0	40
MAR	0	0	0	0	0	0	0	29	58	69	86	96	96	96	93	77	75	61	4	0	0	0	0	0	71
APR	0	0	0	0	0	0	11	36	75	81	92	92	95	93	93	89	86	73	28	0	0	0	0	0	78
MAY	0	0	0	0	0	0	37	84	88	98	98	99	99	100	100	100	90	85	66	0	0	0	0	0	87
JUN	0	0	0	0	0	0	37	75	90	96	98	98	94	93	93	93	89	89	73	0	0	0	0	0	85
JUL	0	0	0	0	0	0	23	77	88	85	92	96	100	100	98	93	89	91	61	0	0	0	0	0	85
AUG	0	0	0	0	0	0	14	73	87	87	100	100	100	100	100	98	95	93	48	0	0	0	0	0	86
SEP	0	0	0	0	0	0	0	48	77	83	98	98	98	93	95	86	84	55	0	0	0	0	0	0	78
OCT	0	0	0	0	0	0	0	30	60	60	73	75	69	71	60	53	62	5	0	0	0	0	0	0	53
NOV	0	0	0	0	0	0	0	0	26	37	52	48	56	60	53	45	32	0	0	0	0	0	0	0	36
DEC	0	0	0	0	0	0	0	0	10	34	52	54	51	54	50	36	30	0	0	0	0	0	0	0	33
Annual	0	0	0	0	0	0	10	62	59	66	78	80	81	81	80	72	67	40	10	0	0	0	0	0	64

South

Month	1	2	3	4	5	6	7	8	9	10	11	12	13	14	15	16	17	18	19	20	21	22	23	24	Hours
JAN	0	0	0	0	0	0	0	0	52	50	69	73	75	77	81	76	62	23	0	0	0	0	0	0	56
FEB	0	0	0	0	0	0	0	0	44	61	61	74	79	81	79	82	74	45	0	0	0	0	0	0	59
MAR	0	0	0	0	0	0	0	45	63	71	86	96	96	96	93	80	77	63	9	0	0	0	0	0	73
APR	0	0	0	0	0	0	6	38	77	81	92	92	95	95	93	89	86	72	25	0	0	0	0	0	78
MAY	0	0	0	0	0	0	26	84	88	98	98	99	99	100	100	100	90	84	40	0	0	0	0	0	87
JUN	0	0	0	0	0	0	25	71	90	96	98	98	94	93	93	93	89	89	43	0	0	0	0	0	85
JUL	0	0	0	0	0	0	6	77	88	85	92	96	100	100	98	93	89	91	32	0	0	0	0	0	84
AUG	0	0	0	0	0	0	2	73	89	87	100	100	100	100	100	98	95	93	37	0	0	0	0	0	86
SEP	0	0	0	0	0	0	0	63	81	83	98	98	98	93	95	86	86	59	0	0	0	0	0	0	80
OCT	0	0	0	0	0	0	0	67	86	92	94	100	100	97	90	93	88	30	0	0	0	0	0	0	80
NOV	0	0	0	0	0	0	0	16	57	74	78	78	87	92	87	84	66	0	0	0	0	0	0	0	62
DEC	0	0	0	0	0	0	0	0	67	71	83	83	77	83	84	70	68	0	0	0	0	0	0	0	61
Annual	0	0	0	0	0	0	5	68	74	79	88	91	92	92	91	87	81	47	8	0	0	0	0	0	74

East

Month	1	2	3	4	5	6	7	8	9	10	11	12	13	14	15	16	17	18	19	20	21	22	23	24	Hours
JAN	0	0	0	0	0	0	0	0	52	50	69	73	54	51	59	43	31	2	0	0	0	0	0	0	44
FEB	0	0	0	0	0	0	0	6	46	61	61	74	77	67	66	55	39	19	0	0	0	0	0	0	50
MAR	0	0	0	0	0	0	0	51	63	71	87	96	96	96	93	75	73	41	0	0	0	0	0	0	70
APR	0	0	0	0	0	0	35	38	77	81	92	92	95	95	93	89	86	71	11	0	0	0	0	0	78
MAY	0	0	0	0	0	0	74	86	90	98	98	99	99	100	100	100	90	84	40	0	0	0	0	0	88
JUN	0	0	0	0	0	0	65	89	92	96	98	98	94	93	93	98	89	86	37	0	0	0	0	0	87
JUL	0	0	0	0	0	0	61	85	88	87	94	96	100	100	98	93	87	84	32	0	0	0	0	0	85
AUG	0	0	0	0	0	0	49	77	89	87	100	100	100	100	100	98	95	63	27	0	0	0	0	0	86
SEP	0	0	0	0	0	0	6	65	82	83	98	98	98	93	95	86	79	36	0	0	0	0	0	0	79
OCT	0	0	0	0	0	0	0	72	88	90	98	100	98	90	72	55	45	0	0	0	0	0	0	0	71
NOV	0	0	0	0	0	0	0	28	57	74	78	74	56	60	53	45	32	0	0	0	0	0	0	0	48
DEC	0	0	0	0	0	0	0	0	73	71	83	77	53	54	52	36	32	0	0	0	0	0	0	0	48
Annual	0	0	0	0	0	0	24	75	75	79	88	90	85	83	82	73	65	33	5	0	0	0	0	0	70

West

Month	1	2	3	4	5	6	7	8	9	10	11	12	13	14	15	16	17	18	19	20	21	22	23	24	Hours
JAN	0	0	0	0	0	0	0	0	21	25	42	52	53	63	81	76	62	38	0	0	0	0	0	0	44
FEB	0	0	0	0	0	0	0	0	20	33	44	61	69	81	79	82	76	51	0	0	0	0	0	0	51
MAR	0	0	0	0	0	0	0	19	50	65	87	96	96	96	96	80	77	63	30	0	0	0	0	0	72
APR	0	0	0	0	0	0	0	23	73	81	92	92	95	95	93	89	86	78	58	0	0	0	0	0	79
MAY	0	0	0	0	0	0	18	76	90	98	98	99	99	100	100	100	92	85	81	0	0	0	0	0	87
JUN	0	0	0	0	0	0	25	71	89	96	98	98	94	93	93	98	89	89	80	12	0	0	0	0	85
JUL	0	0	0	0	0	0	3	75	88	85	94	96	100	100	98	93	91	93	76	0	0	0	0	0	85
AUG	0	0	0	0	0	0	0	37	87	87	100	100	100	100	100	98	98	98	77	0	0	0	0	0	83
SEP	0	0	0	0	0	0	0	31	77	83	98	98	98	93	95	86	86	79	10	0	0	0	0	0	77
OCT	0	0	0	0	0	0	0	19	42	62	88	96	98	97	90	93	90	56	0	0	0	0	0	0	69
NOV	0	0	0	0	0	0	0	0	26	39	52	50	58	92	84	87	66	9	0	0	0	0	0	0	49
DEC	0	0	0	0	0	0	0	0	12	34	54	60	53	78	84	73	72	0	0	0	0	0	0	0	45
Annual	0	0	0	0	0	0	4	49	57	66	79	83	85	91	91	88	82	54	20	1	0	0	0	0	69

Core (Top-lit)

Month	1	2	3	4	5	6	7	8	9	10	11	12	13	14	15	16	17	18	19	20	21	22	23	24	Hours
JAN	0	0	0	0	0	0	0	0	0	25	63	71	69	68	69	33	7	0	0	0	0	0	0	0	36
FEB	0	0	0	0	0	0	0	0	0	28	59	72	66	71	76	71	34	0	0	0	0	0	0	0	42
MAR	0	0	0	0	0	0	0	0	29	69	75	92	96	94	89	77	68	25	0	0	0	0	0	0	63
APR	0	0	0	0	0	0	0	17	68	79	90	90	93	93	93	86	84	36	0	0	0	0	0	0	72
MAY	0	0	0	0	0	0	0	42	88	90	98	99	99	100	100	100	90	42	0	0	0	0	0	0	80
JUN	0	0	0	0	0	0	0	31	83	92	98	94	94	93	93	93	87	67	0	0	0	0	0	0	78
JUL	0	0	0	0	0	0	0	36	85	85	92	96	100	100	98	93	84	70	0	0	0	0	0	0	79
AUG	0	0	0	0	0	0	0	23	83	87	100	100	100	100	100	98	95	48	0	0	0	0	0	0	79
SEP	0	0	0	0	0	0	0	0	57	81	86	98	98	93	89	84	66	5	0	0	0	0	0	0	66
OCT	0	0	0	0	0	0	0	0	35	83	92	100	100	97	90	81	38	0	0	0	0	0	0	0	62
NOV	0	0	0	0	0	0	0	0	4	41	72	78	85	89	82	34	0	0	0	0	0	0	0	0	43
DEC	0	0	0	0	0	0	0	0	0	34	59	81	77	76	66	36	0	0	0	0	0	0	0	0	38
Annual	0	0	0	0	0	0	0	21	45	67	82	89	90	89	87	74	55	19	0	0	0	0	0	0	62

Percent Power Reduction: Chicago

For a typical two-story office building with 15'-0"-deep perimeter zones and a top-lit core zone.

Weather Data:	Chicago (TMY)	Glass Type: ¼" solar bronze tinted (single pane)	
% Opening:	37.5% WWR (windows)	(SC = 0.57; VT = 0.47)	
	4% of roof area (skylights)		
Overhangs:	2'-3" (horizontal)		
Lighting Control Type:	Stepped (two steps)		
Lighting Set Point:	50 footcandles		
No. of Ref. Points:	One (2'-6" high in the center of zone)		

North

Month	1	2	3	4	5	6	7	8	9	10	11	12	13	14	15	16	17	18	19	20	21	22	23	24	Hours
JAN	0	0	0	0	0	0	0	0	29	32	40	39	40	40	35	30	0	0	0	0	0	0	0	0	26
FEB	0	0	0	0	0	0	0	11	26	46	50	46	48	46	50	34	18	0	0	0	0	0	0	0	33
MAR	0	0	0	0	0	0	11	39	69	71	84	84	83	79	68	61	52	11	0	0	0	0	0	0	59
APR	0	0	0	0	0	5	48	37	73	90	92	96	94	94	82	73	57	45	0	0	0	0	0	0	72
MAY	0	0	0	0	0	48	74	82	80	92	92	92	92	95	93	73	75	48	8	0	0	0	0	0	79
JUN	0	0	0	0	0	60	68	81	83	92	94	95	97	98	98	86	80	70	30	0	0	0	0	0	83
JUL	0	0	0	0	0	48	82	92	96	96	98	98	98	98	98	95	95	84	31	0	0	0	0	0	89
AUG	0	0	0	0	0	0	55	75	85	98	98	100	100	100	98	86	79	62	0	0	0	0	0	0	83
SEP	0	0	0	0	0	0	40	69	79	85	90	95	96	93	89	77	59	14	0	0	0	0	0	0	74
OCT	0	0	0	0	0	0	2	40	42	56	58	63	69	55	38	31	12	0	0	0	0	0	0	0	41
NOV	0	0	0	0	0	0	0	8	28	39	46	48	51	47	34	13	0	0	0	0	0	0	0	0	28
DEC	0	0	0	0	0	0	0	0	12	23	36	39	34	24	27	0	0	0	0	0	0	0	0	0	18
Annual	0	0	0	0	0	14	32	70	59	69	74	74	75	72	68	56	45	21	2	0	0	0	0	0	57

South

Month	1	2	3	4	5	6	7	8	9	10	11	12	13	14	15	16	17	18	19	20	21	22	23	24	Hours
JAN	0	0	0	0	0	0	0	4	61	73	75	73	68	70	71	66	13	0	0	0	0	0	0	0	51
FEB	0	0	0	0	0	0	0	40	52	74	76	72	71	70	77	63	52	0	0	0	0	0	0	0	54
MAR	0	0	0	0	0	0	17	58	81	79	90	90	91	81	75	70	61	15	0	0	0	0	0	0	66
APR	0	0	0	0	0	2	53	39	75	90	92	92	96	94	94	82	77	64	45	0	0	0	0	0	73
MAY	0	0	0	0	0	29	73	82	80	92	92	92	92	92	95	93	73	75	48	0	0	0	0	0	79
JUN	0	0	0	0	0	32	68	83	83	92	94	95	97	98	98	86	82	68	8	0	0	0	0	0	83
JUL	0	0	0	0	0	26	87	92	96	96	98	98	98	98	98	95	95	66	11	0	0	0	0	0	88
AUG	0	0	0	0	0	0	64	83	92	98	98	100	100	100	98	88	83	48	0	0	0	0	0	0	85
SEP	0	0	0	0	0	0	60	79	85	85	90	95	98	93	91	86	70	16	0	0	0	0	0	0	78
OCT	0	0	0	0	0	0	15	68	79	77	73	83	84	69	70	58	33	0	0	0	0	0	0	0	61
NOV	0	0	0	0	0	0	0	48	69	78	76	78	80	80	76	50	0	0	0	0	0	0	0	0	53
DEC	0	0	0	0	0	0	0	3	38	50	63	63	61	52	54	36	0	0	0	0	0	0	0	0	38
Annual	0	0	0	0	0	7	37	78	75	82	85	86	86	83	82	71	53	20	0	0	0	0	0	0	68

East

Month	1	2	3	4	5	6	7	8	9	10	11	12	13	14	15	16	17	18	19	20	21	22	23	24	Hours
JAN	0	0	0	0	0	0	0	9	59	71	73	69	43	43	35	30	0	0	0	0	0	0	0	0	39
FEB	0	0	0	0	0	0	0	48	52	74	76	72	62	46	50	34	18	0	0	0	0	0	0	0	44
MAR	0	0	0	0	0	0	30	58	81	79	92	90	89	81	75	59	36	4	0	0	0	0	0	0	62
APR	0	0	0	0	0	13	55	39	77	90	92	96	94	94	82	75	57	24	0	0	0	0	0	0	71
MAY	0	0	0	0	0	64	84	82	82	92	92	92	92	95	93	76	73	28	0	0	0	0	0	0	78
JUN	0	0	0	0	0	72	80	83	85	92	94	95	97	98	98	84	77	57	8	0	0	0	0	0	83
JUL	0	0	0	0	0	82	92	92	96	96	98	98	98	98	98	95	93	70	11	0	0	0	0	0	89
AUG	0	0	0	0	0	19	68	87	92	100	98	100	100	100	98	86	65	34	0	0	0	0	0	0	83
SEP	0	0	0	0	0	0	70	79	85	90	95	98	93	89	77	38	7	0	0	0	0	0	0	0	74
OCT	0	0	0	0	0	0	34	68	79	77	73	81	77	62	48	29	7	0	0	0	0	0	0	0	53
NOV	0	0	0	0	0	0	0	50	67	76	76	54	52	47	34	13	0	0	0	0	0	0	0	0	39
DEC	0	0	0	0	0	0	0	9	36	48	59	50	39	24	27	0	0	0	0	0	0	0	0	0	26
Annual	0	0	0	0	0	21	43	78	75	82	85	83	79	73	69	55	39	14	0	0	0	0	0	0	62

West

Month	1	2	3	4	5	6	7	8	9	10	11	12	13	14	15	16	17	18	19	20	21	22	23	24	Hours
JAN	0	0	0	0	0	0	0	0	31	34	42	42	66	70	71	68	24	0	0	0	0	0	0	0	39
FEB	0	0	0	0	0	0	0	11	26	48	52	54	71	70	77	66	63	0	0	0	0	0	0	0	46
MAR	0	0	0	0	0	0	5	29	59	73	90	90	89	81	75	70	68	39	0	0	0	0	0	0	65
APR	0	0	0	0	0	0	25	36	71	90	92	96	94	94	82	77	68	53	0	0	0	0	0	0	73
MAY	0	0	0	0	0	24	64	82	80	92	92	92	92	95	93	76	80	63	27	0	0	0	0	0	80
JUN	0	0	0	0	0	32	65	81	83	92	94	95	97	100	98	86	84	77	65	0	0	0	0	0	84
JUL	0	0	0	0	0	24	74	87	94	96	98	98	98	98	98	95	95	93	69	0	0	0	0	0	89
AUG	0	0	0	0	0	0	32	71	81	100	98	100	100	100	98	93	95	76	5	0	0	0	0	0	85
SEP	0	0	0	0	0	0	27	48	73	85	90	95	98	93	91	86	73	42	0	0	0	0	0	0	75
OCT	0	0	0	0	0	0	0	32	42	64	66	77	82	69	70	63	45	0	0	0	0	0	0	0	53
NOV	0	0	0	0	0	0	0	8	28	41	48	52	79	80	73	65	2	0	0	0	0	0	0	0	41
DEC	0	0	0	0	0	0	0	0	15	23	38	40	59	52	54	47	0	0	0	0	0	0	0	0	29
Annual	0	0	0	0	0	7	25	64	58	70	76	77	85	83	82	75	59	29	4	0	0	0	0	0	64

Core (Top-lit)

Month	1	2	3	4	5	6	7	8	9	10	11	12	13	14	15	16	17	18	19	20	21	22	23	24	Hours
JAN	0	0	0	0	0	0	0	0	0	32	52	65	63	47	33	0	0	0	0	0	0	0	0	0	27
FEB	0	0	0	0	0	0	0	0	15	52	74	72	69	70	63	26	0	0	0	0	0	0	0	0	40
MAR	0	0	0	0	0	0	0	11	61	77	79	86	83	74	73	48	16	0	0	0	0	0	0	0	54
APR	0	0	0	0	0	0	10	32	73	79	92	96	94	91	75	75	32	0	0	0	0	0	0	0	64
MAY	0	0	0	0	0	0	32	82	78	92	92	92	92	95	81	68	65	8	0	0	0	0	0	0	74
JUN	0	0	0	0	0	0	35	79	81	92	94	95	97	98	98	80	77	34	0	0	0	0	0	0	80
JUL	0	0	0	0	0	0	44	83	94	96	98	98	98	98	95	95	91	43	0	0	0	0	0	0	85
AUG	0	0	0	0	0	0	11	60	79	96	98	100	100	100	95	88	58	5	0	0	0	0	0	0	77
SEP	0	0	0	0	0	0	0	35	79	79	85	91	94	93	89	70	20	0	0	0	0	0	0	0	65
OCT	0	0	0	0	0	0	0	17	50	75	73	77	80	67	48	22	0	0	0	0	0	0	0	0	45
NOV	0	0	0	0	0	0	0	0	22	48	71	71	76	55	31	0	0	0	0	0	0	0	0	0	34
DEC	0	0	0	0	0	0	0	0	0	21	32	56	46	22	4	0	0	0	0	0	0	0	0	0	17
Annual	0	0	0	0	0	0	11	57	53	70	78	83	83	76	66	48	30	5	0	0	0	0	0	0	55

Percent Power Reduction: Denver

For a typical two-story office building with 15'-0"-deep perimeter zones and a top-lit core zone.

Weather Data:	Denver (TMY)	Glass Type: ¼" solar bronze tinted (single pane)
% Opening:	37.5% WWR (windows)	(SC = 0.57; VT = 0.47)
	4% of roof area (skylights)	
Overhangs:	2'-3" (horizontal)	
Lighting Control Type:	Stepped (two steps)	
Lighting Set Point:	50 footcandles	
No. of Ref. Points:	One (2'-6" high in the center of zone)	

North

Month	1	2	3	4	5	6	7	8	9	10	11	12	13	14	15	16	17	18	19	20	21	22	23	24	Hours
JAN	0	0	0	0	0	0	0	2	29	33	15	8	6	7	0	31	0	0	0	0	0	0	0	0	12
FEB	0	0	0	0	0	0	0	40	56	44	48	52	42	15	16	0	23	0	0	0	0	0	0	0	28
MAR	0	0	0	0	0	0	44	73	83	77	69	64	59	44	28	18	57	22	0	0	0	0	0	0	48
APR	0	0	0	0	0	20	82	87	89	94	94	92	74	69	59	37	27	32	0	0	0	0	0	0	63
MAY	0	0	0	0	0	78	90	92	98	98	100	100	95	85	75	55	45	26	19	0	0	0	0	0	77
JUN	0	0	0	0	0	78	88	90	98	98	98	98	100	84	62	59	46	30	30	0	0	0	0	0	77
JUL	0	0	0	0	0	80	90	96	100	100	100	100	94	70	70	54	52	35	21	0	0	0	0	0	77
AUG	0	0	0	0	0	18	87	90	96	98	98	100	82	65	58	36	34	45	0	0	0	0	0	0	70
SEP	0	0	0	0	0	0	78	87	96	92	90	80	57	54	23	14	32	22	0	0	0	0	0	0	58
OCT	0	0	0	0	0	0	23	79	58	58	54	50	33	9	5	0	24	0	0	0	0	0	0	0	33
NOV	0	0	0	0	0	0	0	37	46	48	31	17	12	13	3	8	4	0	0	0	0	0	0	0	17
DEC	0	0	0	0	0	0	0	0	31	31	10	4	2	0	0	5	0	0	0	0	0	0	0	0	8
Annual	0	0	0	0	0	23	49	86	74	73	68	63	55	43	33	27	29	14	2	0	0	0	0	0	48

South

Month	1	2	3	4	5	6	7	8	9	10	11	12	13	14	15	16	17	18	19	20	21	22	23	24	Hours
JAN	0	0	0	0	0	0	0	36	81	85	89	89	87	91	86	72	27	0	0	0	0	0	0	0	64
FEB	0	0	0	0	0	0	0	65	87	87	87	89	89	88	87	92	55	0	0	0	0	0	0	0	68
MAR	0	0	0	0	0	0	50	89	96	96	96	96	96	96	73	86	86	39	0	0	0	0	0	0	77
APR	0	0	0	0	0	12	83	87	89	94	94	98	98	86	68	57	73	31	0	0	0	0	0	0	73
MAY	0	0	0	0	0	64	90	92	98	98	100	100	100	90	80	62	70	41	2	0	0	0	0	0	81
JUN	0	0	0	0	0	72	88	90	98	98	98	98	100	96	64	59	50	44	0	0	0	0	0	0	79
JUL	0	0	0	0	0	45	92	98	100	100	100	100	100	91	73	57	55	46	0	0	0	0	0	0	80
AUG	0	0	0	0	0	8	87	92	96	98	98	100	100	88	62	53	86	47	0	0	0	0	0	0	80
SEP	0	0	0	0	0	0	87	94	96	100	100	100	99	86	54	77	79	26	0	0	0	0	0	0	80
OCT	0	0	0	0	0	0	46	95	96	96	96	96	77	86	86	38	0	0	0	0	0	0	0	0	75
NOV	0	0	0	0	0	0	6	78	94	100	98	98	97	97	92	63	22	0	0	0	0	0	0	0	69
DEC	0	0	0	0	0	0	0	46	89	90	90	92	94	94	93	75	19	0	0	0	0	0	0	0	66
Annual	0	0	0	0	0	17	53	92	93	95	96	96	96	90	76	70	55	19	0	0	0	0	0	0	74

East

Month	1	2	3	4	5	6	7	8	9	10	11	12	13	14	15	16	17	18	19	20	21	22	23	24	Hours
JAN	0	0	0	0	0	0	0	32	81	85	87	71	6	7	5	31	0	0	0	0	0	0	0	0	36
FEB	0	0	0	0	0	0	0	65	82	87	87	69	45	15	18	0	21	0	0	0	0	0	0	0	40
MAR	0	0	0	0	0	0	56	90	96	96	96	81	62	44	30	18	48	2	0	0	0	0	0	0	53
APR	0	0	0	0	0	34	85	88	89	94	94	98	91	71	59	32	16	19	0	0	0	0	0	0	63
MAY	0	0	0	0	0	84	95	96	98	98	100	100	100	85	75	57	45	18	2	0	0	0	0	0	78
JUN	0	0	0	0	10	85	92	92	98	98	98	98	100	84	62	59	37	29	0	0	0	0	0	0	76
JUL	0	0	0	0	4	86	93	98	100	100	100	100	98	73	70	54	47	23	0	0	0	0	0	0	77
AUG	0	0	0	0	0	45	92	94	96	98	98	100	95	65	58	33	14	28	0	0	0	0	0	0	70
SEP	0	0	0	0	0	10	87	94	100	100	100	90	63	57	27	11	13	15	0	0	0	0	0	0	61
OCT	0	0	0	0	0	0	58	95	96	96	92	59	39	9	5	0	7	0	0	0	0	0	0	0	46
NOV	0	0	0	0	0	0	9	82	93	96	91	33	12	13	3	8	2	0	0	0	0	0	0	0	34
DEC	0	0	0	0	0	0	0	48	87	90	90	68	4	0	0	9	0	0	0	0	0	0	0	0	33
Annual	0	0	0	0	1	29	56	93	93	95	95	80	60	44	35	27	21	8	0	0	0	0	0	0	56

West

Month	1	2	3	4	5	6	7	8	9	10	11	12	13	14	15	16	17	18	19	20	21	22	23	24	Hours
JAN	0	0	0	0	0	0	0	2	31	34	15	8	30	88	86	79	41	0	0	0	0	0	0	0	35
FEB	0	0	0	0	0	0	0	34	54	48	48	52	48	49	92	94	63	4	0	0	0	0	0	0	48
MAR	0	0	0	0	0	0	30	69	81	79	75	67	64	65	84	93	88	69	0	0	0	0	0	0	68
APR	0	0	0	0	0	9	77	87	89	94	94	94	94	89	93	91	89	55	4	0	0	0	0	0	80
MAY	0	0	0	0	0	56	87	92	98	98	100	100	100	98	100	93	83	50	45	0	0	0	0	0	87
JUN	0	0	0	0	0	72	87	90	98	98	98	98	100	96	93	91	87	72	63	0	0	0	0	0	88
JUL	0	0	0	0	0	46	87	96	100	100	100	100	100	95	93	89	82	87	55	0	0	0	0	0	89
AUG	0	0	0	0	0	7	82	88	96	98	98	100	100	95	98	95	97	76	5	0	0	0	0	0	88
SEP	0	0	0	0	0	0	65	85	94	94	90	87	80	82	91	91	88	63	0	0	0	0	0	0	81
OCT	0	0	0	0	0	0	13	69	62	63	62	52	53	50	84	86	60	3	0	0	0	0	0	0	55
NOV	0	0	0	0	0	0	0	35	48	48	37	22	56	95	95	84	30	0	0	0	0	0	0	0	45
DEC	0	0	0	0	0	0	0	0	32	38	12	4	94	94	91	80	20	0	0	0	0	0	0	0	40
Annual	0	0	0	0	0	16	44	84	74	75	70	65	77	83	92	89	69	33	5	0	0	0	0	0	67

Core (Top-lit)

Month	1	2	3	4	5	6	7	8	9	10	11	12	13	14	15	16	17	18	19	20	21	22	23	24	Hours
JAN	0	0	0	0	0	0	0	0	17	54	83	89	85	84	48	9	0	0	0	0	0	0	0	0	43
FEB	0	0	0	0	0	0	0	11	52	82	85	87	89	88	84	34	0	0	0	0	0	0	0	0	54
MAR	0	0	0	0	0	0	6	45	94	96	96	96	96	96	93	66	32	0	0	0	0	0	0	0	69
APR	0	0	0	0	0	0	40	86	89	89	94	96	96	98	93	86	36	1	0	0	0	0	0	0	72
MAY	0	0	0	0	0	10	74	88	98	98	100	100	100	100	100	93	55	10	0	0	0	0	0	0	83
JUN	0	0	0	0	0	35	85	90	96	98	98	98	98	96	91	91	75	22	0	0	0	0	0	0	84
JUL	0	0	0	0	0	2	71	98	100	100	100	100	100	98	98	86	78	14	0	0	0	0	0	0	86
AUG	0	0	0	0	0	0	42	92	96	98	98	100	100	100	100	95	57	7	0	0	0	0	0	0	83
SEP	0	0	0	0	0	0	30	83	98	100	100	100	99	100	95	70	16	0	0	0	0	0	0	0	77
OCT	0	0	0	0	0	0	0	45	92	96	96	96	96	91	79	19	0	0	0	0	0	0	0	0	63
NOV	0	0	0	0	0	0	0	5	50	89	91	98	93	84	39	0	0	0	0	0	0	0	0	0	50
DEC	0	0	0	0	0	0	0	0	23	44	83	88	89	69	30	0	0	0	0	0	0	0	0	0	39
Annual	0	0	0	0	0	4	29	81	76	87	94	96	95	92	79	55	30	3	0	0	0	0	0	0	67

Percent Power Reduction (Based on Maximum Illumination for Each Space): Denver

For a typical two-story office building with 15'-0"-deep perimeter zones and a top-lit core zone.

Weather Data:	Denver (TMY)	Glass Type: ¼" solar bronze tinted (single pane)
% Opening:	37.5% WWR (windows)	(SC = 0.57; VT = 0.47)
	4% of roof area (skylights)	
Overhangs:	2'-3" (horizontal)	
Lighting Control Type:	Continuous	
No. of Ref. Points:	One (2'-6" high in the center of zone)	
Max. Illum.:	118 footcandles	

North

Month	1	2	3	4	5	6	7	8	9	10	11	12	13	14	15	16	17	18	19	20	21	22	23	24	Hours
JAN	0	0	0	0	0	0	0	8	22	22	20	16	15	13	9	24	9	0	0	0	0	0	0	0	14
FEB	0	0	0	0	0	0	0	26	34	33	32	31	27	20	16	10	20	2	0	0	0	0	0	0	21
MAR	0	0	0	0	0	0	27	44	46	43	41	39	35	30	24	18	34	19	0	0	0	0	0	0	30
APR	0	0	0	0	0	13	60	61	55	52	50	49	46	41	35	28	21	25	2	0	0	0	0	0	38
MAY	0	0	0	0	0	52	73	68	64	63	61	58	57	50	42	35	27	24	16	0	0	0	0	0	49
JUN	0	0	0	0	4	59	77	70	67	64	60	58	54	47	39	34	28	28	22	0	0	0	0	0	49
JUL	0	0	0	0	1	50	78	73	68	62	56	53	48	43	40	33	28	25	19	0	0	0	0	0	47
AUG	0	0	0	0	0	15	66	67	60	55	52	50	46	40	33	27	23	32	5	0	0	0	0	0	43
SEP	0	0	0	0	0	3	50	55	52	49	48	43	37	30	23	18	24	19	0	0	0	0	0	0	35
OCT	0	0	0	0	0	0	18	44	38	37	35	30	24	18	13	9	19	1	0	0	0	0	0	0	24
NOV	0	0	0	0	0	0	2	25	28	27	25	21	18	14	10	14	9	0	0	0	0	0	0	0	15
DEC	0	0	0	0	0	0	0	10	22	22	19	14	12	10	6	17	6	0	0	0	0	0	0	0	12
Annual	0	0	0	0	0	16	38	61	47	44	42	38	35	30	24	22	21	12	2	0	0	0	0	0	31

South

Max. Illum.: 763 footcandles

Month	1	2	3	4	5	6	7	8	9	10	11	12	13	14	15	16	17	18	19	20	21	22	23	24	Hours
JAN	0	0	0	0	0	0	0	3	21	41	37	31	28	30	29	11	3	0	0	0	0	0	0	0	21
FEB	0	0	0	0	0	0	0	12	28	32	19	19	19	16	18	18	6	0	0	0	0	0	0	0	16
MAR	0	0	0	0	0	0	6	33	38	16	16	17	15	13	9	13	12	4	0	0	0	0	0	0	14
APR	0	0	0	0	0	2	16	25	12	11	10	10	9	7	7	5	9	4	0	0	0	0	0	0	8
MAY	0	0	0	0	0	5	18	17	12	11	11	11	10	8	7	6	7	4	2	0	0	0	0	0	9
JUN	0	0	0	0	0	6	15	12	11	11	11	10	10	8	7	6	5	6	2	0	0	0	0	0	8
JUL	0	0	0	0	0	5	16	18	12	11	10	10	9	7	6	5	5	6	2	0	0	0	0	0	9
AUG	0	0	0	0	0	2	19	30	12	11	10	10	9	7	6	5	10	5	1	0	0	0	0	0	10
SEP	0	0	0	0	0	0	16	44	21	12	11	11	9	7	5	13	9	3	0	0	0	0	0	0	13
OCT	0	0	0	0	0	0	5	58	39	21	22	23	20	14	17	21	4	0	0	0	0	0	0	0	21
NOV	0	0	0	0	0	0	1	18	43	39	25	20	22	26	23	11	2	0	0	0	0	0	0	0	19
DEC	0	0	0	0	0	0	0	5	34	38	41	37	37	37	28	8	2	0	0	0	0	0	0	0	24
Annual	0	0	0	0	0	2	9	28	23	21	19	18	16	15	13	10	6	2	0	0	0	0	0	0	14

East

Month	1	2	3	4	5	6	7	8	9	10	11	12	13	14	15	16	17	18	19	20	21	22	23	24	Hours
JAN	0	0	0	0	0	0	0	3	25	32	21	7	2	2	1	4	1	0	0	0	0	0	0	0	9
FEB	0	0	0	0	0	0	0	11	32	28	11	6	4	3	3	2	3	0	0	0	0	0	0	0	9
MAR	0	0	0	0	0	0	7	28	39	23	10	7	6	5	4	3	5	2	0	0	0	0	0	0	10
APR	0	0	0	0	0	4	26	41	22	18	10	9	8	7	6	4	3	3	0	0	0	0	0	0	9
MAY	0	0	0	0	0	14	40	34	23	14	12	10	9	8	7	5	4	3	2	0	0	0	0	0	12
JUN	0	0	0	0	1	21	48	32	26	14	12	10	9	7	6	5	4	3	2	0	0	0	0	0	12
JUL	0	0	0	0	0	18	48	43	29	15	12	9	8	7	6	5	4	3	2	0	0	0	0	0	13
AUG	0	0	0	0	0	5	35	46	29	15	11	8	6	5	4	3	4	1	0	0	0	0	0	0	13
SEP	0	0	0	0	0	1	21	44	31	20	11	8	6	5	4	3	3	2	0	0	0	0	0	0	13
OCT	0	0	0	0	0	0	7	39	44	21	9	5	4	3	2	1	3	0	0	0	0	0	0	0	12
NOV	0	0	0	0	0	0	1	17	33	26	11	4	3	2	2	2	1	0	0	0	0	0	0	0	8
DEC	0	0	0	0	0	0	0	5	27	26	18	7	2	2	1	3	1	0	0	0	0	0	0	0	8
Annual	0	0	0	0	0	5	20	38	30	21	12	8	6	5	4	3	3	1	0	0	0	0	0	0	11

West

Max. Illum.: 520 footcandles

Month	1	2	3	4	5	6	7	8	9	10	11	12	13	14	15	16	17	18	19	20	21	22	23	24	Hours
JAN	0	0	0	0	0	0	0	2	5	5	5	4	6	24	39	25	6	0	0	0	0	0	0	0	10
FEB	0	0	0	0	0	0	0	5	7	8	8	7	7	7	24	41	11	1	0	0	0	0	0	0	10
MAR	0	0	0	0	0	0	5	8	10	10	9	9	9	9	17	33	31	9	0	0	0	0	0	0	13
APR	0	0	0	0	0	2	10	11	11	12	12	12	12	11	17	16	33	10	1	0	0	0	0	0	13
MAY	0	0	0	0	0	8	11	12	13	14	14	14	14	13	13	18	24	13	6	0	0	0	0	0	14
JUN	0	0	0	0	1	8	11	12	13	14	14	14	14	13	12	22	22	26	9	0	0	0	0	0	14
JUL	0	0	0	0	0	7	11	12	13	13	13	12	12	12	11	18	19	23	8	0	0	0	0	0	13
AUG	0	0	0	0	0	2	10	11	12	12	12	12	12	11	11	24	33	14	2	0	0	0	0	0	14
SEP	0	0	0	0	0	1	8	10	11	11	11	10	10	10	18	35	31	9	0	0	0	0	0	0	14
OCT	0	0	0	0	0	0	3	9	9	9	8	7	7	7	36	38	10	1	0	0	0	0	0	0	12
NOV	0	0	0	0	0	0	1	5	7	6	6	5	7	27	44	19	5	0	0	0	0	0	0	0	11
DEC	0	0	0	0	0	0	0	2	5	5	4	3	11	39	35	13	4	0	0	0	0	0	0	0	10
Annual	0	0	0	0	0	2	6	11	10	10	10	9	10	15	23	25	19	7	1	0	0	0	0	0	12

Core (Top-lit)

Month	1	2	3	4	5	6	7	8	9	10	11	12	13	14	15	16	17	18	19	20	21	22	23	24	Hours
JAN	0	0	0	0	0	0	0	3	11	21	30	36	35	29	18	10	3	0	0	0	0	0	0	0	18
FEB	0	0	0	0	0	0	0	9	19	32	42	46	46	40	30	14	6	0	0	0	0	0	0	0	25
MAR	0	0	0	0	0	0	6	18	36	53	63	64	60	51	40	24	14	5	0	0	0	0	0	0	37
APR	0	0	0	0	0	3	16	34	49	61	69	71	68	60	47	32	15	7	1	0	0	0	0	0	44
MAY	0	0	0	0	0	11	24	42	58	70	77	78	72	63	51	36	20	9	4	0	0	0	0	0	51
JUN	0	0	0	0	1	12	26	47	64	77	84	84	79	71	59	44	27	11	4	0	0	0	0	0	57
JUL	0	0	0	0	0	9	24	47	67	81	88	90	85	74	55	39	26	11	4	0	0	0	0	0	59
AUG	0	0	0	0	0	3	18	36	57	70	78	80	76	68	56	39	21	9	1	0	0	0	0	0	52
SEP	0	0	0	0	0	1	13	27	46	61	70	73	70	60	44	26	11	5	0	0	0	0	0	0	44
OCT	0	0	0	0	0	0	4	20	33	48	55	56	52	42	28	11	5	0	0	0	0	0	0	0	31
NOV	0	0	0	0	0	0	1	9	19	30	38	40	37	28	15	6	3	0	0	0	0	0	0	0	20
DEC	0	0	0	0	0	0	0	3	12	21	28	32	31	24	13	6	2	0	0	0	0	0	0	0	15
Annual	0	0	0	0	0	3	11	36	40	52	61	62	60	51	38	24	13	4	0	0	0	0	0	0	38

Percent Power Reduction: Los Angeles

For a typical two-story office building with 15'-0"-deep perimeter zones and a top-lit core zone.

Weather Data:	Los Angeles (TMY)	Glass Type: ¼" solar bronze tinted (single pane)
% Opening:	37.5% WWR (windows)	(SC = 0.57; VT = 0.47)
	4% of roof area (skylights)	
Overhangs:	2'-3" (horizontal)	
Lighting Control Type:	Stepped (two steps)	
Lighting Set Point:	50 footcandles	
No. of Ref. Points:	One (2'-6" high in the center of zone)	

North

Month	1	2	3	4	5	6	7	8	9	10	11	12	13	14	15	16	17	18	19	20	21	22	23	24	Hours
JAN	0	0	0	0	0	0	0	0	39	46	52	56	56	52	48	43	7	0	0	0	0	0	0	0	36
FEB	0	0	0	0	0	0	0	37	54	54	61	67	69	70	66	50	42	0	0	0	0	0	0	0	48
MAR	0	0	0	0	0	0	0	53	67	100	100	100	100	100	100	96	91	88	70	0	0	0	0	0	80
APR	0	0	0	0	0	0	53	67	100	100	100	100	100	100	100	98	88	70	0	0	0	0	0	0	86
MAY	0	0	0	0	0	11	40	94	100	100	100	100	100	100	100	100	98	88	0	0	0	0	0	0	90
JUN	0	0	0	0	0	18	45	87	100	100	100	100	100	100	100	100	93	84	26	0	0	0	0	0	90
JUL	0	0	0	0	0	2	64	87	100	98	98	100	100	100	100	100	96	93	19	0	0	0	0	0	90
AUG	0	0	0	0	0	0	56	83	94	100	100	100	100	98	100	100	95	83	0	0	0	0	0	0	89
SEP	0	0	0	0	0	0	17	69	85	100	100	100	100	100	98	96	84	23	0	0	0	0	0	0	83
OCT	0	0	0	0	0	0	3	37	63	73	79	77	74	67	57	69	36	0	0	0	0	0	0	0	55
NOV	0	0	0	0	0	0	0	35	46	46	57	61	59	56	50	45	0	0	0	0	0	0	0	0	38
DEC	0	0	0	0	0	0	0	0	42	48	52	50	53	52	48	41	0	0	1	0	0	0	0	0	35
Annual	0	0	0	0	0	3	24	75	76	81	84	84	85	83	81	79	62	30	1	0	0	0	0	0	69

South

Month	1	2	3	4	5	6	7	8	9	10	11	12	13	14	15	16	17	18	19	20	21	22	23	24	Hours
JAN	0	0	0	0	0	0	0	48	87	90	92	96	97	91	95	86	45	0	0	0	0	0	0	0	70
FEB	0	0	0	0	0	0	0	82	91	96	100	100	100	100	100	97	83	0	0	0	0	0	0	0	78
MAR	0	0	0	0	0	0	11	79	85	100	100	100	100	100	100	96	93	31	0	0	0	0	0	0	81
APR	0	0	0	0	0	0	53	68	100	100	100	100	100	100	100	98	91	83	0	0	0	0	0	0	87
MAY	0	0	0	0	0	0	40	94	100	100	100	100	100	100	100	100	98	90	0	0	0	0	0	0	91
JUN	0	0	0	0	0	0	47	87	100	100	100	100	100	100	100	100	93	84	0	0	0	0	0	0	90
JUL	0	0	0	0	0	0	64	89	100	98	98	100	100	100	100	100	96	73	0	0	0	0	0	0	89
AUG	0	0	0	0	0	0	56	85	96	100	100	100	100	98	100	100	98	63	0	0	0	0	0	0	88
SEP	0	0	0	0	0	0	22	77	85	100	100	100	100	100	100	98	93	31	0	0	0	0	0	0	85
OCT	0	0	0	0	0	0	17	70	88	96	100	100	100	100	100	95	71	0	0	0	0	0	0	0	80
NOV	0	0	0	0	0	0	0	78	85	89	96	98	98	98	95	90	14	0	0	0	0	0	0	0	68
DEC	0	0	0	0	0	0	0	63	92	90	92	94	96	98	93	89	8	0	0	0	0	0	0	0	68
Annual	0	0	0	0	0	0	26	83	92	97	98	99	99	99	99	96	74	31	0	0	0	0	0	0	81

East

Month	1	2	3	4	5	6	7	8	9	10	11	12	13	14	15	16	17	18	19	20	21	22	23	24	Hours
JAN	0	0	0	0	0	0	0	70	85	87	90	63	56	52	48	43	7	0	0	0	0	0	0	0	49
FEB	0	0	0	0	0	0	0	84	91	91	100	100	84	80	68	50	42	0	0	0	0	0	0	0	64
MAR	0	0	0	0	0	0	25	82	94	100	100	100	100	100	100	93	64	5	0	0	0	0	0	0	77
APR	0	0	0	0	0	6	57	97	100	100	100	100	100	100	100	98	86	41	0	0	0	0	0	0	84
MAY	0	0	0	0	0	32	64	100	100	100	100	100	100	100	100	100	95	45	0	0	0	0	0	0	90
JUN	0	0	0	0	0	40	73	87	100	100	100	100	100	100	100	100	91	66	0	0	0	0	0	0	89
JUL	0	0	0	0	0	17	85	100	100	98	98	100	100	100	100	100	93	64	0	0	0	0	0	0	90
AUG	0	0	0	0	0	7	58	89	100	100	100	100	100	98	100	100	90	43	0	0	0	0	0	0	88
SEP	0	0	0	0	0	0	37	79	85	100	100	100	100	100	98	91	50	11	0	0	0	0	0	0	81
OCT	0	0	0	0	0	0	31	78	90	100	100	100	88	81	57	50	24	0	0	0	0	0	0	0	68
NOV	0	0	0	0	0	0	6	78	85	89	96	61	59	58	50	45	0	0	0	0	0	0	0	0	50
DEC	0	0	0	0	0	0	0	74	92	90	92	54	57	52	48	41	0	0	0	0	0	0	0	0	49
Annual	0	0	0	0	0	9	37	89	94	96	98	89	87	85	81	76	54	17	0	0	0	0	0	0	73

West

Month	1	2	3	4	5	6	7	8	9	10	11	12	13	14	15	16	17	18	19	20	21	22	23	24	Hours
JAN	0	0	0	0	0	0	0	0	39	46	52	56	57	91	90	88	64	0	0	0	0	0	0	0	51
FEB	0	0	0	0	0	0	0	34	50	59	76	83	100	100	100	97	89	7	0	0	0	0	0	0	67
MAR	0	0	0	0	0	0	3	48	83	100	100	100	100	100	100	100	98	67	0	0	0	0	0	0	84
APR	0	0	0	0	0	0	27	67	100	100	100	100	100	100	100	100	93	86	0	0	0	0	0	0	87
MAY	0	0	0	0	0	0	31	86	100	100	100	100	100	100	100	100	100	95	14	0	0	0	0	0	90
JUN	0	0	0	0	0	0	37	83	100	100	100	100	100	100	100	100	100	93	64	0	0	0	0	0	91
JUL	0	0	0	0	0	0	47	83	100	98	98	100	100	100	100	100	98	96	53	0	0	0	0	0	90
AUG	0	0	0	0	0	0	27	81	98	100	100	100	100	98	100	100	100	93	0	0	0	0	0	0	89
SEP	0	0	0	0	0	0	8	61	85	100	100	100	100	100	100	100	98	96	60	0	0	0	0	0	85
OCT	0	0	0	0	0	0	0	30	60	77	90	92	100	100	100	100	100	90	0	0	0	0	0	0	72
NOV	0	0	0	0	0	0	0	33	46	48	59	61	86	98	97	95	41	0	0	0	0	0	0	0	55
DEC	0	0	0	0	0	0	0	0	42	48	56	52	59	96	93	89	26	0	0	0	0	0	0	0	49
Annual	0	0	0	0	0	0	15	69	76	82	86	87	92	98	98	97	83	41	3	0	0	0	0	0	76

Core (Top-lit)

Month	1	2	3	4	5	6	7	8	9	10	11	12	13	14	15	16	17	18	19	20	21	22	23	24	Hours
JAN	0	0	0	0	0	0	0	0	33	60	90	94	95	91	74	26	0	0	0	0	0	0	0	0	51
FEB	0	0	0	0	0	0	0	0	46	91	96	100	100	98	95	58	3	0	0	0	0	0	0	0	62
MAR	0	0	0	0	0	0	0	24	85	100	100	100	100	100	100	96	43	0	0	0	0	0	0	0	74
APR	0	0	0	0	0	0	5	63	94	100	100	100	100	100	100	93	54	0	0	0	0	0	0	0	77
MAY	0	0	0	0	0	0	19	72	100	100	100	100	100	100	100	100	92	15	0	0	0	0	0	0	85
JUN	0	0	0	0	0	0	23	71	100	100	100	100	100	100	100	100	91	41	0	0	0	0	0	0	87
JUL	0	0	0	0	0	0	27	85	100	98	98	100	100	100	100	100	93	48	0	0	0	0	0	0	88
AUG	0	0	0	0	0	0	6	69	90	100	100	100	100	98	100	100	81	5	0	0	0	0	0	0	83
SEP	0	0	0	0	0	0	0	44	79	100	100	100	100	100	100	100	98	32	0	0	0	0	0	0	75
OCT	0	0	0	0	0	0	0	22	75	94	100	100	100	100	100	57	0	0	0	0	0	0	0	0	66
NOV	0	0	0	0	0	0	0	0	46	85	93	96	95	93	63	8	0	0	0	0	0	0	0	0	52
DEC	0	0	0	0	0	0	0	0	42	67	88	92	93	94	48	0	0	0	0	0	0	0	0	0	48
Annual	0	0	0	0	0	0	7	59	75	91	97	98	99	98	90	70	42	6	0	0	0	0	0	0	71

Percent Power Reduction: New York

For a typical two-story office building with 15'-0"-deep perimeter zones and a top-lit core zone.

Weather Data:	New York (TMY)	Glass Type: ¼" solar bronze tinted (single pane)
% Opening:	37.5% WWR (windows)	(SC = 0.57; VT = 0.47)
	4% of roof area (skylights)	
Overhangs:	2'-3" (horizontal)	
Lighting Control Type:	Stepped (two steps)	
Lighting Set Point:	50 footcandles	
No. of Ref. Points:	One (2'-6" high in the center of zone)	

North

Month	1	2	3	4	5	6	7	8	9	10	11	12	13	14	15	16	17	18	19	20	21	22	23	24	Hours
JAN	0	0	0	0	0	0	0	12	21	21	25	25	25	23	24	19	13	0	0	0	0	0	0	0	18
FEB	0	0	0	0	0	0	0	21	24	28	26	31	35	39	32	29	29	12	0	0	0	0	0	0	25
MAR	0	0	0	0	0	0	23	29	29	33	54	67	70	66	39	30	23	20	0	0	0	0	0	0	39
APR	0	0	0	0	0	25	45	58	56	71	73	75	71	73	73	59	57	50	18	0	0	0	0	0	60
MAY	0	0	0	0	0	50	58	73	86	82	90	91	86	89	84	69	74	65	43	0	0	0	0	0	76
JUN	0	0	0	0	20	53	57	58	79	81	85	84	91	91	86	84	61	61	60	16	0	0	0	0	74
JUL	0	0	0	0	13	56	61	73	88	88	87	85	76	82	77	80	75	73	73	15	0	0	0	0	76
AUG	0	0	0	0	0	57	76	83	89	83	92	94	91	91	88	88	84	79	57	0	0	0	0	0	82
SEP	0	0	0	0	0	18	68	75	78	86	85	86	83	86	86	75	70	61	8	0	0	0	0	0	75
OCT	0	0	0	0	0	0	36	64	60	71	81	79	78	78	64	57	63	7	0	0	0	0	0	0	61
NOV	0	0	0	0	0	0	0	6	23	28	35	54	52	40	45	29	26	17	0	0	0	0	0	0	29
DEC	0	0	0	0	0	0	0	0	14	23	25	25	27	29	28	21	14	7	0	0	0	0	0	0	18
Annual	0	0	0	0	3	22	36	68	56	59	65	66	65	66	59	53	48	27	8	3	0	0	0	0	53

South

Month	1	2	3	4	5	6	7	8	9	10	11	12	13	14	15	16	17	18	19	20	21	22	23	24	Hours
JAN	0	0	0	0	0	0	0	28	54	58	54	54	53	52	55	50	28	0	0	0	0	0	0	0	41
FEB	0	0	0	0	0	0	0	47	55	61	55	59	69	69	69	69	53	19	0	0	0	0	0	0	51
MAR	0	0	0	0	0	0	36	58	58	60	65	85	83	81	59	62	46	39	0	0	0	0	0	0	57
APR	0	0	0	0	0	15	47	71	61	75	79	81	78	82	84	64	70	55	12	0	0	0	0	0	66
MAY	0	0	0	0	0	21	61	73	88	86	90	91	91	92	84	71	74	61	22	0	0	0	0	0	77
JUN	0	0	0	0	9	43	57	58	81	81	85	89	93	91	88	84	61	61	45	7	0	0	0	0	75
JUL	0	0	0	0	5	44	64	73	90	88	87	91	84	82	80	82	75	71	56	7	0	0	0	0	77
AUG	0	0	0	0	0	45	77	85	90	90	94	96	93	93	91	88	88	81	43	0	0	0	0	0	84
SEP	0	0	0	0	0	17	70	79	81	86	88	91	86	88	86	82	75	63	5	0	0	0	0	0	77
OCT	0	0	0	0	0	0	51	79	77	75	90	88	85	88	71	76	74	12	0	0	0	0	0	0	70
NOV	0	0	0	0	0	0	13	68	78	69	80	78	61	75	74	63	36	0	0	0	0	0	0	0	55
DEC	0	0	0	0	0	0	0	40	62	58	58	62	58	57	53	46	20	0	0	0	0	0	0	0	43
Annual	0	0	0	0	1	15	40	73	73	74	77	80	78	79	75	70	59	31	6	1	0	0	0	0	65

East

Month	1	2	3	4	5	6	7	8	9	10	11	12	13	14	15	16	17	18	19	20	21	22	23	24	Hours
JAN	0	0	0	0	0	0	0	33	52	54	54	44	42	23	24	19	13	0	0	0	0	0	0	0	30
FEB	0	0	0	0	0	0	0	54	55	59	55	57	52	55	32	29	26	9	0	0	0	0	0	0	39
MAR	0	0	0	0	0	0	46	60	58	62	81	79	75	70	43	30	23	17	0	0	0	0	0	0	49
APR	0	0	0	0	0	40	55	81	69	81	79	79	73	73	70	52	41	26	10	0	0	0	0	0	60
MAY	0	0	0	0	0	61	63	77	88	90	90	91	86	89	84	66	61	53	22	0	0	0	0	0	76
JUN	0	0	0	0	23	60	63	62	81	81	86	84	91	91	86	82	61	57	45	7	0	0	0	0	74
JUL	0	0	0	0	15	69	68	73	92	90	90	89	76	82	77	80	75	66	56	7	0	0	0	0	77
AUG	0	0	0	0	0	61	84	89	94	92	96	94	91	91	88	88	81	70	41	0	0	0	0	0	84
SEP	0	0	0	0	0	21	73	81	82	86	88	88	86	86	86	75	68	48	4	0	0	0	0	0	76
OCT	0	0	0	0	0	0	55	79	75	75	90	85	80	78	64	57	35	6	0	0	0	0	0	0	63
NOV	0	0	0	0	0	0	14	67	71	67	74	59	45	49	32	26	17	0	0	0	0	0	0	0	40
DEC	0	0	0	0	0	0	0	46	58	56	54	52	37	31	21	14	7	0	0	0	0	0	0	0	31
Annual	0	0	0	0	3	26	44	75	73	75	78	75	70	68	59	52	43	22	5	1	0	0	0	0	58

West

Month	1	2	3	4	5	6	7	8	9	10	11	12	13	14	15	16	17	18	19	20	21	22	23	24	Hours
JAN	0	0	0	0	0	0	0	12	21	21	25	44	44	51	57	55	32	0	0	0	0	0	0	0	31
FEB	0	0	0	0	0	0	0	21	24	28	33	50	59	67	71	71	69	24	0	0	0	0	0	0	43
MAR	0	0	0	0	0	0	21	29	29	35	71	73	78	81	61	64	55	47	0	0	0	0	0	0	52
APR	0	0	0	0	0	15	22	27	54	71	73	77	75	80	84	68	77	71	26	0	0	0	0	0	65
MAY	0	0	0	0	0	21	45	65	80	82	90	91	91	92	92	74	77	76	54	0	0	0	0	0	76
JUN	0	0	0	0	9	43	53	54	79	81	85	84	91	93	88	84	72	68	67	19	0	0	0	0	75
JUL	0	0	0	0	5	44	60	73	85	88	87	85	78	82	80	84	78	78	81	18	0	0	0	0	76
AUG	0	0	0	0	0	29	66	79	89	83	92	94	91	95	95	91	91	91	61	0	0	0	0	0	83
SEP	0	0	0	0	0	9	62	71	78	86	85	88	86	86	86	84	77	68	9	0	0	0	0	0	76
OCT	0	0	0	0	0	0	24	59	60	71	85	83	80	85	74	81	77	13	0	0	0	0	0	0	66
NOV	0	0	0	0	0	0	5	23	28	46	59	54	46	73	74	69	42	0	0	0	0	0	0	0	43
DEC	0	0	0	0	0	0	0	14	23	25	35	40	53	57	55	53	22	0	0	0	0	0	0	0	32
Annual	0	0	0	0	1	13	30	64	55	60	68	72	73	78	76	73	64	37	10	3	0	0	0	0	60

Core (Top-lit)

Month	1	2	3	4	5	6	7	8	9	10	11	12	13	14	15	16	17	18	19	20	21	22	23	24	Hours
JAN	0	0	0	0	0	0	0	0	0	21	40	44	42	37	22	0	0	0	0	0	0	0	0	0	19
FEB	0	0	0	0	0	0	0	0	15	30	48	57	59	64	42	21	0	0	0	0	0	0	0	0	30
MAR	0	0	0	0	0	0	0	0	29	56	65	67	68	64	57	37	14	0	0	0	0	0	0	0	41
APR	0	0	0	0	0	0	0	25	59	58	79	81	78	80	66	59	30	0	0	0	0	0	0	0	53
MAY	0	0	0	0	0	0	19	60	75	86	90	91	91	92	84	69	54	21	0	0	0	0	0	0	70
JUN	0	0	0	0	0	17	26	54	79	81	85	84	91	91	88	72	59	30	0	0	0	0	0	0	70
JUL	0	0	0	0	0	0	27	69	88	88	87	85	76	82	80	64	71	34	21	0	0	0	0	0	71
AUG	0	0	0	0	0	0	27	62	83	90	92	94	91	91	91	79	65	34	0	0	0	0	0	0	75
SEP	0	0	0	0	0	0	27	40	78	86	88	88	86	86	86	75	34	17	0	0	0	0	0	0	67
OCT	0	0	0	0	0	0	0	32	60	71	88	85	80	73	64	29	12	0	0	0	0	0	0	0	52
NOV	0	0	0	0	0	0	0	0	24	46	61	65	45	49	29	13	0	0	0	0	0	0	0	0	30
DEC	0	0	0	0	0	0	0	0	6	21	35	40	43	33	14	0	0	0	0	0	0	0	0	0	18
Annual	0	0	0	0	0	1	11	50	50	62	72	73	71	70	61	44	29	7	1	0	0	0	0	0	50

Percent Power Reduction: Seattle

For a typical two-story office building with 15'-0"-deep perimeter zones and a top-lit core zone.

Weather Data:	Seattle (TMY)	Glass Type: ¼" solar bronze tinted (single pane)
% Opening:	37.5% WWR (windows)	(SC = 0.57; VT = 0.47)
	4% of roof area (skylights)	
Overhangs:	2'-3" (horizontal)	
Lighting Control Type:	Stepped (two steps)	
Lighting Set Point:	50 footcandles	
No. of Ref. Points:	One (2'-6" high in the center of zone)	

North

Month	1	2	3	4	5	6	7	8	9	10	11	12	13	14	15	16	17	18	19	20	21	22	23	24	Hours
JAN	0	0	0	0	0	0	0	0	0	13	19	31	32	32	23	12	0	0	0	0	0	0	0	0	14
FEB	0	0	0	0	0	0	0	0	9	24	43	48	42	42	34	19	5	0	0	0	0	0	0	0	24
MAR	0	0	0	0	0	6	21	40	44	64	73	75	69	73	59	46	16	0	0	0	0	0	0	0	50
APR	0	0	0	0	0	1	37	79	71	87	90	94	92	91	91	77	65	41	6	0	0	0	0	0	73
MAY	0	0	0	0	0	27	44	62	66	82	92	90	95	90	83	70	58	47	40	0	0	0	0	0	72
JUN	0	0	0	0	0	20	43	61	84	92	94	86	87	87	87	84	80	67	55	5	0	0	0	0	78
JUL	0	0	0	0	0	34	48	64	81	90	92	100	100	95	93	89	84	83	66	3	0	0	0	0	82
AUG	0	0	0	0	0	0	39	71	81	88	94	97	97	95	86	81	78	27	0	0	0	0	0	0	81
SEP	0	0	0	0	0	0	17	46	54	71	79	81	82	82	75	70	59	29	0	0	0	0	0	0	63
OCT	0	0	0	0	0	0	0	15	21	44	52	54	60	48	41	27	10	0	0	0	0	0	0	0	33
NOV	0	0	0	0	0	0	0	0	13	26	39	41	44	28	16	10	0	0	0	0	0	0	0	0	20
DEC	0	0	0	0	0	0	0	0	0	6	13	21	17	21	9	0	0	0	0	0	0	0	0	0	8
Annual	0	0	0	0	0	7	20	53	44	56	65	68	69	65	61	51	41	22	5	1	0	0	0	0	50

South

Month	1	2	3	4	5	6	7	8	9	10	11	12	13	14	15	16	17	18	19	20	21	22	23	24	Hours
JAN	0	0	0	0	0	0	0	0	19	31	40	48	49	49	45	31	7	0	0	0	0	0	0	0	29
FEB	0	0	0	0	0	0	0	0	32	43	65	67	58	66	63	47	24	0	0	0	0	0	0	0	42
MAR	0	0	0	0	0	0	6	32	48	54	68	77	82	75	80	71	61	29	0	0	0	0	0	0	57
APR	0	0	0	0	0	0	38	80	73	88	92	96	94	91	93	81	72	47	0	0	0	0	0	0	75
MAY	0	0	0	0	0	11	45	62	74	82	92	90	95	90	85	73	61	49	24	0	0	0	0	0	73
JUN	0	0	0	0	0	10	40	61	84	94	96	89	91	91	93	89	82	64	37	0	0	0	0	0	80
JUL	0	0	0	0	0	15	50	66	83	90	94	100	100	98	98	95	89	88	45	0	0	0	0	0	84
AUG	0	0	0	0	0	0	48	81	85	94	100	100	100	100	97	88	95	83	23	0	0	0	0	0	86
SEP	0	0	0	0	0	0	38	54	61	77	85	89	89	88	88	81	72	35	0	0	0	0	0	0	70
OCT	0	0	0	0	0	0	0	44	60	54	65	69	69	61	53	48	29	0	0	0	0	0	0	0	48
NOV	0	0	0	0	0	0	0	2	54	56	57	65	59	54	45	36	0	0	0	0	0	0	0	0	38
DEC	0	0	0	0	0	0	0	0	14	31	35	37	43	44	28	7	0	0	0	0	0	0	0	0	21
Annual	0	0	0	0	0	3	22	60	57	67	74	77	78	76	73	63	50	25	3	0	0	0	0	0	59

East

Month	1	2	3	4	5	6	7	8	9	10	11	12	13	14	15	16	17	18	19	20	21	22	23	24	Hours
JAN	0	0	0	0	0	0	0	0	25	31	40	44	36	38	26	12	0	0	0	0	0	0	0	0	23
FEB	0	0	0	0	0	0	0	0	35	43	63	65	52	47	40	19	5	0	0	0	0	0	0	0	33
MAR	0	0	0	0	0	0	13	39	54	54	68	77	75	71	73	59	43	7	0	0	0	0	0	0	52
APR	0	0	0	0	0	4	47	80	75	88	92	96	94	91	91	75	61	28	0	0	0	0	0	0	72
MAY	0	0	0	0	0	40	55	64	76	82	92	90	95	90	83	70	56	42	23	0	0	0	0	0	72
JUN	0	0	0	0	1	33	52	69	86	94	96	91	89	89	87	80	77	54	33	0	0	0	0	0	79
JUL	0	0	0	0	0	55	61	67	83	90	94	100	100	95	93	87	77	63	39	0	0	0	0	0	81
AUG	0	0	0	0	0	15	60	85	85	94	100	100	98	98	95	83	76	58	8	0	0	0	0	0	83
SEP	0	0	0	0	0	0	46	54	63	79	85	87	87	86	75	70	52	16	0	0	0	0	0	0	66
OCT	0	0	0	0	0	0	3	49	60	52	64	61	60	50	43	27	10	0	0	0	0	0	0	0	42
NOV	0	0	0	0	0	0	0	3	48	52	54	56	46	28	18	10	0	0	0	0	0	0	0	0	29
DEC	0	0	0	0	0	0	0	0	14	29	31	31	19	23	9	0	0	0	0	0	0	0	0	0	14
Annual	0	0	0	0	0	12	28	63	59	66	73	74	71	67	62	50	39	16	3	0	0	0	0	0	54

West

Month	1	2	3	4	5	6	7	8	9	10	11	12	13	14	15	16	17	18	19	20	21	22	23	24	Hours
JAN	0	0	0	0	0	0	0	0	0	13	19	33	43	47	45	33	7	0	0	0	0	0	0	0	21
FEB	0	0	0	0	0	0	0	0	9	24	45	52	55	56	66	50	35	0	0	0	0	0	0	0	34
MAR	0	0	0	0	0	0	3	16	40	46	64	75	75	75	80	73	66	51	0	0	0	0	0	0	57
APR	0	0	0	0	0	0	22	68	71	87	90	96	94	91	93	81	74	54	22	0	0	0	0	0	75
MAY	0	0	0	0	0	11	37	60	68	82	92	90	95	90	85	73	66	64	61	6	0	0	0	0	73
JUN	0	0	0	0	0	10	33	58	84	92	94	91	91	91	93	93	84	73	68	34	0	0	0	0	81
JUL	0	0	0	0	0	15	32	54	77	88	94	100	100	98	100	98	91	91	79	28	0	0	0	0	83
AUG	0	0	0	0	0	0	24	62	73	88	98	100	98	100	98	90	95	90	67	0	0	0	0	0	83
SEP	0	0	0	0	0	0	10	33	52	71	79	84	89	91	88	88	75	59	5	0	0	0	0	0	68
OCT	0	0	0	0	0	0	0	12	21	44	54	56	65	58	56	51	41	1	0	0	0	0	0	0	40
NOV	0	0	0	0	0	0	0	0	13	26	41	43	54	54	45	42	0	0	0	0	0	0	0	0	28
DEC	0	0	0	0	0	0	0	0	0	6	15	23	30	36	28	12	0	0	0	0	0	0	0	0	13
Annual	0	0	0	0	0	3	14	46	43	56	66	70	74	74	73	66	53	32	10	6	0	0	0	0	55

Core (Top-lit)

Month	1	2	3	4	5	6	7	8	9	10	11	12	13	14	15	16	17	18	19	20	21	22	23	24	Hours
JAN	0	0	0	0	0	0	0	0	0	2	17	23	29	21	14	0	0	0	0	0	0	0	0	0	9
FEB	0	0	0	0	0	0	0	0	0	19	45	52	51	49	32	8	0	0	0	0	0	0	0	0	23
MAR	0	0	0	0	0	0	0	5	27	54	60	71	75	71	75	52	18	0	0	0	0	0	0	0	45
APR	0	0	0	0	0	0	2	53	69	85	90	96	94	91	88	72	50	11	0	0	0	0	0	0	68
MAY	0	0	0	0	0	0	19	56	72	80	86	86	95	90	83	73	56	21	2	0	0	0	0	0	69
JUN	0	0	0	0	0	0	20	50	79	94	94	91	94	93	93	93	80	39	7	0	0	0	0	0	77
JUL	0	0	0	0	0	0	26	60	77	90	94	100	100	98	100	98	89	55	3	0	0	0	0	0	82
AUG	0	0	0	0	0	0	5	50	79	89	100	100	100	100	98	88	83	35	0	0	0	0	0	0	79
SEP	0	0	0	0	0	0	0	23	57	69	85	82	89	88	86	77	29	0	0	0	0	0	0	0	60
OCT	0	0	0	0	0	0	0	0	21	44	60	66	65	54	36	14	0	0	0	0	0	0	0	0	32
NOV	0	0	0	0	0	0	0	0	0	22	30	43	41	20	13	0	0	0	0	0	0	0	0	0	15
DEC	0	0	0	0	0	0	0	0	0	0	8	15	18	12	0	0	0	0	0	0	0	0	0	0	5
Annual	0	0	0	0	0	0	6	40	41	55	65	68	71	65	61	49	34	9	0	0	0	0	0	0	47

Appendix F.5   Average Illuminance Summary

Average Illuminance (Footcandles): Atlanta

For a typical two-story office building with 15'-0"-deep perimeter zones and a top-lit core zone.

Weather Data:	Atlanta (TMY)
% Opening:	37.5% WWR (windows)
	4% of roof area (skylights)
Overhangs:	2'-3" (horizontal)
Lighting Control Type:	Continuous
No. of Ref. Points:	One (2'-6" high in the center of zone)

Glass Type: ¼" solar bronze tinted (single pane)
(SC = 0.57; VT = 0.47)

North

Month	1	2	3	4	5	6	7	8	9	10	11	12	13	14	15	16	17	18	19	20	21	22	23	24	Hours
JAN	0	0	0	0	0	0	0	0	13	19	25	29	29	29	28	24	19	9	0	0	0	0	0	0	20
FEB	0	0	0	0	0	0	0	2	18	24	29	32	32	33	33	31	25	19	1	0	0	0	0	0	24
MAR	0	0	0	0	0	0	0	17	28	33	35	37	37	37	36	35	32	27	8	0	0	0	0	0	30
APR	0	0	0	0	0	0	11	23	32	35	37	37	37	38	37	36	36	32	21	0	0	0	0	0	32
MAY	0	0	0	0	0	1	26	35	37	37	38	39	39	39	39	39	37	36	29	2	0	0	0	0	35
JUN	0	0	0	0	0	1	25	34	36	37	38	37	38	38	37	37	36	35	31	6	0	0	0	0	34
JUL	0	0	0	0	0	0	19	34	35	36	37	38	39	39	39	37	36	36	29	3	0	0	0	0	34
AUG	0	0	0	0	0	0	15	31	35	37	38	39	39	39	39	39	37	37	30	0	0	0	0	0	34
SEP	0	0	0	0	0	0	3	24	32	35	37	38	38	37	37	36	35	26	6	0	0	0	0	0	32
OCT	0	0	0	0	0	0	0	18	29	32	37	38	38	37	35	33	32	13	0	0	0	0	0	0	29
NOV	0	0	0	0	0	0	0	7	19	23	27	30	31	31	28	27	20	3	0	0	0	0	0	0	21
DEC	0	0	0	0	0	0	0	1	14	20	26	29	28	28	25	21	15	2	0	0	0	0	0	0	19
Annual	0	0	0	0	0	0	8	28	28	31	34	35	35	35	35	33	30	20	7	1	0	0	0	0	29

South

Month	1	2	3	4	5	6	7	8	9	10	11	12	13	14	15	16	17	18	19	20	21	22	23	24	Hours
JAN	0	0	0	0	0	0	0	0	29	41	48	49	49	51	51	48	44	18	0	0	0	0	0	0	38
FEB	0	0	0	0	0	0	0	4	31	41	45	50	51	53	52	53	48	30	0	0	0	0	0	0	40
MAR	0	0	0	0	0	0	0	24	45	49	52	58	58	59	57	54	51	43	10	0	0	0	0	0	47
APR	0	0	0	0	0	0	10	26	48	54	57	57	58	60	58	59	56	48	19	0	0	0	0	0	50
MAY	0	0	0	0	0	0	19	48	58	60	59	63	65	65	63	63	58	53	24	1	0	0	0	0	54
JUN	0	0	0	0	0	1	17	43	51	60	59	62	62	61	60	59	55	48	25	4	0	0	0	0	52
JUL	0	0	0	0	0	0	12	44	52	57	55	58	60	62	59	55	55	50	23	2	0	0	0	0	51
AUG	0	0	0	0	0	0	11	37	53	55	59	64	63	66	62	65	61	51	27	0	0	0	0	0	53
SEP	0	0	0	0	0	0	3	30	50	53	57	61	61	60	58	58	54	34	6	0	0	0	0	0	48
OCT	0	0	0	0	0	0	0	34	53	60	63	64	65	64	62	62	60	23	0	0	0	0	0	0	51
NOV	0	0	0	0	0	0	0	13	42	47	52	51	57	60	56	55	46	5	0	0	0	0	0	0	42
DEC	0	0	0	0	0	0	0	2	44	50	54	55	53	55	54	49	43	3	0	0	0	0	0	0	41
Annual	0	0	0	0	0	0	6	37	47	52	55	57	59	60	58	57	52	30	7	1	0	0	0	0	48

East

Month	1	2	3	4	5	6	7	8	9	10	11	12	13	14	15	16	17	18	19	20	21	22	23	24	Hours
JAN	0	0	0	0	0	0	0	1	29	32	37	40	36	31	29	24	20	8	0	0	0	0	0	0	26
FEB	0	0	0	0	0	0	0	6	29	34	37	41	41	37	36	34	25	16	0	0	0	0	0	0	29
MAR	0	0	0	0	0	0	0	28	36	40	42	45	46	46	43	39	33	24	6	0	0	0	0	0	35
APR	0	0	0	0	0	0	21	28	41	43	45	46	46	47	47	43	40	31	15	0	0	0	0	0	39
MAY	0	0	0	0	0	1	39	44	46	47	47	48	48	49	49	47	42	36	22	1	0	0	0	0	43
JUN	0	0	0	0	0	2	34	44	46	47	48	47	48	47	47	47	41	37	23	4	0	0	0	0	43
JUL	0	0	0	0	0	0	35	43	44	45	45	47	48	48	48	45	41	35	20	2	0	0	0	0	41
AUG	0	0	0	0	0	0	29	41	44	44	48	48	49	49	49	46	39	32	22	0	0	0	0	0	41
SEP	0	0	0	0	0	0	6	35	41	43	46	46	47	46	43	40	34	21	4	0	0	0	0	0	39
OCT	0	0	0	0	0	0	0	37	43	46	48	48	44	41	36	34	26	11	0	0	0	0	0	0	36
NOV	0	0	0	0	0	0	0	18	33	38	41	40	34	32	28	25	18	3	0	0	0	0	0	0	26
DEC	0	0	0	0	0	0	0	2	37	39	42	43	32	29	26	22	15	1	0	0	0	0	0	0	26
Annual	0	0	0	0	0	0	14	39	39	41	43	45	43	42	41	37	32	18	5	1	0	0	0	0	36

West

Month	1	2	3	4	5	6	7	8	9	10	11	12	13	14	15	16	17	18	19	20	21	22	23	24	Hours
JAN	0	0	0	0	0	0	0	0	13	20	26	30	32	40	41	39	34	22	0	0	0	0	0	0	26
FEB	0	0	0	0	0	0	0	2	17	24	31	36	37	41	41	43	39	27	1	0	0	0	0	0	29
MAR	0	0	0	0	0	0	0	0	15	27	34	39	44	46	46	45	43	41	35	18	0	0	0	0	36
APR	0	0	0	0	0	0	8	21	35	40	44	46	46	48	47	45	44	41	34	0	0	0	0	0	40
MAY	0	0	0	0	0	0	18	33	41	46	47	48	48	49	48	48	47	45	41	3	0	0	0	0	41
JUN	0	0	0	0	0	1	17	33	40	46	48	48	48	47	47	46	46	45	41	11	0	0	0	0	41
JUL	0	0	0	0	0	0	12	32	39	42	45	47	48	48	48	46	46	46	40	6	0	0	0	0	41
AUG	0	0	0	0	0	0	10	25	34	41	46	48	48	49	49	48	48	48	41	0	0	0	0	0	40
SEP	0	0	0	0	0	0	2	19	32	39	43	46	47	48	46	45	44	41	11	0	0	0	0	0	37
OCT	0	0	0	0	0	0	0	15	27	36	40	43	46	48	47	47	46	33	0	0	0	0	0	0	36
NOV	0	0	0	0	0	0	0	6	18	25	29	31	36	46	43	43	36	8	0	0	0	0	0	0	27
DEC	0	0	0	0	0	0	0	1	14	21	28	30	31	43	42	39	37	4	0	0	0	0	0	0	25
Annual	0	0	0	0	0	0	6	25	28	34	39	41	43	46	46	44	43	29	11	0	0	0	0	0	35

Core (Top-lit)

Month	1	2	3	4	5	6	7	8	9	10	11	12	13	14	15	16	17	18	19	20	21	22	23	24	Hours
JAN	0	0	0	0	0	0	0	0	9	20	33	36	38	37	36	29	16	4	0	0	0	0	0	0	23
FEB	0	0	0	0	0	0	0	1	12	25	33	39	38	39	39	36	25	10	0	0	0	0	0	0	26
MAR	0	0	0	0	0	0	0	9	24	36	40	44	44	44	43	40	36	18	3	0	0	0	0	0	33
APR	0	0	0	0	0	0	4	18	36	40	42	43	44	44	44	42	41	26	8	0	0	0	0	0	36
MAY	0	0	0	0	0	0	8	30	42	44	45	45	46	46	46	46	44	34	12	1	0	0	0	0	39
JUN	0	0	0	0	0	0	8	28	41	44	45	44	44	44	44	42	38	16	2	0	0	0	0	0	38
JUL	0	0	0	0	0	0	6	27	41	42	44	44	46	46	45	43	42	39	15	1	0	0	0	0	38
AUG	0	0	0	0	0	0	5	20	40	43	46	46	46	46	45	44	31	12	0	0	0	0	0	0	38
SEP	0	0	0	0	0	0	1	14	34	40	44	45	45	44	43	42	37	16	2	0	0	0	0	0	34
OCT	0	0	0	0	0	0	0	9	27	41	44	46	46	45	44	42	24	5	0	0	0	0	0	0	32
NOV	0	0	0	0	0	0	0	3	15	30	37	40	42	43	40	28	13	1	0	0	0	0	0	0	25
DEC	0	0	0	0	0	0	0	1	10	22	36	39	40	38	36	23	10	1	0	0	0	0	0	0	23
Annual	0	0	0	0	0	0	3	21	28	36	41	42	43	43	42	38	31	16	3	0	0	0	0	0	33

Average Illuminance (Footcandles): Chicago

For a typical two-story office building with 15'-0"-deep perimeter zones and a top-lit core zone.

Weather Data:	Chicago (TMY)
% Opening:	37.5% WWR (windows)
	4% of roof area (skylights)
Overhangs:	2'-3" (horizontal)
Lighting Control Type:	Continuous
No. of Ref. Points:	One (2'-6" high in the center of zone)

Glass Type: ¼" solar bronze tinted (single pane)
(SC = 0.57; VT = 0.47)

North

Month	1	2	3	4	5	6	7	8	9	10	11	12	13	14	15	16	17	18	19	20	21	22	23	24	Hours
JAN	0	0	0	0	0	0	0	3	15	20	22	24	24	24	21	17	5	0	0	0	0	0	0	0	16
FEB	0	0	0	0	0	0	0	13	21	27	31	31	31	30	28	24	16	1	0	0	0	0	0	0	21
MAR	0	0	0	0	0	0	12	26	32	34	33	33	33	32	32	29	26	12	0	0	0	0	0	0	27
APR	0	0	0	0	0	0	6	24	32	32	34	35	35	34	33	32	27	21	1	0	0	0	0	0	29
MAY	0	0	0	0	1	24	31	33	33	34	34	34	35	34	33	31	31	24	10	0	0	0	0	0	31
JUN	0	0	0	0	4	26	29	32	33	34	34	35	35	35	35	33	32	29	24	0	0	0	0	0	31
JUL	0	0	0	0	2	28	32	34	35	34	35	35	35	35	35	34	32	23	0	0	0	0	0	0	32
AUG	0	0	0	0	0	8	26	31	33	35	35	35	34	35	34	34	32	27	2	0	0	0	0	0	31
SEP	0	0	0	0	0	2	23	29	32	33	33	34	35	34	34	32	27	13	0	0	0	0	0	0	29
OCT	0	0	0	0	0	0	8	23	26	29	30	33	32	30	27	22	12	0	0	0	0	0	0	0	23
NOV	0	0	0	0	0	0	1	11	19	23	25	25	26	24	21	12	2	0	0	0	0	0	0	0	16
DEC	0	0	0	0	0	0	0	3	12	17	20	22	22	20	17	9	0	0	0	0	0	0	0	0	13
Annual	0	0	0	0	1	8	16	29	27	30	31	31	31	31	29	26	21	11	2	0	0	0	0	0	25

South

Month	1	2	3	4	5	6	7	8	9	10	11	12	13	14	15	16	17	18	19	20	21	22	23	24	Hours
JAN	0	0	0	0	0	0	0	7	42	49	49	49	48	48	48	46	11	0	0	0	0	0	0	0	35
FEB	0	0	0	0	0	0	0	28	41	49	52	51	50	49	51	46	32	2	0	0	0	0	0	0	38
MAR	0	0	0	0	0	0	15	43	51	53	53	54	54	53	51	47	45	14	0	0	0	0	0	0	43
APR	0	0	0	0	0	5	32	32	49	53	55	56	55	54	53	50	44	24	0	0	0	0	0	0	45
MAY	0	0	0	0	1	20	44	53	54	52	55	57	57	56	53	48	46	25	7	0	0	0	0	0	48
JUN	0	0	0	0	3	20	43	50	56	54	60	60	62	61	57	54	50	33	15	0	0	0	0	0	51
JUL	0	0	0	0	1	19	46	54	60	56	63	65	65	61	60	63	57	39	14	0	0	0	0	0	55
AUG	0	0	0	0	0	7	33	48	53	62	63	65	64	65	61	57	54	33	1	0	0	0	0	0	53
SEP	0	0	0	0	0	2	29	49	53	57	58	59	63	62	56	54	44	14	0	0	0	0	0	0	49
OCT	0	0	0	0	0	0	13	44	51	51	50	55	54	48	46	39	20	0	0	0	0	0	0	0	40
NOV	0	0	0	0	0	0	1	29	48	49	49	50	52	51	49	33	3	0	0	0	0	0	0	0	35
DEC	0	0	0	0	0	0	0	6	29	37	41	43	41	39	40	23	0	0	0	0	0	0	0	0	27
Annual	0	0	0	0	0	6	22	48	49	52	54	55	55	54	52	47	34	12	1	0	0	0	0	0	44

East

Month	1	2	3	4	5	6	7	8	9	10	11	12	13	14	15	16	17	18	19	20	21	22	23	24	Hours
JAN	0	0	0	0	0	0	0	8	34	38	39	37	26	24	21	18	5	0	0	0	0	0	0	0	22
FEB	0	0	0	0	0	0	0	26	33	39	42	40	34	32	29	23	14	1	0	0	0	0	0	0	26
MAR	0	0	0	0	0	0	19	36	42	43	43	44	40	39	36	30	22	9	0	0	0	0	0	0	32
APR	0	0	0	0	0	11	33	27	41	44	43	46	45	43	40	36	29	16	1	0	0	0	0	0	35
MAY	0	0	0	0	2	34	43	43	43	45	44	45	46	43	36	34	23	6	0	0	0	0	0	0	39
JUN	0	0	0	0	7	37	41	43	44	46	46	47	48	47	47	41	35	28	15	0	0	0	0	0	41
JUL	0	0	0	0	3	42	46	46	48	48	48	48	48	48	47	44	38	30	15	0	0	0	0	0	43
AUG	0	0	0	0	0	17	37	43	46	48	48	48	48	48	44	39	33	21	1	0	0	0	0	0	41
SEP	0	0	0	0	0	4	37	41	43	43	45	45	46	43	39	34	23	10	0	0	0	0	0	0	36
OCT	0	0	0	0	0	0	20	37	41	41	39	39	36	32	27	21	10	0	0	0	0	0	0	0	29
NOV	0	0	0	0	0	0	1	29	36	39	39	32	29	26	21	15	1	0	0	0	0	0	0	0	22
DEC	0	0	0	0	0	0	0	6	24	29	33	29	22	20	16	10	0	0	0	0	0	0	0	0	17
Annual	0	0	0	0	1	12	23	41	40	42	43	41	39	37	34	29	20	9	1	0	0	0	0	0	32

West

Month	1	2	3	4	5	6	7	8	9	10	11	12	13	14	15	16	17	18	19	20	21	22	23	24	Hours
JAN	0	0	0	0	0	0	0	3	15	22	25	25	35	37	36	36	15	0	0	0	0	0	0	0	22
FEB	0	0	0	0	0	0	0	11	20	28	34	34	40	39	40	36	32	3	0	0	0	0	0	0	27
MAR	0	0	0	0	0	0	10	22	32	38	39	41	44	42	41	38	36	22	0	0	0	0	0	0	34
APR	0	0	0	0	0	4	21	22	35	41	45	45	46	44	43	42	36	30	1	0	0	0	0	0	36
MAY	0	0	0	0	1	19	31	38	41	43	45	46	46	46	44	41	41	34	18	0	0	0	0	0	39
JUN	0	0	0	0	2	19	30	36	41	44	46	46	48	48	48	44	43	41	35	0	0	0	0	0	41
JUL	0	0	0	0	1	19	32	38	43	47	47	48	48	48	48	48	48	46	38	0	0	0	0	0	43
AUG	0	0	0	0	0	6	21	31	39	45	48	48	48	49	48	46	46	40	4	0	0	0	0	0	41
SEP	0	0	0	0	0	1	17	27	35	39	43	46	47	47	46	43	39	23	0	0	0	0	0	0	37
OCT	0	0	0	0	0	0	7	20	28	34	34	38	41	39	36	34	26	0	0	0	0	0	0	0	29
NOV	0	0	0	0	0	0	1	11	20	25	27	28	40	40	39	35	4	0	0	0	0	0	0	0	22
DEC	0	0	0	0	0	0	0	2	12	18	21	23	32	31	32	25	0	0	0	0	0	0	0	0	17
Annual	0	0	0	0	0	6	14	31	30	35	38	39	43	42	42	39	31	16	3	0	0	0	0	0	32

Core (Top-lit)

Month	1	2	3	4	5	6	7	8	9	10	11	12	13	14	15	16	17	18	19	20	21	22	23	24	Hours
JAN	0	0	0	0	0	0	0	1	12	23	33	34	33	31	23	13	2	0	0	0	0	0	0	0	18
FEB	0	0	0	0	0	0	7	19	33	38	38	38	36	35	21	10	1	0	0	0	0	0	0	0	24
MAR	0	0	0	0	0	0	5	19	34	40	42	42	42	40	38	33	18	5	0	0	0	0	0	0	30
APR	0	0	0	0	0	3	16	24	38	42	42	44	43	42	40	38	29	11	0	0	0	0	0	0	33
MAY	0	0	0	0	1	10	27	39	40	42	42	42	43	44	42	38	33	16	3	0	0	0	0	0	36
JUN	0	0	0	0	1	12	29	39	42	42	43	44	44	45	44	41	38	23	8	0	0	0	0	0	38
JUL	0	0	0	0	1	9	29	41	44	44	45	45	45	45	44	44	44	25	7	0	0	0	0	0	40
AUG	0	0	0	0	0	3	18	34	40	45	45	46	46	46	45	43	35	16	1	0	0	0	0	0	38
SEP	0	0	0	0	0	1	11	29	39	41	42	43	44	44	42	37	20	5	0	0	0	0	0	0	34
OCT	0	0	0	0	0	0	3	18	33	37	37	40	40	36	31	19	7	0	0	0	0	0	0	0	27
NOV	0	0	0	0	0	0	0	8	20	32	36	36	38	34	23	10	1	0	0	0	0	0	0	0	21
DEC	0	0	0	0	0	0	0	1	10	18	26	30	28	23	15	7	0	0	0	0	0	0	0	0	14
Annual	0	0	0	0	0	3	12	33	31	36	39	40	40	38	35	29	20	7	1	0	0	0	0	0	30

Average Illuminance (Footcandles): Denver

For a typical two-story office building with 15'-0"-deep perimeter zones and a top-lit core zone.

Weather Data:	Denver (TMY)
% Opening:	37.5% WWR (windows)
	4% of roof area (skylights)
Overhangs:	2'-3" (horizontal)
Lighting Control Type:	Continuous
No. of Ref. Points:	One (2'-6" high in the center of zone)

Glass Type: ¼" solar bronze tinted (single pane)
(SC = 0.57; VT = 0.47)

North

Month	1	2	3	4	5	6	7	8	9	10	11	12	13	14	15	16	17	18	19	20	21	22	23	24	Hours
JAN	0	0	0	0	0	0	0	8	19	21	20	19	18	15	11	20	9	0	0	0	0	0	0	0	14
FEB	0	0	0	0	0	0	0	21	27	30	30	30	26	22	17	11	20	2	0	0	0	0	0	0	20
MAR	0	0	0	0	0	0	20	31	34	34	34	34	32	28	24	19	28	19	0	0	0	0	0	0	26
APR	0	0	0	0	0	12	31	33	33	34	35	35	35	35	32	27	25	22	3	0	0	0	0	0	29
MAY	0	0	0	0	0	30	34	34	35	35	35	35	35	35	34	31	28	22	17	0	0	0	0	0	31
JUN	0	0	0	0	4	31	33	34	35	35	35	35	35	35	34	32	28	26	23	0	0	0	0	0	31
JUL	0	0	0	0	2	30	33	35	35	35	35	35	35	35	35	31	28	27	20	0	0	0	0	0	31
AUG	0	0	0	0	0	15	33	34	34	35	35	35	35	35	32	27	27	27	5	0	0	0	0	0	31
SEP	0	0	0	0	0	4	32	34	35	35	35	35	34	31	24	19	25	20	0	0	0	0	0	0	28
OCT	0	0	0	0	0	0	16	34	32	33	33	30	26	20	15	12	19	1	0	0	0	0	0	0	23
NOV	0	0	0	0	0	0	3	22	24	26	25	22	19	16	10	12	10	0	0	0	0	0	0	0	15
DEC	0	0	0	0	0	0	0	9	19	21	19	16	15	12	8	17	6	0	0	0	0	0	0	0	12
Annual	0	0	0	0	1	10	20	33	30	31	31	30	29	27	23	22	21	12	2	0	0	0	0	0	24

South

Month	1	2	3	4	5	6	7	8	9	10	11	12	13	14	15	16	17	18	19	20	21	22	23	24	Hours
JAN	0	0	0	0	0	0	0	22	104	114	114	120	118	116	114	64	20	0	0	0	0	0	0	0	80
FEB	0	0	0	0	0	0	0	46	102	114	110	116	116	110	110	114	34	2	0	0	0	0	0	0	84
MAR	0	0	0	0	0	0	30	88	126	114	118	112	108	92	76	86	66	24	0	0	0	0	0	0	84
APR	0	0	0	0	0	10	62	90	82	78	68	76	70	54	52	46	60	24	2	0	0	0	0	0	56
MAY	0	0	0	0	0	30	72	82	78	68	66	70	68	52	46	42	40	22	12	0	0	0	0	0	56
JUN	0	0	0	0	2	28	64	70	74	64	66	60	60	50	40	42	34	30	14	0	0	0	0	0	52
JUL	0	0	0	0	0	26	68	94	82	68	62	68	60	50	38	40	32	24	14	0	0	0	0	0	54
AUG	0	0	0	0	0	12	74	102	88	78	68	78	72	52	48	48	60	30	4	0	0	0	0	0	64
SEP	0	0	0	0	0	4	62	112	106	94	98	102	96	74	62	74	52	22	0	0	0	0	0	0	80
OCT	0	0	0	0	0	0	26	124	128	126	128	124	120	108	106	98	30	2	0	0	0	0	0	0	96
NOV	0	0	0	0	0	0	4	72	122	126	122	126	126	120	112	58	16	0	0	0	0	0	0	0	84
DEC	0	0	0	0	0	0	0	28	112	122	126	126	130	130	126	52	12	0	0	0	0	0	0	0	84
Annual	0	0	0	0	0	10	38	94	100	96	96	100	96	84	76	64	38	12	2	0	0	0	0	0	72

East

Month	1	2	3	4	5	6	7	8	9	10	11	12	13	14	15	16	17	18	19	20	21	22	23	24	Hours
JAN	0	0	0	0	0	0	0	20	51	53	54	47	17	16	10	21	9	0	0	0	0	0	0	0	26
FEB	0	0	0	0	0	0	0	41	54	56	54	50	28	23	18	11	19	2	0	0	0	0	0	0	29
MAR	0	0	0	0	0	0	37	57	61	61	61	56	36	31	23	16	24	15	0	0	0	0	0	0	36
APR	0	0	0	0	0	23	54	55	57	58	59	55	45	40	33	25	16	20	2	0	0	0	0	0	39
MAY	0	0	0	0	0	54	60	59	59	61	61	59	54	48	39	31	22	19	11	0	0	0	0	0	46
JUN	0	0	0	0	7	55	59	59	60	61	61	59	53	46	38	30	23	15	14	0	0	0	0	0	46
JUL	0	0	0	0	3	55	59	61	63	62	62	59	50	43	39	31	24	15	14	0	0	0	0	0	46
AUG	0	0	0	0	0	30	59	59	59	61	61	58	47	41	32	25	18	24	4	0	0	0	0	0	43
SEP	0	0	0	0	0	7	57	60	61	62	61	53	39	32	24	17	17	15	0	0	0	0	0	0	40
OCT	0	0	0	0	0	0	35	60	59	59	59	41	27	22	14	9	17	1	0	0	0	0	0	0	33
NOV	0	0	0	0	0	0	6	52	59	59	58	32	20	15	11	9	0	0	0	0	0	0	0	0	26
DEC	0	0	0	0	0	0	0	30	54	58	58	41	15	12	8	17	6	0	0	0	0	0	0	0	25
Annual	0	0	0	0	1	19	36	59	59	59	59	50	36	31	24	21	17	9	1	0	0	0	0	0	36

West

Month	1	2	3	4	5	6	7	8	9	10	11	12	13	14	15	16	17	18	19	20	21	22	23	24	Hours
JAN	0	0	0	0	0	0	0	7	19	22	20	19	32	38	37	35	25	0	0	0	0	0	0	0	22
FEB	0	0	0	0	0	0	0	19	29	31	32	31	35	37	40	40	30	5	0	0	0	0	0	0	28
MAR	0	0	0	0	0	0	17	30	37	38	38	38	39	39	41	40	38	32	0	0	0	0	0	0	34
APR	0	0	0	0	0	9	31	37	39	40	41	41	41	41	40	38	28	4	0	0	0	0	0	0	35
MAY	0	0	0	0	0	28	38	39	41	41	42	42	42	42	42	41	37	28	24	0	0	0	0	0	38
JUN	0	0	0	0	2	29	37	40	41	41	41	42	41	41	40	40	38	34	32	0	0	0	0	0	38
JUL	0	0	0	0	1	25	37	41	42	42	42	42	42	42	41	41	39	39	37	30	0	0	0	0	38
AUG	0	0	0	0	0	10	34	40	40	41	41	42	42	42	42	41	41	37	10	0	0	0	0	0	38
SEP	0	0	0	0	0	2	28	37	40	41	41	41	41	41	41	39	38	30	0	0	0	0	0	0	37
OCT	0	0	0	0	0	0	13	32	34	35	35	32	37	38	39	38	32	2	0	0	0	0	0	0	31
NOV	0	0	0	0	0	0	2	20	25	26	25	22	39	40	40	37	20	0	0	0	0	0	0	0	24
DEC	0	0	0	0	0	0	0	9	20	22	20	17	40	40	40	37	16	0	0	0	0	0	0	0	22
Annual	0	0	0	0	0	8	20	37	34	35	35	34	40	40	40	39	33	16	3	0	0	0	0	0	32

Core (Top-lit)

Month	1	2	3	4	5	6	7	8	9	10	11	12	13	14	15	16	17	18	19	20	21	22	23	24	Hours
JAN	0	0	0	0	0	0	0	5	19	36	47	50	49	47	30	17	5	0	0	0	0	0	0	0	27
FEB	0	0	0	0	0	0	0	15	32	47	50	50	51	51	47	25	11	1	0	0	0	0	0	0	33
MAR	0	0	0	0	0	0	10	30	53	54	54	54	54	54	53	42	24	8	0	0	0	0	0	0	41
APR	0	0	0	0	0	5	26	50	51	52	53	54	54	54	54	50	26	12	1	0	0	0	0	0	42
MAY	0	0	0	0	0	18	41	51	54	55	56	56	56	56	54	50	34	15	6	0	0	0	0	0	47
JUN	0	0	0	0	1	21	45	52	54	54	55	55	55	54	52	50	44	18	7	0	0	0	0	0	48
JUL	0	0	0	0	0	16	42	54	56	56	56	56	56	54	53	49	42	18	7	0	0	0	0	0	48
AUG	0	0	0	0	0	5	30	52	54	54	55	56	56	56	53	35	14	2	0	0	0	0	0	0	47
SEP	0	0	0	0	0	1	22	46	54	55	56	56	55	55	54	42	18	8	0	0	0	0	0	0	44
OCT	0	0	0	0	0	0	7	34	51	54	54	54	54	51	45	19	10	1	0	0	0	0	0	0	38
NOV	0	0	0	0	0	0	2	16	33	49	53	54	53	46	26	11	5	0	0	0	0	0	0	0	30
DEC	0	0	0	0	0	0	0	6	21	35	47	50	50	41	22	10	3	0	0	0	0	0	0	0	26
Annual	0	0	0	0	0	6	19	47	45	50	53	54	54	51	46	35	22	6	1	0	0	0	0	0	39

Average Illuminance (Footcandles): Los Angeles

For a typical two-story office building with 15'-0"-deep perimeter zones and a top-lit core zone.

Weather Data: Los Angeles (TMY)

% Opening: 37.5% WWR (windows)

4% of roof area (skylights)

Overhangs: 2'-3" (horizontal)

Lighting Control Type: Continuous

No. of Ref. Points: One (2'-6" high in the center of zone)

Glass Type: ¼" solar bronze tinted (single pane)

(SC = 0.57; VT = 0.47)

North

Month	1	2	3	4	5	6	7	8	9	10	11	12	13	14	15	16	17	18	19	20	21	22	23	24	Hours
JAN	0	0	0	0	0	0	0	11	20	23	25	26	26	25	22	20	12	0	0	0	0	0	0	0	18
FEB	0	0	0	0	0	0	0	18	28	31	35	35	35	35	32	28	23	3	0	0	0	0	0	0	25
MAR	0	0	0	0	0	0	8	29	34	37	39	39	39	39	38	37	36	15	0	0	0	0	0	0	31
APR	0	0	0	0	0	3	24	29	37	39	39	39	39	39	39	37	35	29	0	0	0	0	0	0	33
MAY	0	0	0	0	0	10	24	35	38	39	39	39	39	39	39	39	37	35	6	0	0	0	0	0	35
JUN	0	0	0	0	0	13	26	34	37	39	39	39	39	39	39	38	36	35	17	0	0	0	0	0	35
JUL	0	0	0	0	0	7	29	35	37	38	38	39	39	39	39	39	37	36	14	0	0	0	0	0	35
AUG	0	0	0	0	0	3	25	33	36	39	39	39	39	38	39	38	37	32	1	0	0	0	0	0	34
SEP	0	0	0	0	0	1	13	28	35	38	39	39	39	39	38	37	35	15	0	0	0	0	0	0	33
OCT	0	0	0	0	0	0	8	22	29	34	37	37	37	36	32	32	20	0	0	0	0	0	0	0	28
NOV	0	0	0	0	0	0	2	18	23	26	28	30	29	28	25	20	8	0	0	0	0	0	0	0	19
DEC	0	0	0	0	0	0	0	11	19	22	25	26	26	25	21	17	5	0	0	0	0	0	0	0	17
Annual	0	0	0	0	0	3	13	31	31	34	35	35	35	35	34	32	27	13	1	0	0	0	0	0	29

South

Month	1	2	3	4	5	6	7	8	9	10	11	12	13	14	15	16	17	18	19	20	21	22	23	24	Hours
JAN	0	0	0	0	0	0	0	27	74	77	78	79	79	79	79	75	30	0	0	0	0	0	0	0	59
FEB	0	0	0	0	0	0	0	43	79	79	82	82	79	83	81	82	57	4	0	0	0	0	0	0	64
MAR	0	0	0	0	0	0	9	52	68	66	74	74	70	77	77	79	74	20	0	0	0	0	0	0	61
APR	0	0	0	0	0	3	26	44	55	60	57	59	60	59	65	60	66	31	0	0	0	0	0	0	51
MAY	0	0	0	0	0	7	26	46	59	59	59	64	62	60	62	57	56	33	4	0	0	0	0	0	52
JUN	0	0	0	0	0	9	29	39	51	56	59	64	61	57	56	52	53	34	10	0	0	0	0	0	49
JUL	0	0	0	0	0	5	29	51	49	53	55	57	59	56	55	55	60	40	9	0	0	0	0	0	49
AUG	0	0	0	0	0	3	27	53	55	59	56	60	59	56	61	60	64	34	0	0	0	0	0	0	52
SEP	0	0	0	0	0	0	14	51	57	68	68	64	65	72	70	78	60	18	0	0	0	0	0	0	59
OCT	0	0	0	0	0	0	12	47	66	68	78	82	85	83	85	85	38	0	0	0	0	0	0	0	62
NOV	0	0	0	0	0	0	3	49	73	75	75	77	79	79	81	73	16	0	0	0	0	0	0	0	56
DEC	0	0	0	0	0	3	0	34	77	79	79	79	82	85	82	70	10	0	0	0	0	0	0	0	59
Annual	0	0	0	0	0	3	14	48	64	66	68	70	70	70	72	69	49	14	0	0	0	0	0	0	56

East

Month	1	2	3	4	5	6	7	8	9	10	11	12	13	14	15	16	17	18	19	20	21	22	23	24	Hours
JAN	0	0	0	0	0	0	0	34	43	43	44	39	28	26	23	21	12	0	0	0	0	0	0	0	26
FEB	0	0	0	0	0	0	0	42	46	46	47	46	38	37	34	27	20	2	0	0	0	0	0	0	32
MAR	0	0	0	0	0	0	15	41	44	46	48	48	47	45	41	36	29	12	0	0	0	0	0	0	36
APR	0	0	0	0	0	5	32	39	46	48	48	49	49	48	44	39	32	20	0	0	0	0	0	0	39
MAY	0	0	0	0	0	18	32	47	48	48	49	49	49	49	48	43	36	25	4	0	0	0	0	0	42
JUN	0	0	0	0	0	24	36	44	46	48	49	49	49	49	47	42	34	29	11	0	0	0	0	0	42
JUL	0	0	0	0	0	14	41	45	47	47	48	49	49	49	46	41	35	28	9	0	0	0	0	0	41
AUG	0	0	0	0	0	6	32	43	47	48	49	48	49	48	46	40	33	20	1	0	0	0	0	0	41
SEP	0	0	0	0	0	1	22	40	43	48	49	49	48	45	41	34	28	11	0	0	0	0	0	0	39
OCT	0	0	0	0	0	0	19	36	44	46	48	44	40	37	34	28	17	0	0	0	0	0	0	0	33
NOV	0	0	0	0	0	0	5	41	42	43	43	34	30	29	25	20	7	0	0	0	0	0	0	0	25
DEC	0	0	0	0	0	0	0	38	46	45	46	34	28	27	21	18	5	0	0	0	0	0	0	0	25
Annual	0	0	0	0	0	6	20	43	45	46	48	45	42	41	38	32	24	10	1	0	0	0	0	0	35

West

Month	1	2	3	4	5	6	7	8	9	10	11	12	13	14	15	16	17	18	19	20	21	22	23	24	Hours
JAN	0	0	0	0	0	0	0	11	20	23	26	27	38	49	49	48	34	0	0	0	0	0	0	0	27
FEB	0	0	0	0	0	0	0	16	27	32	37	39	46	52	53	51	48	7	0	0	0	0	0	0	34
MAR	0	0	0	0	0	0	6	25	34	39	45	48	52	54	54	52	53	36	0	0	0	0	0	0	41
APR	0	0	0	0	0	2	18	27	37	46	49	51	54	53	53	51	51	48	0	0	0	0	0	0	44
MAY	0	0	0	0	0	6	21	34	46	50	52	55	55	55	55	55	53	52	11	0	0	0	0	0	46
JUN	0	0	0	0	0	9	23	34	44	49	53	54	54	54	53	52	51	50	33	0	0	0	0	0	46
JUL	0	0	0	0	0	5	23	34	40	46	50	53	54	54	54	55	53	52	29	0	0	0	0	0	45
AUG	0	0	0	0	0	2	18	29	40	44	49	53	54	52	54	54	54	51	2	0	0	0	0	0	44
SEP	0	0	0	0	0	0	10	25	34	42	47	49	54	55	55	53	53	33	0	0	0	0	0	0	42
OCT	0	0	0	0	0	0	7	20	28	35	41	41	52	54	55	55	48	0	0	0	0	0	0	0	37
NOV	0	0	0	0	0	0	2	16	22	27	30	31	48	51	52	49	23	0	0	0	0	0	0	0	29
DEC	0	0	0	0	0	0	0	11	20	23	27	27	41	51	51	48	14	0	0	0	0	0	0	0	27
Annual	0	0	0	0	0	2	11	29	33	38	42	44	50	53	53	52	44	23	2	0	0	0	0	0	39

Core (Top-lit)

Month	1	2	3	4	5	6	7	8	9	10	11	12	13	14	15	16	17	18	19	20	21	22	23	24	Hours
JAN	0	0	0	0	0	0	0	6	22	40	51	52	53	51	42	22	7	0	0	0	0	0	0	0	30
FEB	0	0	0	0	0	0	0	12	31	51	54	55	54	54	54	38	17	2	0	0	0	0	0	0	37
MAR	0	0	0	0	0	0	5	22	46	54	56	56	56	56	56	53	28	7	0	0	0	0	0	0	42
APR	0	0	0	0	0	2	16	37	51	56	56	56	56	56	56	54	38	15	0	0	0	0	0	0	45
MAY	0	0	0	0	0	4	22	43	55	56	56	56	56	56	56	48	20	2	0	0	0	0	0	0	48
JUN	0	0	0	0	0	6	23	43	54	56	56	56	56	56	55	51	25	6	0	0	0	0	0	0	49
JUL	0	0	0	0	0	3	22	46	54	55	55	56	56	56	56	53	26	6	0	0	0	0	0	0	49
AUG	0	0	0	0	0	2	16	37	53	56	56	56	56	55	56	55	45	18	0	0	0	0	0	0	47
SEP	0	0	0	0	0	0	8	28	49	55	56	56	56	56	56	53	26	6	0	0	0	0	0	0	44
OCT	0	0	0	0	0	0	5	21	42	53	55	56	56	56	54	34	11	0	0	0	0	0	0	0	38
NOV	0	0	0	0	0	0	1	13	31	49	52	54	54	53	41	19	4	0	0	0	0	0	0	0	32
DEC	0	0	0	0	0	0	0	7	22	40	50	53	53	52	34	16	2	0	0	0	0	0	0	0	30
Annual	0	0	0	0	0	2	10	36	42	52	54	55	55	54	51	42	28	8	0	0	0	0	0	0	41

Average Illuminance (Footcandles): New York

For a typical two-story office building with 15'-0"-deep perimeter zones and a top-lit core zone.

Weather Data:	New York (TMY)	Glass Type: ¼" solar bronze tinted (single pane)
% Opening:	37.5% WWR (windows)	(SC = 0.57; VT = 0.47)
	4% of roof area (skylights)	
Overhangs:	2'-3" (horizontal)	
Lighting Control Type:	Continuous	
No. of Ref. Points:	One (2'-6" high in the center of zone)	

North

Month	1	2	3	4	5	6	7	8	9	10	11	12	13	14	15	16	17	18	19	20	21	22	23	24	Hours
JAN	0	0	0	0	0	0	0	9	15	20	21	23	22	21	20	14	10	0	0	0	0	0	0	0	15
FEB	0	0	0	0	0	0	0	17	18	21	24	27	28	25	23	19	15	7	0	0	0	0	0	0	19
MAR	0	0	0	0	0	0	18	21	23	27	32	33	33	31	27	23	20	18	0	0	0	0	0	0	24
APR	0	0	0	0	0	16	21	29	31	33	36	36	36	35	34	33	31	25	10	0	0	0	0	0	30
MAY	0	0	0	0	0	26	31	36	37	38	41	42	40	40	38	36	36	33	24	0	0	0	0	0	36
JUN	0	0	0	0	10	28	32	34	37	39	41	42	42	41	40	38	34	33	31	8	0	0	0	0	36
JUL	0	0	0	0	7	30	33	38	40	41	42	41	40	40	39	37	38	35	35	8	0	0	0	0	37
AUG	0	0	0	0	0	29	36	39	39	40	42	43	43	42	42	38	40	38	28	0	0	0	0	0	38
SEP	0	0	0	0	0	9	33	37	38	39	39	40	40	41	40	38	36	29	4	0	0	0	0	0	36
OCT	0	0	0	0	0	0	19	31	33	36	38	36	36	36	32	30	28	5	0	0	0	0	0	0	29
NOV	0	0	0	0	0	0	5	18	21	26	28	27	26	26	22	20	13	0	0	0	0	0	0	0	19
DEC	0	0	0	0	0	0	0	12	16	21	23	25	23	21	18	13	7	0	0	0	0	0	0	0	15
Annual	0	0	0	0	1	12	19	34	29	32	34	34	34	33	31	29	25	15	5	1	0	0	0	0	28

South

Month	1	2	3	4	5	6	7	8	9	10	11	12	13	14	15	16	17	18	19	20	21	22	23	24	Hours
JAN	0	0	0	0	0	0	0	21	44	46	49	49	48	46	49	38	21	0	0	0	0	0	0	0	36
FEB	0	0	0	0	0	0	0	35	46	53	49	55	60	58	54	55	31	12	0	0	0	0	0	0	43
MAR	0	0	0	0	0	0	21	38	49	53	56	60	60	59	52	48	41	23	0	0	0	0	0	0	45
APR	0	0	0	0	0	13	28	43	46	47	52	55	53	52	52	49	46	24	8	0	0	0	0	0	44
MAY	0	0	0	0	0	21	32	49	56	52	59	64	61	60	56	54	49	33	17	0	0	0	0	0	51
JUN	0	0	0	0	7	22	38	46	52	58	58	61	66	61	59	55	46	35	26	6	0	0	0	0	52
JUL	0	0	0	0	5	23	39	55	62	62	63	61	58	55	55	54	55	41	29	6	0	0	0	0	54
AUG	0	0	0	0	0	28	45	58	63	61	67	70	68	67	64	60	60	47	26	0	0	0	0	0	59
SEP	0	0	0	0	0	9	41	63	64	66	63	68	66	66	64	66	59	35	3	0	0	0	0	0	59
OCT	0	0	0	0	0	0	37	60	63	66	69	67	63	66	62	61	51	7	0	0	0	0	0	0	55
NOV	0	0	0	0	0	0	8	45	58	58	63	63	54	61	60	54	28	0	0	0	0	0	0	0	45
DEC	0	0	0	0	0	0	0	31	46	51	51	52	53	52	48	39	14	0	0	0	0	0	0	0	37
Annual	0	0	0	0	1	9	24	54	54	56	59	60	59	59	56	53	41	17	3	1	0	0	0	0	48

East

Month	1	2	3	4	5	6	7	8	9	10	11	12	13	14	15	16	17	18	19	20	21	22	23	24	Hours
JAN	0	0	0	0	0	0	0	21	37	38	41	35	25	23	19	14	9	0	0	0	0	0	0	0	23
FEB	0	0	0	0	0	0	0	33	39	42	41	41	31	28	22	19	14	6	0	0	0	0	0	0	26
MAR	0	0	0	0	0	0	29	41	42	45	47	43	35	32	29	22	16	14	0	0	0	0	0	0	30
APR	0	0	0	0	0	25	36	48	47	46	47	44	40	39	34	33	25	18	7	0	0	0	0	0	35
MAY	0	0	0	0	0	40	44	51	54	54	52	49	47	43	37	31	23	17	0	0	0	0	0	0	43
JUN	0	0	0	0	14	40	44	46	50	50	52	52	53	51	49	43	34	30	26	5	0	0	0	0	44
JUL	0	0	0	0	10	44	45	51	56	56	55	50	48	47	44	42	42	34	31	5	0	0	0	0	46
AUG	0	0	0	0	0	41	53	56	57	56	57	55	53	51	49	43	41	32	23	0	0	0	0	0	48
SEP	0	0	0	0	0	14	48	51	55	54	53	53	50	49	48	42	36	23	3	0	0	0	0	0	45
OCT	0	0	0	0	0	0	36	51	51	52	54	49	41	40	33	28	23	4	0	0	0	0	0	0	38
NOV	0	0	0	0	0	0	9	42	48	46	47	35	30	27	22	19	12	0	0	0	0	0	0	0	26
DEC	0	0	0	0	0	0	0	30	40	40	41	32	25	22	18	14	6	0	0	0	0	0	0	0	22
Annual	0	0	0	0	2	17	29	50	48	49	49	45	40	38	34	30	24	12	4	1	0	0	0	0	35

West

Month	1	2	3	4	5	6	7	8	9	10	11	12	13	14	15	16	17	18	19	20	21	22	23	24	Hours
JAN	0	0	0	0	0	0	0	9	16	21	23	26	32	36	40	33	21	0	0	0	0	0	0	0	22
FEB	0	0	0	0	0	0	0	15	17	23	25	31	37	45	47	48	41	16	0	0	0	0	0	0	29
MAR	0	0	0	0	0	0	14	17	23	28	32	35	42	47	45	44	36	29	0	0	0	0	0	0	32
APR	0	0	0	0	0	11	15	21	28	33	37	41	43	48	50	48	49	44	16	0	0	0	0	0	38
MAY	0	0	0	0	0	20	23	33	39	43	47	51	51	54	55	51	52	50	36	0	0	0	0	0	43
JUN	0	0	0	0	7	23	29	37	41	46	50	52	55	55	55	52	50	46	43	12	0	0	0	0	46
JUL	0	0	0	0	5	23	30	40	49	50	51	50	49	50	49	50	53	50	50	12	0	0	0	0	46
AUG	0	0	0	0	0	24	33	41	46	49	53	56	55	57	57	55	59	57	40	0	0	0	0	0	49
SEP	0	0	0	0	0	7	26	36	44	46	47	52	52	54	53	55	50	43	5	0	0	0	0	0	45
OCT	0	0	0	0	0	0	19	28	35	39	41	42	49	53	50	52	50	8	0	0	0	0	0	0	38
NOV	0	0	0	0	0	0	4	16	23	27	31	30	38	49	50	43	27	0	0	0	0	0	0	0	28
DEC	0	0	0	0	0	0	0	13	17	21	23	26	37	41	37	33	15	0	0	0	0	0	0	0	23
Annual	0	0	0	0	1	9	16	34	32	36	39	41	45	49	49	47	41	23	6	2	0	0	0	0	36

Core (Top-lit)

Month	1	2	3	4	5	6	7	8	9	10	11	12	13	14	15	16	17	18	19	20	21	22	23	24	Hours
JAN	0	0	0	0	0	0	0	5	12	20	25	26	25	24	20	11	5	0	0	0	0	0	0	0	15
FEB	0	0	0	0	0	0	0	8	15	26	28	30	31	31	28	19	10	3	0	0	0	0	0	0	20
MAR	0	0	0	0	0	0	6	13	25	30	32	33	33	32	30	25	14	7	0	0	0	0	0	0	23
APR	0	0	0	0	0	5	11	24	30	32	34	34	34	35	33	31	24	12	3	0	0	0	0	0	27
MAY	0	0	0	0	0	9	19	32	34	36	36	37	37	37	36	33	31	19	8	0	0	0	0	0	31
JUN	0	0	0	0	3	14	24	29	33	35	36	36	37	37	36	34	30	24	13	3	0	0	0	0	31
JUL	0	0	0	0	2	14	25	32	36	36	37	37	36	35	34	33	33	28	17	3	0	0	0	0	32
AUG	0	0	0	0	0	11	24	32	36	36	37	38	37	37	37	35	34	25	12	0	0	0	0	0	33
SEP	0	0	0	0	0	3	18	31	34	35	35	36	36	36	34	34	29	15	1	0	0	0	0	0	31
OCT	0	0	0	0	0	0	9	23	31	34	36	35	35	34	31	27	17	2	0	0	0	0	0	0	26
NOV	0	0	0	0	0	0	2	13	21	27	31	32	29	29	25	15	6	0	0	0	0	0	0	0	19
DEC	0	0	0	0	0	0	0	7	14	22	25	26	26	24	17	10	3	0	0	0	0	0	0	0	15
Annual	0	0	0	0	1	5	12	29	27	31	32	34	33	32	30	26	20	8	2	1	0	0	0	0	25

Average Illuminance (Footcandles): Seattle

For a typical two-story office building with 15'-0"-deep perimeter zones and a top-lit core zone.

Weather Data:	Seattle (TMY)	Glass Type: ¼" solar bronze tinted (single pane)	
% Opening:	37.5% WWR (windows)	(SC = 0.57; VT = 0.47)	
	4% of roof area (skylights)		
Overhangs:	2'-3" (horizontal)		
Lighting Control Type:	Continuous		
No. of Ref. Points:	One (2'-6" high in the center of zone)		

North

Month	1	2	3	4	5	6	7	8	9	10	11	12	13	14	15	16	17	18	19	20	21	22	23	24	Hours
JAN	0	0	0	0	0	0	0	0	6	14	20	23	23	23	18	11	3	0	0	0	0	0	0	0	13
FEB	0	0	0	0	0	0	0	2	13	20	25	27	27	27	24	18	11	1	0	0	0	0	0	0	17
MAR	0	0	0	0	0	0	6	16	22	26	30	32	33	31	31	28	23	15	0	0	0	0	0	0	24
APR	0	0	0	0	0	4	19	31	32	33	34	35	35	34	34	33	29	23	8	0	0	0	0	0	29
MAY	0	0	0	0	0	15	24	29	31	33	34	34	35	34	32	30	28	25	22	4	0	0	0	0	29
JUN	0	0	0	0	2	14	23	29	33	35	35	34	34	35	35	34	32	30	26	11	0	0	0	0	31
JUL	0	0	0	0	1	18	24	28	32	33	35	35	35	35	35	34	33	29	9	0	0	0	0	0	32
AUG	0	0	0	0	0	7	23	30	33	34	35	35	35	35	35	34	33	31	19	1	0	0	0	0	31
SEP	0	0	0	0	0	0	12	23	27	31	33	33	34	34	32	31	27	17	2	0	0	0	0	0	28
OCT	0	0	0	0	0	0	2	13	18	24	27	28	29	27	23	18	12	1	0	0	0	0	0	0	19
NOV	0	0	0	0	0	0	0	2	12	19	23	24	23	21	17	10	1	0	0	0	0	0	0	0	14
DEC	0	0	0	0	0	0	0	0	4	10	15	17	15	15	11	4	0	0	0	0	0	0	0	0	8
Annual	0	0	0	0	0	5	11	25	22	26	29	30	30	29	27	24	20	12	4	2	0	0	0	0	23

South

Month	1	2	3	4	5	6	7	8	9	10	11	12	13	14	15	16	17	18	19	20	21	22	23	24	Hours
JAN	0	0	0	0	0	0	0	0	13	22	28	30	31	31	29	21	6	0	0	0	0	0	0	0	19
FEB	0	0	0	0	0	0	0	3	22	27	36	37	36	36	36	30	20	1	0	0	0	0	0	0	25
MAR	0	0	0	0	0	0	6	22	29	32	37	41	42	41	41	39	33	21	0	0	0	0	0	0	32
APR	0	0	0	0	0	3	23	41	41	43	45	46	47	44	45	42	37	27	6	0	0	0	0	0	38
MAY	0	0	0	0	0	13	29	35	39	43	44	45	46	45	43	39	34	29	20	2	0	0	0	0	38
JUN	0	0	0	0	1	11	25	34	41	46	46	46	46	46	46	44	41	37	21	7	0	0	0	0	41
JUL	0	0	0	0	1	13	29	35	41	45	47	48	48	48	48	46	44	25	6	0	0	0	0	0	42
AUG	0	0	0	0	0	5	25	38	42	45	48	48	48	48	48	44	44	40	16	1	0	0	0	0	41
SEP	0	0	0	0	0	0	15	30	34	40	43	44	46	45	45	44	38	23	1	0	0	0	0	0	37
OCT	0	0	0	0	0	0	3	24	31	32	36	38	38	35	33	28	20	1	0	0	0	0	0	0	27
NOV	0	0	0	0	0	0	0	4	28	32	34	36	33	33	29	22	1	0	0	0	0	0	0	0	22
DEC	0	0	0	0	0	0	0	0	10	20	24	25	25	26	18	8	0	0	0	0	0	0	0	0	14
Annual	0	0	0	0	0	4	13	32	31	36	39	40	41	40	39	34	27	15	3	1	0	0	0	0	32

East

Month	1	2	3	4	5	6	7	8	9	10	11	12	13	14	15	16	17	18	19	20	21	22	23	24	Hours
JAN	0	0	0	0	0	0	0	0	15	21	27	27	24	24	19	10	3	0	0	0	0	0	0	0	16
FEB	0	0	0	0	0	0	0	4	23	27	33	34	30	30	25	19	10	1	0	0	0	0	0	0	21
MAR	0	0	0	0	0	0	9	23	29	32	36	38	38	36	36	30	23	13	0	0	0	0	0	0	28
APR	0	0	0	0	0	7	26	39	39	41	42	44	44	42	41	36	30	20	5	0	0	0	0	0	34
MAY	0	0	0	0	0	22	31	34	38	41	42	42	43	42	40	36	31	25	18	3	0	0	0	0	36
JUN	0	0	0	0	3	20	29	36	40	44	44	43	42	43	41	38	36	30	22	7	0	0	0	0	38
JUL	0	0	0	0	1	28	32	36	40	42	44	46	45	45	44	42	38	33	23	6	0	0	0	0	39
AUG	0	0	0	0	0	13	31	40	42	44	45	46	44	44	44	39	35	29	12	1	0	0	0	0	38
SEP	0	0	0	0	0	1	23	30	34	38	41	42	42	40	36	33	25	13	1	0	0	0	0	0	33
OCT	0	0	0	0	0	0	4	28	30	31	33	34	33	30	25	19	11	1	0	0	0	0	0	0	24
NOV	0	0	0	0	0	0	0	6	29	29	31	29	27	23	18	10	1	0	0	0	0	0	0	0	18
DEC	0	0	0	0	0	0	0	0	10	18	21	21	16	16	11	4	0	0	0	0	0	0	0	0	10
Annual	0	0	0	0	1	8	16	33	31	34	36	37	36	34	32	27	21	10	3	1	0	0	0	0	28

West

Month	1	2	3	4	5	6	7	8	9	10	11	12	13	14	15	16	17	18	19	20	21	22	23	24	Hours
JAN	0	0	0	0	0	0	0	0	6	14	20	24	26	30	29	21	7	0	0	0	0	0	0	0	16
FEB	0	0	0	0	0	0	0	1	12	19	27	30	32	36	35	31	23	1	0	0	0	0	0	0	22
MAR	0	0	0	0	0	0	4	15	23	27	35	40	42	42	42	40	37	28	0	0	0	0	0	0	31
APR	0	0	0	0	0	2	17	36	37	42	45	47	48	45	46	43	39	33	15	0	0	0	0	0	39
MAY	0	0	0	0	0	12	24	32	37	41	44	45	46	46	45	40	37	36	34	7	0	0	0	0	37
JUN	0	0	0	0	1	12	21	32	40	45	46	46	46	48	48	48	44	41	37	22	0	0	0	0	41
JUL	0	0	0	0	1	12	21	30	37	42	47	49	50	50	50	49	48	46	42	19	0	0	0	0	42
AUG	0	0	0	0	0	4	18	32	37	42	48	48	50	49	49	47	48	46	36	1	0	0	0	0	41
SEP	0	0	0	0	0	0	9	22	28	35	40	42	46	47	46	45	40	32	4	0	0	0	0	0	35
OCT	0	0	0	0	0	0	1	12	19	27	30	32	37	35	33	30	24	2	0	0	0	0	0	0	24
NOV	0	0	0	0	0	0	0	2	12	19	24	26	30	32	30	24	1	0	0	0	0	0	0	0	17
DEC	0	0	0	0	0	0	0	0	4	11	14	17	20	24	18	9	0	0	0	0	0	0	0	0	11
Annual	0	0	0	0	0	4	10	26	24	31	35	37	40	40	40	36	30	18	6	4	0	0	0	0	30

Core (Top-lit)

Month	1	2	3	4	5	6	7	8	9	10	11	12	13	14	15	16	17	18	19	20	21	22	23	24	Hours
JAN	0	0	0	0	0	0	0	0	4	12	19	23	25	22	16	8	1	0	0	0	0	0	0	0	12
FEB	0	0	0	0	0	0	0	1	9	19	28	32	33	31	26	16	7	1	0	0	0	0	0	0	18
MAR	0	0	0	0	0	0	2	10	21	29	34	38	39	37	38	33	19	7	0	0	0	0	0	0	27
APR	0	0	0	0	0	1	11	34	38	41	43	44	44	42	43	39	31	16	3	0	0	0	0	0	34
MAY	0	0	0	0	0	7	20	32	38	40	42	43	44	42	40	37	31	21	10	1	0	0	0	0	35
JUN	0	0	0	0	1	8	19	32	40	44	44	43	43	44	44	44	40	31	16	4	0	0	0	0	38
JUL	0	0	0	0	0	8	20	33	39	42	44	46	46	46	46	46	43	36	16	3	0	0	0	0	39
AUG	0	0	0	0	0	3	14	32	41	44	46	46	46	46	46	43	40	25	7	0	0	0	0	0	38
SEP	0	0	0	0	0	0	6	20	31	36	40	41	42	42	41	39	24	8	1	0	0	0	0	0	32
OCT	0	0	0	0	0	0	1	10	19	28	33	34	35	31	25	16	7	1	0	0	0	0	0	0	21
NOV	0	0	0	0	0	0	0	1	10	20	25	29	27	23	16	7	0	0	0	0	0	0	0	0	14
DEC	0	0	0	0	0	0	0	0	3	8	14	16	16	14	9	3	0	0	0	0	0	0	0	0	8
Annual	0	0	0	0	0	2	8	26	25	31	34	36	36	35	33	28	21	9	1	1	0	0	0	0	27

Postoccupancy Visual Comfort Evaluation Form

Questionnaire for Daylighted Spaces (Uncontrolled Cases)

Space I.D. and respondent _____

Date _____ Time _____

Weather conditions (clear, partly cloudy, or cloudy) _____

Number of persons occupying the space _____

Location of respondent's work area (check one):

_____ center of room and along wall
_____ along wall opposite window
_____ along side wall
_____ along wall at window

Please **circle** the appropriate responses describing the conditions in your office at the **present time:**

Electric light sensor: On/Off
Position of miniblinds: fully raised/partially raised/completely lowered
Angle of partially raised or lowered miniblinds: closed up/45-degree angled up/90-degree open/45-degree angled down/closed down
Position of door: open/closed

The following questions ask you to provide perceptual responses to lighting levels for a variety of everyday tasks you carry out in your office: **desk work, computer work, filing tasks,** and **social meetings.** For each task, please answer the full set of questions and provide comments as you like. Brief definitions of several lighting terms have been included at the end of the questionnaire should you have any questions regarding terminology. **Thanks for your help!**

1. Your impressions of the space at this time:

very unpleasant	○	○	○	○	○	very pleasant
not enough light to work	○	○	○	○	○	too much light to work
room too dark	○	○	○	○	○	room too light

Take a little time to adapt to each of the following five tasks **before** responding to the questions about lighting in these areas:

2. Desk work—writing and paperwork at main desk area:

   A. Is the lighting adequate?

     totally inadequate   ○   ○   ○   ○   ○   completely adequate

   B. Are there reflections on your work surface?

     many   ○   ○   ○   ○   ○   none

   C. And are they annoying?

     very annoying   ○   ○   ○   ○   ○   not at all

   D. Is the brightness of this work area in relation to the rest of the room

     too bright?   ○   ○   ○   ○   ○   too dark?

3. Desk work—reading papers or a book at main desk area:

   A. Is the lighting adequate?

     totally inadequate   ○   ○   ○   ○   ○   completely adequate

   B. Are there reflections on your work surface?

     many   ○   ○   ○   ○   ○   none

   C. And are they annoying?

     very annoying   ○   ○   ○   ○   ○   not at all

   D. Is the brightness of this work in relation to the rest of the room

     too bright?   ○   ○   ○   ○   ○   too dark?

4. Computer work—data entry looking at desktop near computer:

   A. Is the lighting adequate?

     totally inadequate   ○   ○   ○   ○   ○   completely adequate

   B. Are there reflections on your work surface?

     many   ○   ○   ○   ○   ○   none

   C. And are they annoying?

     very annoying   ○   ○   ○   ○   ○   not at all

   D. Is the brightness of this work in relation to the rest of the room

     too bright?   ○   ○   ○   ○   ○   too dark?

5. Computer work—data editing looking at the computer screen:

   A. Is the lighting adequate?

     totally inadequate   ○   ○   ○   ○   ○   completely adequate

   B. Are there reflections on your work surface?

     many   ○   ○   ○   ○   ○   none

C. And are they annoying?

very annoying   ○   ○   ○   ○   ○   not at all

D. Is the brightness of this work in relation to the rest of the room

too bright?   ○   ○   ○   ○   ○   too dark?

6. Filing:

A. Is the lighting adequate?

totally inadequate   ○   ○   ○   ○   ○   completely adequate

B. Are there reflections on your work surface?

many   ○   ○   ○   ○   ○   none

C. And are they annoying?

very annoying   ○   ○   ○   ○   ○   not at all

D. Is the brightness of this work in relation to the rest of the room

too bright?   ○   ○   ○   ○   ○   too dark?

7. Is there anything in the room which is very bright and, if so, what is it?

Is this

very distracting?   ○   ○   ○   ○   ○   not distracting?

8. Is there glare from the windows?

intolerable glare   ○   ○   ○   ○   ○   no glare

9. Is there a brightness contrast between the room and what you see through the window?

great contrast   ○   ○   ○   ○   ○   no contrast

10. Is the amount of view through the window

inadequate?   ○   ○   ○   ○   ○   adequate?

11. Is the quality of the view through the window

unpleasant?   ○   ○   ○   ○   ○   pleasant?

Please **take the place** of someone who would be sitting in your office to visit or work; where are you located?

_____ opposite the window
_____ facing the wall
_____ facing both window and wall at an angle

12. Facing the direction where you would normally sit to meet with someone, is the view comfortable in terms of glare?

uncomfortable   ○   ○   ○   ○   ○   comfortable

13. From this position are the two areas of your office indicated below decidedly dark or bright?

wall perpendicular to window

too dark   ○   ○   ○   ○   ○   too bright

wall opposite window

too dark   ○   ○   ○   ○   ○   too bright

Do you have any **comments** on the quality of light in your office at this time?

Thanks for your cooperation!

Daylighting Design
Web Resources

The following are Web sites that may be useful sources of additional information on techniques and products for green design.

ORGANIZATIONS

http://research.gsd.harvard.edu/envelopes/index1.htm
Building Envelopes.org is based at the MIT architecture school and provides an online resource offering information on advanced facades and innovative HVAC and lighting systems to support preliminary design of energy-efficient buildings. A worldwide consortium of professionals, universities, and research organizations supports this effort and provides information for the site.

www.daylighting.org
Energy Center of Wisconsin
Daylighting Collaborative
595 Science Drive
Madison, WI 53711
The Daylighting Collaborative is a program started by utilities and the state of Wisconsin to incorporate daylighting into mainstream design and construction.

http://www.energyefficiencycenter.com/index.html
The Energy-Efficiency Center is a collaborative effort of the energy education centers of Pacific Gas & Electric Company; Southern California Edison; and Southern California Gas Company, a Sempra Energy Company.

http://www.greenseal.org/recommendations.htm#product
Green Seal provides recommendations of environmentally preferable products, published as *Choose Green Reports*, giving environmental criteria for the category, rationales for them, the product recommendations, and sources for recommended products.

http://www.h-m-g.com/
Heschong Mahone Group is a professional consulting firm that focuses on the field of building energy efficiency. It has published a groundbreaking study on the effects of daylighting on productivity in public schools.

http://www.isdesignet.com/ed/greenlinks.html
Interiors and Sources publishes the magazine *EnvironDesign Journal*. Its Web site lists many organizations under "Green Gateways on the Internet."

http://www.iaeel.org/
The International Association for Energy-Efficient Lighting (IAEEL) is a global contact network and an information resource for high-quality, energy-efficient lighting. Here you can read all IAEEL newsletter issues, visit the far-reaching "Lighting Crossroads" resource index, check out "Lighting and Energy Meetings & Events," and search for background information in the IAEEL archives.

www.northwestlighting.com
Lighting Design Lab
400 East Pine Street, #100
Seattle, WA 98122
Phone: (206) 352-9711; Fax: (206) 329-9532
The LDL has a daylighting element that supports the implementation of architectural daylighting design strategies across the Pacific Northwest.

http://lighting.lrc.rpi.edu/
The Lighting Research Center, part of Rensselaer Polytechnic Institute's School of Architecture, is the world's largest university-based center for lighting education and research.

www.pge.com/003_save_energy/003c_edu_train/pec/003c1_pac_energy.shtml
Pacific Gas & Electric
Pacific Energy Center
The Pacific Energy Center has a daylighting initiative, which is a source of information on daylighting design practice, case studies, and reports, many of which are available on its Web site.

http://www.peci.org/cx/index.html
Portland Energy Conservation, Inc., conducts building commissioning services. It offers a model commissioning plan and guide specifications.

http://www.sce.com/ctac/index.shtml
Southern California Edison offers energy management solutions through training courses at its Customer Technology Assistance Center (CTAC) and technical consulting through the Savings by Design and the Design and Engineering Services groups.

http://www.worldbuild.com/services.htm
WorldBuild provides high-level green building strategy services for cities, states, developers, and design professionals to design green building programs and to help plan specific green building projects.

http://windows.lbl.gov
Windows and Daylighting Group
Building Technologies Program
Energy and Environment Division
Lawrence Berkeley National Laboratory
Mail Stop 90-3111, 1 Cyclotron Road
Berkeley, CA 94720
Phone: (510) 486-5605; Fax: (510) 486-4089
The Windows and Daylighting Group has various resources for daylighting design, including software.

PRODUCTS AND MANUFACTURERS

General

http://www.archrecord.com/green/green.asp
Architectural Record offers a green building products directory arranged in CSI format, along with articles on green building.

www.buildinggreen.com
Environmental Building News offers a green product directory and guideline specifications.

http://oikos.com/products/
Oikos is a Web site devoted to serving professionals whose work promotes sustainable design and construction. It offers a listing of green products.

http://www.energystar.gov/products/
U.S. Department of Energy
The Energy Star Web site lists products by manufacturer that meet the requirements for the Energy Star label. Includes roofing, windows, appliances, HVAC, lighting, office equipment, etc.

Controls

http://content.honeywell.com/yourhome/
Honeywell offers a wide range of building controls.

http://www.johnsoncontrols.com/cg/
Johnson Controls produces systems to control HVAC, lighting, security, and fire safety in commercial buildings.

http://www.novitas.com/
Novitas developed the first occupancy sensors and manufactures infrared and photocell controls.

http://www2.landisstaefa.com/default_e.asp
Siemens' Landis & Staefa Division offers building energy management systems.

http://www.wattstopper.com/cgi-bin/2/webc.cgi/home.htm
Wattstopper offers a range of lighting control products for all types of buildings—from offices to schools to retail to warehouses—with occupancy sensors, control panels, plug load controls, daylighting, etc.

HVAC Equipment

http://www.carrier-commercial.com/
Carrier is a manufacturer of commercial HVAC equipment.

http://www.ariprimenet.org/ari-prog/direct.nsf?open
PrimeNet is the Air Conditioning and Refrigeration Institute's (ARI) applied and unitary certified performance ratings directory database for air conditioners, heat pumps, and other HVAC equipment.

http://www.trane.com/commercial/equipment/index.asp
Trane is a manufacturer of commercial HVAC equipment.

Lighting

http://www.lightsite.net/
LightSite is a resource for energy-efficient lighting information and products. The site will provide you with detailed information on lighting: bulbs, fixtures, the Energy Star® Program, new innovations, a new featured product each month, and a bounty of historical information. You can also purchase products.

http://www.lightsofamerica.com/
Lights of America is a manufacturer of environmentally friendly lighting products.

http://www.ruudlighting.com/
Ruud Lighting develops, manufactures, and sells lighting fixtures, focusing on metal halide systems.

Paints

www.lifepaint.com
Life Paint Corp. offers a line of paints with a thermally resistant additive that works like low-e window coatings to reflect the infrared heat rays of the sun.

Recycled Materials

http://www.ciwmb.ca.gov/rcp/
California Integrated Waste Management Board. Contains a recycled-content product database.
www.ciwmb.ca.gov/calmax
California Materials Exchange offers info on recycled materials.

Skylights

http://www.solatube.com/home.htm
Solatube is a manufacturerer of light pipe daylighting luminaires.

http://www.bristolite.com/
Bristolite is a skylight manufacturer. It makes an Energy Star skylight often specified for daylighting applications.

http://www.dayliteco.com/
Dayliteco is a development and manufacturing company of hybrid lighting systems, conducting research, design, construction, and installation of energy-efficient solar/electric lighting products. Manufacturer of light systems, including light pipes, that maximize the transmission and distribution of natural light, thereby significantly reducing electric lighting costs while dramatically improving light quality.

http://www.sunoptics.com/
Sunoptics produces a prismatic skylight with thousands of tiny prisms—over 8,000 per square foot. The prisms refract sunlight into micro light beams, directed throughout the room, creating a soft, natural light.

Tools

http://www.eren.doe.gov/buildings/tools_directory/
U.S. DOE, Office of Building Technologies
State and Community Programs
Described here are 220 energy-related public-domain software tools for buildings, with an emphasis on using renewable energy and achieving energy efficiency and sustainability in buildings.

http://windows.lbl.gov/software/default.htm
U.S. DOE, Windows and Daylighting Group
Building Technologies Program
Energy and Environment Division
Lawrence Berkeley National Laboratory
Window-related public-domain software tools for analyzing energy use in buildings.

http://www.lighting-technologies.com/
Lighting Technologies, Inc. (LTI) is a leading provider of lighting software, optical design services, and custom software solutions worldwide. Software products include Lumen Micro for lighting design, analysis, and specification; Photopia luminaire design software; Simply Lighting for luminaire design; and the Lightscape rendering engine.

http://www.energydesignresources.com/tools.html
Energy Design Resources is funded by California utility customers and administered by Pacific Gas & Electric Company, San Diego Gas & Electric, and Southern California Edison, under the auspices of the California Public Utilities Commission. It offers a palette of energy design tools that make it easier to design and build energy-efficient commercial and industrial buildings in California. Software tools include the skylight design tool SkyCalc, the DOE2-based building energy analysis tool eQuest, and the life-cycle cost-analysis tool eVALUator.

Windows

http://www.afgd.com/
AFGD Glass offers a complete range of high-performance architectural glass products, including low-e and solar control glazing.

http://www.guardian.com/archglass_productlist.asp
Guardian offers a complete range of high-performance architectural glass products, including low-e and solar control glazing.

http://www.glasssentinel.com
Glass Sentinel produces a window film product that is applied with a chemical acrylic adhesive that actually absorbs into glass, making it stronger. The film also has low-e properties, allowing the use of single glazing in place of laminated or double-glazed window glass.

http://www.pilkington.com/
Pilkington manufactures glass products worldwide, including low-e and solar control glazing, and owns Libbey-Owens-Ford in the United States. See http://www.lof.com.

http://www.ppg.com/gls_commercial/default.htm
PPG is a major U.S. glass manufacturer. Products include Solarban® 80, PPG's newest architectural glass designed to address the need for a single product of superior solar control, visible light transmittance, and aesthetic appeal.

http://www.southwall.com/
Southwall manufactures Heat Mirror insulating glass, using a clear, colorless, coated film that is permanently suspended between two panes of glass. This suspended film divides the space into two smaller compartments, which, in turn, provide additional insulation and thermal performance. It also makes V-Kool, a low-e window film that can be applied to existing window glass. See http://www.v-kool-usa.com/.

http://www.viracon.com/
Viracon offers a very complete range of high-performance architectural glass products, including low-e and solar control glazing.

http://www.visionwall.com/
Visionwall supplies high-performance window assemblies with a combination of high thermal insulation, low shading coefficient, high visible light transmission, and excellent sound attenuation.

Wood

http://www.certifiedwood.org
The Certified Forest Products Council Web site has a searchable directory of certified sustainably harvested wood products suppliers.

http://www.ecotimber.com
EcoTimber offers a complete line of ecologically sound wood flooring, including woods from certified well-managed forests and reclaimed sources, as well as innovative wood alternatives such as bamboo.

http://www.forestworld.com
Forest World offers certified wood procurement services.

Absorptance. The ratio of the luminous flux absorbed by the body to the flux it receives.

Absorption. Transformation of radiant energy to a different form of energy by the intervention of matter.

Acrylic glazing. A glazing material that is softer than glass.

Altitude. The angular distance of the sun measured upward from the horizon on that vertical plane that passes through the sun. It is measured positively from horizon to zenith from 0 to 90 degrees.

Ambient lighting. Lighting throughout an area that produces general illumination.

Angle of incidence. The angle between a ray of light falling on a surface and a line normal (perpendicular) to the surface. The angle of incidence for specific conditions can be obtained with the use of the LOF Sun Angle Calculator. To calculate angle of incidence on a vertical window (ai), find solar altitude (at) and window azimuth orientation from sun (az).

Angle-selective coating. Coatings that can block or filter light.

Azimuth. The azimuth of the sun is the angle between the vertical plane containing sun and the plane of the horizon.

Ballast. A device used with a fluorescent lamp to obtain the necessary circuit conditions for starting and operating.

Blinding glare. Glare so intense that for an appreciable time no object can be seen.

Brightness. The subjective attribute of any light sensation giving rise to the perception of luminous intensity—a subjective sensation. (The preferable term for photometric, or measurable, quantity is *luminance.*)

Candela. The unit of luminous intensity. The magnitude of the candela is such that the luminance of a full radiator at the temperature of solidification of platinum is 60 candelas/cm^2.

Candela per square meter. A unit of luminance recommended by the CIE.

Circadian rhythms. Biological activity or functions occurring within 24-hour periods.

Clear sky. A sky that has less than 30% cloud cover.

Clerestory. That part of a building rising clear of the roof or other parts whose walls contain windows for lighting of interiors.

Cloudy sky. A sky having more than 70% cloud cover.

Coefficient of utilization (cu). The ratio of the luminous flux (lumens) for a light source (luminaire, window, skylight, etc.) received on the work plane to the lumens emitted by the light source.

Contrast. The degree of difference between the lightest and darkest element of an object.

Daylight. The light from the sun and sky.

Daylight factor. The ratio of the daylight illuminance at a point on a given plane due to the light received directly or indirectly from a sky of assumed or known luminance distribution to the illumination on a horizontal plane due to an unobstructed hemisphere of this sky. Direct sunlight is excluded for both values of illumination.

Daylight saturation. The condition where the interior daylight illuminance level equals or exceeds the specified design illuminance level and the lighting control system thus provides maximum lighting energy savings. At saturation, any further increase in daylight illuminance will not produce additional lighting energy savings.

Daylight tracking and reflecting system. Devices that have the potential to enhance performance by actively tracking and reflecting daylight.

Diffuse. A device used to alter the spatial distribution of the luminous flux from a source and depending essentially on the phenomenon of diffusion.

Diffuse reflection. Diffusion by reflection in which, on the macroscopic scale, there is no direct reflection.

Diffuse transmission. Transmission in which light is scattered in many directions and, on the macroscopic scale, independent of the laws of refraction.

Diffuse transmittance. The ratio of the luminous flux diffusely transmitted in all directions (other than that of direct transmission) to the total incident flux.

Diffusion. Alteration of the spatial distribution of a beam of light, which, after reflection at a surface or passage through a medium, travels on in numerous directions.

Direct glare. Glare due to a luminous object situated in the same or nearly the same direction as the object viewed.

Direct reflectance. The ratio of the luminous flux, reflected in accordance with the laws of regular reflection, to the total incident flux.

Direct (regular or specular) reflection. Reflection in accordance with the laws of optical reflection (e.g., in a mirror).

Direct transmittance. The ratio of the luminous flux transmitted in accordance with the laws of direct transmission to the total incident flux.

Disability glare. Excessive contrast, especially to the extent that visibility of one part of the field is obscured by the attempt by the eye to adapt to the brightness of the other part.

Discomfort glare. Glare that causes discomfort without necessarily impairing the vision of objects.

Effective aperture (EA). A measure of the light-transmitting ability of a fenestration system. Effective aperture is the product of the skylight-to-floor ratio (SFR) and the visible transmittance (VT). EA values range from 0 to 1.0 and are typically less than 0.1 for most practical skylight systems.

Electrochromic material. A dynamic glazing system that changes properties by modulating voltage.

Emission. Release of radiant energy.

Equivalent room. A theoretical room whose dimensions are adjusted to compensate for the effects of special conditions in an actual room. A room with an overhanging window shading device has some of the same coefficients of utilization as a larger room without such overhang.

External obstruction. An element near fenestration that may affect the amount of daylight.

Fenestration. Any opening or arrangement of openings for the admission of daylight or air.

Footcandle. The illumination on a surface 1 square foot in area on which there is a uniformly distributed flux of 1 lumen:

$$1 \, fc = 10.76 \, lux = 10.76 \, lumens/m^2$$

Footlambert. A unit of luminance equal to the uniform luminance of a perfectly diffusing surface emitting or reflecting light at the rate of 1 lumen per square foot; or the average luminance of any surface emitting or reflecting light at that rate.

Glare. The effect of luminance or luminance differences within the visual field sufficiently high to cause annoyance, discomfort, or loss in visual performance. *Direct glare* is glare resulting from high-luminance or insufficiently shielded light sources in the field of view, or reflecting areas of high luminance and large area. *Reflected glare* is glare resulting from reflections of high-luminance sources by surfaces in the field of view.

Holographic film. A directionally selective glazing that diffracts light.

Horizontal louver. Horizontal elements installed to control direct beam daylight.

Illuminance (illumination). The density of luminous flux (light) incident on a surface.

Illumination. Light falling on a surface.

Illumination at a point of a surface. The quotient of the luminous flux incident on an infinitesimal element of surface containing the point under consideration by the area of that element.

Indirect glare. Glare due to a luminous object situated in a direction other than that of the object viewed.

Insulated plastic panel. Multilayer of plastic used for fenestration.

Latitude. The geographical latitude of a point is the angle measured in the plane of the local meridian between the equator and a line perpendicular to the surface of the earth through the point in question.

Light. For the purpose of illuminating engineering, light is radiant energy evaluated according to its capacity to produce visual sensation. *Skylight* is visible radiation from the sun redirected by the atmosphere. *Sunlight* is direct visible radiation from the sun.

Lighting power density (LPD). A measure of the amount of electric lighting installed in a building. Expressed as the number of watts of lighting power required for the luminaires and lamps installed in a building, divided by the gross number of square feet in the building (watts per square foot).

Light-loss factor. The ratio of the light transmission or utilization after a designated period of time to the initial light transmission or utilization. This is a measure of deterioration because of accumulation of dust or dirt.

Light shelf. A horizontal device located near the window used to reduce window brightness and to increase room brightness.

Light wells. Light wells are extensively used to bring light through the roof structure and help control light distribution. Local solar geometry (altitude and azimuth of the sun change hourly and seasonally), surface reflectance of the well (influenced by structural material and paint color), and wall slope are basic considerations.

Longitude. The angular distance measure along the earth's equator from the meridian through Greenwich, England, to the local meridian through the point in question. Longitude is measured either east or west from Greenwich through 180 degrees or 12 hours.

Low-emissivity (low-e) coating. Spectrally selective coatings.

Lumen. The unit of luminous flux. It is equal to the flux through a unit of solid angle (steradian) from a uniform point source of 1 candela; or the flux on a unit surface all points of which are at a unit distance from a uniform point of 1 candela.

Luminaire. A complete lighting unit consisting of a lamp, or lamps, together with parts designed to distribute the light, to position and protect the lamps, and to connect the lamps to the power supply.

Luminance (photometric brightness). The luminous intensity of any surface in a given direction per unit or projected area of the surface as viewed from that direction.

Luminous efficacy (K_e). A measure of the luminous efficiency of a radiant flux, expressed in lumens per watt. For daylighting, this is the ratio of visible flux incident on a surface divided by the radiant flux on that surface. For electric sources, it is the ratio of the total luminous flux emitted divided by the total lamp or luminaire power input.

Luminous efficacy constant (K_e). The coolness index indicating a window's relative performance in rejecting solar heat while transmitting daylight.

Luminous flux. The quantity characteristic of radiant flux which expresses its capacity to produce a luminous sensation evaluated according to the values of relative luminous efficiency. Unless otherwise indicated, the luminous flux in question relates to photopic vision and is connected with the radian flux in accordance with the formula adopted in 1948 by the CIE. (International Lighting Vocabulary tabulates the relative luminous efficiency of radiation in terms of this agreed formula.)

Lux. The International System (SI) unit of illumination. It is the illumination on a surface 1 square meter in area on which there is a uniformly distributed flux of 1 lumen.

Mean radiant temperature (MRT). Having to do with the temperatures of surrounding surfaces within a space.

Mean spherical intensity. The average value of the luminous intensity of a source in all directions. Note: It is also the quotient of the total luminous flux by the total solid angle, 4π steradians.

Melatonin. A hormone that is secreted in the brain at night.

Mixed reflection. The simultaneous occurrence of regular reflection and of diffuse reflection.

Multivariate linear regression analysis. An analysis technique that uses dependent and independent variables.

Optical density. The logarithm to the base 10 of the reciprocal of the transmission factor.

Overcast sky. Sky completely covered by clouds, with no sun visible.

Overhang. A horizontal shading device.

Perfect diffuser. An ideal uniform diffuser with zero absorption factor. (Note: Practical uniform diffusers always have an absorption factor greater than zero.)

Perfect diffusion. Ideal diffusion in which the whole of the incident light is redistributed uniformly in all possible directions in such a way that the luminance is the same in all directions. (Note: A surface possessing this property is sometimes called "perfectly matte.")

Photochromic material. Dynamic glazing that changes properties as a function of light intensity.

Point source. Source of radiant energy of dimensions negligible compared with the distance between source and receptor.

Polycarbonate glazing. Similar to acrylic glazing with harder properties.

Prismatic system. A system that redirects light.

Profile angle. The projection of the true solar altitude angle on a vertical plane perpendicular to a wall.

Protective glazing. A glazing system used to protect property.

Pyrolytic coating. A metallic oxide coating applied to glass.

Quantity of light. The product of luminous flux and the time during which it is maintained. (Note: The lumen-hour and lumen-second are the quantities of light equal to 1 lumen radiated or received for 1 hour and 1 second, respectively.)

Radiation. Energy in the form of electromagnetic waves or particles.

Reflectance. The ratio of light reflected by a body to the incident light; the total reflection factor of a layer of material of such thickness that there is no change of reflection factor with increase in thickness.

Reflected glare. Glare produced by specular reflections of luminous objects, especially reflections appearing on or near the object viewed.

Reflection. Backward reflection of radiation by a surface without change of frequency of the monochromatic components of which the radiation is composed.

Roof monitor. Raised building elements of a roof with vertical or sloped apertures.

***R*-value.** Resistance to heat flow.

Shading. Use of fixed or movable shading devices can help block, diffuse, or redirect incoming light to control unwanted heat gains and glare.

Shading coefficient (SC). The dimensionless ratio of the total solar heat gain from a particular glazing system to that for one sheet of clear 3 mm ($\frac{1}{8}$ in.) double-strength glass. The solar heat gain is the sum of the transmitted solar energy plus that portion of the absorbed solar energy that flows inward.

Site energy. Energy consumed at the building site.

Skylight. Horizontal roof apertures.

Skylight efficacy. Another design parameter, determined by dividing the product of visible transmittance (VT) and well factor (WF) by the shading coefficient, SC (the fraction of solar heat that enters through the skylight glazing).

Skylight-to-floor ratio (SFR). The ratio of skylight opening area to gross daylit floor area.

Solar altitude. The vertical angular distance of the sun in the sky above the horizon.

Solar azimuth. The horizontal angular distance between the vertical plane containing the sun and true south.

Solar heat gain coefficient (SHGC). The fraction of incident solar energy transmitted through a glazing system.

Source energy. Total energy consumed, including transmission losses and power source.

Sputtered coating. A multilayer of metallic material applied to glass.

Suspended coated film (SCF). A selective film suspended between layers of glass.

Thermochromic material. A dynamic glazing system that changes properties as a function of temperature.

(Total) transmission factor of a body (total transmittance). The ratio of the luminous flux transmitted by the body to that which it receives. In mixed transmission, the (total) transmission factor is the sum of two components, the direct transmission factor and the diffuse transmission factor.

Translucent coating. A coating that is not transparent.

Transmission. Passage of radiation through a medium without change of frequency of the monochromatic components of which the radiation is composed.

Transmittance. The ratio of the light transmitted by the material to the incident light. *Regular* or *direct transmittance* is that in which the transmitted light is not diffused. In such transmission, the direction of a transmitted beam of light has a definite geometrical relationship to corresponding incident beam. *Diffuse transmittance* of a material is the ratio of the diffusely transmitted light to the incident light.

Uniform diffuser. A diffuser for which the luminance is the same in all directions regardless of the direction of incidence of the light.

Uniform diffuse reflection. Diffusion by reflection such that the luminance is the same in all directions.

Uniform ground. The average brightness of the ground, including all the various reflectances of different ground materials.

Uniform point source. A point source that emits radiation uniformly in all directions.

U-value. A measure of a material's heat transfer capabilities when placed between two spaces of different temperatures, typically given in Btu/hr-ft^2-°F. The *U*-value is the inverse of the *R*-value, which measures the material's resistance to heat transfer.

Veiling reflection. Regular reflections superimposed on diffuse reflections from an object that partially or totally obscures the details to be seen by reducing the contrast. This is sometimes called reflected glare.

Vertical louver (or fin). Vertical elements used to control direct beam light.

Vertical window. A window system used to introduce light and/or air into spaces.

Visible radiation or radiant energy. Any radiation capable of causing a visual sensation directly. The wavelength range of such radiation can be considered for practical purposes to lie between 380 and 780 nm.

Visible transmittance (VT). The percentage of visible light that passes through a glazing system.

Visual size. Having to do with the physical size of an object.

Well factor (WF). The ratio of the amount of visible light leaving a skylight well to the amount of visible light entering the skylight.

Well index (WI). A parameter used to determine the light well efficiency. Well index is a measure of the geometric shape of the well, and is calculated as follows:

$$\text{Well index} = \frac{\text{Well height (well length + well width)}}{2 \times \text{well length} \times \text{well width}}$$

A light well with proportions of a cube always has a well index of 1.0.

SYMBOLS

DG: Double glazing

EA: Effective aperture

fc: Footcandle

kWh: Kilowatt-hour

LE: Luminous efficacy

lm: Lumen

lm/W: Lumens per watt

LPD: Lighting power density

R: Reflectance

SC: Shading coefficient

SE: Skylight efficacy

SFR: Skylight-to-floor ratio

SG: Single glazing

VDT: Visual display terminal

WF: Well factor

WI: Well index

W/ft^2: Watts per square foot

ANNOTATED BIBLIOGRAPHY

AIA/ACSA Council on Architectural Research, *Energy Tools: New Products for Architects,* National Energy Laboratories, Washington, DC, 1992.

The U.S. Department of Energy operates four laboratories that conduct research on energy-efficient building applications. This document describes each laboratory's activities plus products that were developed to assist building design professionals. These products include handbooks, design manuals, and computer software.

American Institute of Architects, *Architect's Handbook of Energy Practice: Daylighting,* American Institute of Architects, Washington, DC, 1992.

This handbook is part of a series of monographs published by the AIA on energy-conscious design. It is meant to provide architects with the basic concepts of daylighting. The text is supported with case studies of famous buildings that utilize daylighting.

Ander, Gregg D., *The Integration of Architectural Art and Load-Reducing Fenestration: Daylighting Case Studies,* Thermal Performance of the Exterior Envelopes of Buildings IV, ASHRAE, Atlanta, pp. 108–125.

This article contains six case studies of buildings that utilize daylighting to reduce energy consumption. The daylighting strategies were described and results of DOE2 computer models given. Significant savings were shown for each project when compared with a base case building.

Ander, Gregg D., and Wilcox, Joe S., *Fenestration Modeling Techniques,* Research and Design 85 Proceedings, March 1985, American Institute of Architects, Washington, DC, pp. 83–88.

This paper discusses a methodology for analyzing complex fenestration systems and room geometries. This procedure can be used in conjunction with an hourly simulation program to determine the impacts of lighting, mechanical, and peak loads.

Bennett, David J., and Ewadi, David A., Solar Optics: Light as Energy; Energy as Light, *Underground Space,* 4(6):349–354.

This paper reviews the high-technology ideas of beaming light and images to underground spaces. They are state-of-the-art concepts and how they will be tested in a design application being developed for the Civil/Mineral Engineering building at the University of Minnesota.

Bennett, Robert, *Sun Angles for Design,* Robert Bennett, Bala Cynwyd, PA, 1978.

This book contains sun path diagrams in two-degree increments from 0 to 60 degrees north latitude. It includes examples of how to use these diagrams to determine shadow patterns, prepare solar site analyses, and evaluate the effectiveness of shading devices.

Bevington, Rick, and Rosenfeld, Arthur H., Energy for Buildings and Homes, *Scientific American,* September 1990, pp. 77–86.

This article presents and supports an argument that energy conservation in buildings could result in a savings of 50%. The article also describes many of the new technologies available and how they will affect energy usage. The impacts on cost, environment, and thermal comfort are covered in detail.

Boles, Daralice D., Modernism in the City, *Progressive Architecture,* July 1987, pp. 72–79.

The article focuses on the design strategies of the Institut du Monde Arabe (Arab World Institute) in Paris, by French architect Jean Nouvel. It is a building that combines architecture and technology into a unique sun control device. Some attention is paid to daylighting because it had a strong influence on the design. The building's most notable features are the sun-controlling apertures along the south facade. The architect was successful in creating a sun control device that makes a strong architectural statement consistent with the design concept.

Bryan, Harvey, Standard 90.1P—Daylighting: Energy Conservation, *Architectural Record*, June 1988, p. 156.

Standards 90 and 90.1P were prepared by ASHRAE and the Department of Energy and serve as the model energy conservation code for the United States. Standard 90.1P is a much more flexible revision of Standard 90. The article is concerned primarily with describing the various compliance methods as they relate to daylighting.

Bryan, Harvey J., Simplified Procedure for Calculating the Effects of Daylight from Clear Skies, *Journal of IES*, April 1980, pp. 142–151.

Using the Daylight Factor method, Bryan has reworked the method recommended by the CIE for use with clear sky conditions. This has been the major hindrance to the use of the Daylight Factor method in the United States, because the Daylight Factor method was developed using overcast or uniform sky conditions.

Bryan, Harvey, and Clear, Robert. *A Procedure for Calculating Interior Daylight Illumination with a Programmable Hand Calculator*, Fifth National Passive Solar Conference, October 1980, pp. 1192–1196.

A procedure is described for calculating interior daylight illumination using an inexpensive programmable hand calculator. The proposed procedure calculates illumination at any point within a room utilizing sky luminance distribution functions that are consistent with the CIE overcast and clear sky functions. This procedure separates the light reaching the point being considered into three components. Two examples are presented to demonstrate the proposed procedure and indicate the speed with which the calculations may be performed.

Building Research Station (BRS), Estimating Daylighting in Buildings: Parts 1 and 2, *Building Research Station Digest*, 42:1–7, January 1977.

Here the Daylight Factor method of analysis is outlined from the source (BRS). This is an excellent condensation of the very basic principles first presented in Hopkinson's *Daylighting*.

Burt Hill Kosar Rittleman Associates, Constructing a Daylighting Model, *Architectural Technology*, Fall 1983, pp. 50–51.

Written by associates in an architectural firm, this article outlines how to use scale models during the schematic and design development phases of a project. Many good tips on construction and photographic techniques are given.

Burt Hill Kosar Rittleman Associates, Stepping Through Daylighting, *Architectural Technology*, Fall 1983, pp. 36–49.

This article is a step-by-step guide to incorporating daylighting into the different phases of the architectural design process. Each phase is outlined independently, and the means for evaluating the design against a base case are given.

Burt Hill Kosar Rittleman Associates, *Thermal and Optical Performance Characteristics of Reflective Light Shelves in Buildings*, Washington, DC.

This is a study performed with funding provided by the Department of Energy to examine the effectiveness of light shelves for increasing levels of daylight within buildings. The reports concluded that light shelves increase light quality through better distribution but are ineffective at increasing light quantity deep within a space. This conclusion is based on the fact that to increase lighting levels, the light shelves would have to reflect 19% to 24% of the light that hits them. Materials currently being used for reflecting surfaces do not meet these criteria.

Campbell, Robert, Daylighting: Research and Design, *AIA Journal*, June 1983, pp. 63–65.

The author reviewed the 1983 International Conference on Daylighting in Phoenix. Design and research were the two fundamental issues discussed at the conference. The author concluded that the two needed to be more integrated to achieve more successful results.

Dean, Andrea Oppenheimer, Commodity, Firmness, Delight—and Energy, *Architecture*, April 1985, pp. 63–65.

This is an overview of attitudes about energy in the architectural profession. Advances in computer and building technologies, along with a heightened ecological awareness by those entering the profession, are fueling a resurgence in energy conservation through building design. Soon buildings might be judged on the basis of energy conservation along with their aesthetic and functional features.

De Nevi, Donald, Master of Natural Light: Frank Lloyd Wright, *AIA Journal,* September 1979, pp. 63–65.

Early in his career Frank Lloyd Wright realized that glass would become a major building material because it would let different types of light (diffused, reflected, refracted) enter a space. Wright believed that light elevates the human spirit to a higher order. He used ribbon windows, clerestories, corner windows, trellises, overhangs, translucent roofs, skylights, and atriums. Each of these has a different effect on lighting. Wright went to great extremes to integrate electric light near the source of natural light.

Eacret, Keg M., *Beamed Daylighting: Historical Review, Current Testing and Analysis and Design Options,* Fifth National Passive Solar Conference Proceedings, October 1980, pp. 1174–1178.

This paper discusses the results of testing of various beamed daylighting prototypes, the findings of a review of patent documents in the field, and some options for design using beamed daylighting techniques.

Evans, Benjamin H., Basics of Daylighting, *Architecture,* February 1981, pp. 78–85.

The article condenses much of what the author wrote in his book *Daylight in Architecture.* None of the items mentioned can ensure that a building will be well designed; however, when architects combine the natural and built environment through daylighting, the results are generally a more beautiful, stimulating, and humanistic architecture.

Evans, Benjamin H., *Daylight in Architecture,* McGraw-Hill, New York, 1971.

This design-oriented book is intended as a primer. It is strong on basic concepts and model testings and is a good place to start for those entering the field.

Evans, Benjamin H., and Nowak, Matthew, Effects of Direct Sunlight on Building Interiors and Subsequent Skylight Studies, *Illuminating Engineering,* 54:715–721, 1969.

This article discusses an interesting procedure using a sky dome in conjunction with a separate sun machine for the purpose of superimposing results to obtain daylighting predictions.

Hass, Eileen, *Natural Lighting: How to Use Daylight,* SolarVision Publications, Churchill-Harrisville, NH, 1982.

This book offers an overview of the basic concepts and applications of daylighting. It contains input from many of the foremost experts in this field and has interesting sections on analysis methods, daylighting codes, and availability of daylight in urban areas.

Hattrup, M. P., *Daylighting Practices of the Architectural Industry* (baseline results of a national survey), Pacific Northwest Laboratory, Richland, WA.

This report was prepared for the U.S. Department of Energy by the Batelle Memorial Institute and the Pacific Northwest Laboratory. "This survey was conducted to develop a more accurate profile of architects' knowledge, perceptions, and use of daylighting in commercial building design." The profile was required to determine how much DOE-sponsored research has been incorporated into daily practice.

Heerwagen, Judith H., Windowscapes: The Role of Nature in the View from the Window, *Proceedings I, 1986 International Daylighting Conference,* pp. 352–355.

The author conducted research at the University of Washington on "Decor in Windowed and Windowless Offices." People who were in offices that had a view of nature through a window had much less in the way of decor. People in windowless offices tried to compensate for the lack of view by creating a surrogate view. View combined with good daylighting design should provide a more hospitable work environment.

Heerwagen, Judith, and Heerwagen, Dean, Energy and Psychology: Designing for a State of Mind, *AIA Journal,* Spring-Summer 1984, pp. 35–37.

The main point of this article is that once we have a better understanding of the relationship between the built environment and its occupants, we can create the illusion of a better environment. Theoretically, the actual comfort level could be lower than the perceived comfort level. This would be extremely effective for energy conservation measures.

Heschong, Lisa, An Interview with William Lam, *Solar Age*, August 1980, pp. 30, 33.

William Lam has been a lighting design and building systems consultant for years. This article presents several interesting views on daylighting design and resultant environments.

Hopkinson, R. G., Petherbridge, P., and Longmore, J., *Daylighting*, University College, London, 1966.

This text is an excellent resource for daylighting research and design methods, including sections on sky luminance, daylight photometry, models, and artificial skies. It is dated in that it does not include more current IES methods. It contains good bibliographical references at the conclusion of each chapter.

Illuminating Engineering Society of North America, *Recommended Practice of Daylighting*, IES, New York, 1979.

This publication is a very good source for daylighting information. The appendix goes through typical examples of the IES method. Charts and tables required for this procedure are included.

Jewell, J. E., Selkowitz, S., and Verderber, R., Solid-State Ballasts Prove to be Energy Savers, *Lighting Design and Application*, January 1980, pp. 36–42.

This article presents the results of a research project testing solid-state ballasts for fluorescent lighting versus the typically used core-coil ballast. Graphs and tables are used to clarify the conclusions indicating that solid-state ballasts outperform the commonly used core-coil ballasts.

Johnson, Janith E., *Facility Program for a Participatory Environment Responsive Educational Facility*, Master's Thesis, California State Polytechnic University, Pomona, CA, 1987.

This is the programming portion of a master's thesis completed by a graduate student of architecture at the California State Polytechnic University in Pomona. The program is for an educational facility at the San Bernardino Valley College. The program reviews the various energy conservation strategies to be used, along with outlining the space requirements. There is also a brief site analysis that includes the climatic conditions.

Johnson, Janith E., Ander, Gregg D., and Addison, Marlin, *Daylighting Design Analysis: SCAQMD Headquarters Facility, Diamond Bar, California*, Southern California Edison, Rosemead, CA, 1989.

This report makes recommendations on ways of conserving energy through the use of daylighting on the proposed South Coast Air Quality Management District (SCAQMD) Headquarters facility. The conclusions contained within the report are based on the results of daylighting studies conducted on physical and computer (DOE2)-generated models. The report concludes that the building be designed with the combination of a drop ceiling with 4-ft overhangs and 4-ft light shelves.

Johnson, Timothy E., *Low-E Glazing Design Guide*, Butterworth Architecture, Stoneham, MA, 1991.

This text is complete with detailed descriptions of the physical principles by which low-e glazing works, the different types of low-e glazing, how low-e glazing is manufactured, and different design applications for low-e glazing (warm daylighting and cool daylighting). Also included are some very helpful rule-of-thumb calculations such as those for room depth for daylighting applications (p. 86) and for determining aperture size (p. 88).

Kaleidoscope, *AIA Journal*, September 1979, pp. 77–85.

This is a series of brief case studies of some building projects that employ the use of daylighting as a major architectural element. The projects reviewed include Jorn Utzon's church in Bagsvaerd, Denmark; Walter Gropius's last project in the Rosenthal Glass Factory in Amberg, Bavaria; the Mount Vernon College Chapel in Washington, DC, by Hartman-Cox; Canadian architect Arthur Erickson's Museum of Anthropology for the University of British Columbia; the Louisiana Museum of

Modern Art outside of Copenhagen by Vilhelm Wohlert and Jorgen Bo; the library at the Institute for Advanced Studies in Princeton by Harrison and Abramovitz; a translucent roof for a Bullock's Department Store in San Jose, CA; the Auraria Higher Education Center by Helmut Jahn in Denver; and Paul Rudolph's Christian Science Student Center in Urbana, IL.

Kluck, Martin, *Shadow Angle Charts for a North-South Profile,* Fifth National Passive Solar Conference, October 1980, pp. 1188–1191.

A method and charts are presented to help visualize and determine shadow angles in the plane of a north-south cross section through a building.

Knowles, Ralph, Sun's Rhythm as Generator of Form: Student Models, *AIA Journal,* June 1979, pp. 58–69.

Ralph Knowles conducted research on how to make forms that respond to gravity and the sun's daily and seasonal rhythms. Five geometric forms were selected to act as three-dimensional graphs. Results are shown in a series of photographs. The pictures show what could be an aesthetic based on natural conditions.

Lam, William M. C., *Perception and Lighting as Formgivers for Architecture,* McGraw-Hill, New York, 1977.

The psychology of visual perception is a primary thesis in this text. Professional experience is the resource for much of what the author conveys. Many case studies are presented with photographs in the last half of the book.

Lam, William M. C., *Sunlighting as Formgiver for Architecture,* Van Nostrand Reinhold, New York, 1986.

Sunlighting is the use of direct-beam radiation to illuminate interior spaces. Design strategies are thoroughly covered and supported with case studies. The book ends with some examples of how to use physical models as qualitative design tools.

Libbey Owens Ford Company, *How to Predict Interior Daylight Illumination,* LOF, Toledo, OH, 1976.

The lumen or IES method of calculating interior daylighting illumination levels is explained in this publication. This method has become the industry standard. Nine examples are worked out that are useful in clarifying the procedures.

Linn, Charles, Calculating Daylighting for Successful Retail Design, *Architectural Lighting,* January 1987.

The main body of the article describes the energy conservation design process that was used in Salzer's Video Store in Ventura, CA. Much of this information is in the architect's own words. A smaller companion article describes the DOE2 computer energy analysis done by Southern California Edison.

Lord, David, Power Applied to Purpose: Towards a Synthesis of Climate, Energy, and Comfort, *Journal of Architectural Education,* Spring-Summer 1984, pp. 38–42.

There are many examples throughout history in which thermal comfort was achieved without the use of mechanical equipment (comfort in a relative sense; how effective these buildings were is not known). The study of architecture includes a survey of historical accomplishments. Many modern-day masterpieces were derived from architecture from the past. Wright, Le Corbusier, Kahn, and Aalto all used historic precedent. They were also successful in merging art with science to create some "well-tempered environments." It is through the combination of these two diametrically opposed methods of design that well-tempered environments will be achieved.

McCluney, Ross, A Daylighting Checklist, *Solar Age,* April 1985, p. 84.

This one-page outline contains 15 factors to consider when one is using daylighting. It contains good references to other articles that delve into some of the factors in more detail, such as roof monitor design and calculator programs for skylight. The article was taken from the "Notebook" section of *Solar Age* magazine. The author is a principal research scientist at the Florida Solar Energy Center.

McCluney, Ross, and Zdepski, M. Stephen, *Proceedings I, 1986 International Daylighting Conference.* ASHRAE, Atlanta.

This is a bound collection of articles, papers, and abstracts for the 1986 International Daylighting Conference divided into three sections with 17 subsections. At the time of its printing, it represented the most up-to-date publication on the subject of daylighting.

McGuiness, Stein, and Reynolds, John, *Mechanical and Electrical Equipment for Buildings,* 8th edition, John Wiley & Sons, New York, 1986.

This textbook on environmental equipment and systems for buildings includes sections on HVAC, plumbing, vertical transportation, and electrical power distribution.

Matthews, Scott, Proving the Benefits of Daylighting, *Architectural Record,* August 1981, pp. 46–51.

The article describes buildings in which daylighting was used as an energy-conserving strategy. Three buildings were mentioned: the Gregory Bateson Building in Sacramento, CA; the Philippine Government Service Insurance Building in Manila; and the Department of Interior Building in Provo, UT.

Matthews, Scott, and Calthorpe, Peter, Daylight as Central Determinant of Design, *AIA Journal,* September 1979, pp. 86–92.

Much of the article is dedicated to describing the daylighting features of the Tennessee Valley Authority Chattanooga Office Building. The most unique feature is the atrium space with its louvered control system. The rest of the article describes the various analyses used and explains their results.

Meyers, Marshall, Masters of Light: Louis Kahn, *AIA Journal,* September 1979, pp. 60–62.

In the article, attention was given to the design of the reflector positioned below the skylight. Kahn wanted people to be able to see through the skylight while reflecting light onto the ceilings. Kahn was well aware of the psychological aspects of the view, connection to the outdoors, and orientation that comes with the use of daylighting. The design of the reflector was challenging; it needed to be transparent while protecting the art from direct sunlight.

Moore, Fuller, *Concepts and Practice of Architectural Daylighting,* Van Nostrand Reinhold, New York, 1986.

This good text on the fundamentals of daylighting is well supported with graphics. Simpler and more direct to use than other texts on the subject, it covers all of the major issues pertaining to daylighting and includes a glossary and seven appendices to supplement the material given.

Moore, Fuller, Daylighting: Six Aalto Libraries, *AIA Journal,* June 1983, pp. 58–69.

This is a good short article on the aesthetics of daylighting. Aalto used daylight for its aesthetic values. The manner by which he used it resulted in a very unique and humane architecture.

Moore, James, Daylight in Manhattan, *Solar Age,* December-June 1981, pp. 32–36.

New York City's first zoning regulation in 1916 recognized the importance of light reaching the street and lower floors of buildings. The regulation established a series of setbacks and sky planes to control building form and allow sunlight to reach the ground. The set of regulations became the model for many other cities in the United States and Europe. In 1980, the city recognized the need to update the zoning to once again provide sunlight at street level. The best example that they could find was the original New York City Zoning Regulation of 1916. They revised this regulation and also developed a "Daylight Map."

Navvab, Mojiaba, Daylighting Control Techniques, *Architectural Lighting,* October 1988, pp. 44–46.

This article describes daylighting control techniques from a unique perspective. Control techniques are divided into three groups: exterior, glazing, and interior. The pros and cons of each are briefly given. Also discussed is a control concept, the dynamic envelope.

Navvab, Mojiaba, and Selkowitz, Stephen, *Daylighting Data for Atrium Design,* paper presented at the Ninth National Passive Solar Conference, August 1984.

A research report supported by the U.S. Department of Energy, this paper focuses on the architectural design characteristics that affect the admittance of solar gain and daylight in atriums. Testing was done on a series of physical models in a sky simulator located at the Lawrence Berkeley Laboratories. Results are given in terms of geometric factors and sky conditions. The report concludes that many factors are involved in daylighting design and that the presence of an atrium is not sufficient to guarantee adequate amounts of light within buildings.

Ne'eman, Eliyahu, A Comprehensive Approach to the Integration of Daylight and Electric Light in Buildings, *Energy and Buildings*, June 1984, pp. 97–108.

For daylighting to be energy- and cost-efficient, it must be integrated with the space that it will serve. Of the many factors that the designer must consider, human performance is the most important. Energy management is essential for cost savings. Daylighting performance is also evaluated according to its effect on the heating and cooling loads. The selection of a daylighting strategy should be based on the overall performance and the cost benefits.

Olgyay, Aladar, and Olgyay, Victor, *Solar Control and Shading Devices*, Princeton University Press, Princeton, NJ, 1976.

This classic text on designing shading devices begins with a historical overview of indigenous responses to shading and ends by outlining a detailed analysis and design process. Photographs of many different shading devices are used to support the authors' claims.

A Perspective on Daylighting Design, *Architectural Record*, Mid-August 1981, pp. 44–45.

Many design tools are available to assist architects in daylighting design. They range from sophisticated mainframe computer programs to hand-held calculators to three-dimensional models made out of cardboard. The benefits of daylighting beyond the energy conservation aspects were reiterated in this article. They include view, connection to the outdoors, and health.

Peters, Richard P., Masters of Light: Alvar Aalto, *AIA Journal*, September 1979, pp. 53–55.

Alvar Aalto was truly a master when it came to light and architecture. Windows, light scoops, and clerestories were used as major design elements. He used these design elements to control daylighting. Artificial lighting, as well as daylighting, was viewed as an integral part of his building design. His buildings were so well done that the article concludes by saying that "Aalto's architecture is light."

Phillips, D., *Lighting in Architectural Design*, McGraw-Hill, New York, 1969.

This book covers lighting from a design point of view. Principles and criteria useful in establishing design goals are discussed, as well as natural and electrical strategies. Computational techniques are also covered but are dated.

Place, Wayne, and Howard, Thomas C., *Daylighting Multistory Office Buildings*, North Carolina Alternative Energy Corporation, 1990.

This simple, easy-to-follow book offers designers a set of design guidelines for daylighting multistory office buildings. These guidelines include building massing (orientation), light shelves, mirrored systems, tracking systems, interior surfaces, and lighting controls.

Pritchard, M.D.W., *Environmental Physics: Lighting*, American Elsevier Publishing Company, New York, 1969.

Basic fundamentals are thoroughly reviewed. Metric units are used throughout, which may be confusing for those accustomed to English units.

Robbins, Claude L., *Daylighting: Design and Analysis*, Van Nostrand Reinhold, New York, 1986.

This is a valuable two-part handbook that explores the fundamentals of daylighting. The first part presents the principal sources, control devices, and analysis methods used in daylighting. The second part contains reference material needed to supplement the design methodologies given.

Rosenfeld, Arthur H., and Selkowitz, Stephen E., Beam Daylighting: An Alternative Illuminating Technique, *Energy and Building*, January 1977.

This article is concerned with the energy savings and peak power reductions associated with the maximum utilization of natural light. The general characteristics of diffused daylighting are discussed in terms of a standard office plan. An innovative technique of daylighting using direct-beam radiation from the sun is treated in some detail.

Ross and Baruzzina, Inc., *Lighting and Thermal Operations: Energy Conservation Principles Applied to Office Lighting*, Federal Energy Administration, Washington, DC, 1975, ir NTIS PB-244, No. 154.

This report gives a detailed investigation of relationships between office lighting (specifically levels and orientation with respect to task) and visual task performance. Its conclusions are strong arguments for reduced light levels and more careful lighting design.

Ruck, Nancy C., Editor, *Building Design and Human Performance,* Van Nostrand Reinhold, New York, 1989.

Contributing experts explore the interrelationship between the thermal, visual, and acoustic elements of buildings and the occupants within. It includes major sections on daylighting and glazing materials.

Selkowitz, Stephen E., Effective Daylighting in Buildings—Revisited, *Lighting Design and Applications,* March 1986, pp. 34–47.

"Buildings are not designed to save energy; they are built to convert energy and other physical resources to produce a useful output and to provide a pleasant and healthy environment for human activities." Although the main emphasis of this article is on daylighting, the author reminds us that there are other important issues involved in building design.

Selkowitz, Steven E., *Influence of Windows on Building Energy Use,* paper presented at the Windows in Building Design and Maintenance Conference, Gothenburg, Sweden, June 1984.

The article focuses on heat loss, heat gain, and daylighting. The article concludes that cost is assumed to be the driving factor behind the more conservative design approaches, which have a faster return on investment. The text is supported with some good graphs and diagrams in addition to a list of conclusions at the end of the article.

Selkowitz, Stephen, and Johnson, Richard, The Daylighting Solution, *Solar Age,* August 1980, pp. 14–20.

This article reviews the electricity consumed for lighting by residential and office buildings. It looks at the economics involved in saving electricity by reducing lighting loads, and it goes into the control of daylight.

Sobin, Harris, Master of Natural Light: Le Corbusier, *AIA Journal,* September 1979, pp. 56–59.

Le Corbusier believed that "the facade would fulfill its true destiny, it is the provider of light." With this in mind, he created a typology of windows to provide adequate light within a space. Unfortunately, the "window walls" failed because of severe overheating during the summer months. However, Le Corbusier traveled to Africa and became fascinated with the vernacular solutions to his problem. He utilized shade, ventilation, and mass in his new architectural language. Le Corbusier used daylighting to accent, intensify, or delineate space.

State of California, Office of General Services, *Cookbook for Energy-Efficient Classroom Design,* Sacramento, CA, 1984.

Thirty-five recipes for making classrooms more energy efficient are outlined in this book. The format, which is geared to a nontechnical audience, is simple and easy to follow. The purpose of the book is to explain to school district officials different strategies that are known to be both energy efficient and cost-effective.

Stein, Richard G., Observations on Energy Use in Buildings, *Journal of Architectural Education,* February 1977, pp. 36–41.

This article outlines studies that determined where energy is used in buildings and areas in which substantial amounts of energy could be saved. This is a good article to reference for energy use data. Texts and charts support the need for daylighting applications. Of particular interest was the fact that office building lighting systems provide more than 100 footcandles, whereas prefluorescent and English standards show that 30 footcandles are sufficient. This reinforces the theory that lighting levels in the United States are unnecessarily high.

Sweitzer, G., Arasteh, D., and Selkowitz, S., Effects of Low-Emissivity Glazing on Energy Use Patterns in Nonresidential Daylighted Buildings, Low-E Coatings (ASHRAE Symposium on Fenestration Performance, 1987), *ASHRAE Transactions* vol. 93 (part I), 1987.

This paper shows the results of test data on window performance in two climates: Madison, WI, and Lake Charles, LA. The focus on testing was to improve occupant comfort through better fenestration design. The increased *R*-value of the glazing provides significant savings in cold climates (e.g., Madison, WI) and is also beneficial in hot climates.

Technology Pursues, Catches, Daylight, *Architectural Record*, Mid-August 1981, pp. 58–59.

This is a brief case study into the design of the Lockheed Missile and Space Company, Building 157, in Sunnyvale, CA. This building uses a daylighting energy conservation design strategy. Much of the design is standard practice (orientation, model testing, etc.). Two unique features are 12-ft-deep light shelves (which also act as electrical raceways and house air-conditioning ducts) and the "litetrium." DOE2.1 computer energy analysis runs predict energy savings of approximately 50%.

Terman, M., The Photic Environment and Physiological Time-Keeping Light, *Proceedings I, 1986 International Daylighting Conference*, p. 356.

Human physiology evolved to synchronize with the daily solar cycle. Light exposure in the evening inhibits the production of melotonin. Melotonin is a hormone that helps induce sleep. It responds to different light intensities by varying the amount of photoreceptive substance in the retina. Studies have shown that their melotonin production runs free, causing fatigue to occur at varying times of the day. Other studies have shown that without adequate light exposure, humans are vulnerable to insomnia and depression.

Terraced Pods Invite Daylight and Breezes, *Architectural Record*, Mid-August 1981, pp. 53–58.

This is a case study of the Government Service Insurance System Headquarters Building in Manila, by Jorge Y. Ramos. This building has many interesting design features that respond to the natural surroundings. The upper level steps back to facilitate the daylighting aspects of the design. The building is "notched" to break up the mass and direct cooling breezes. The article is well documented with graphics and photographs. This building can serve as a very good prototype for a daylight building in a hot, humid climate.

Turner, D. P., *Windows and Environment*, Pilkington Environmental Advisory Service, Architectural Press, London, 1971.

This book offers excellent qualitative treatment of daylighting in the first part and excellent technical treatment in the second part.

Vezey, E. E., and Evans, B. H., The Study of Natural Illumination by Means of Models Under Artificial Sky, *Illuminating Engineering* 50:3667–3674, 1955.

This article includes a very brief description of the sky dome at the Texas Engineering Experiment Station (19 ft in diameter), and informative explanations of procedures regarding models, instrumentation, and model testing.

Villecco, Marguerite, Natural Light, *AIA Journal*, September 1979, pp. 49–51.

All buildings can benefit from the energy savings and psychological advantages of daylighting; however, daylighting is best suited for buildings with intense daytime use, such as schools and office buildings. Daylighting is one of many energy conservation issues that require buildings to be designed to integrate with the environment. The location and form of buildings have become the focus for energy-conscious design instead of mechanical systems. Architects need to become aware of the delicate balance between the two to design buildings that are energy efficient.

Villecco, M., Selkowitz, S., and Griffith, J. W., Strategies of Daylight Design, *AIA Journal*, September 1979, pp. 68–77, 104, 108, 110, 112.

This is a comprehensive article into daylighting design. It is divided into five parts: introduction, controls, integration, analysis, and codes. Each part focuses on an important aspect of the daylighting design process. The article is a good introduction to principles and concepts due to its scope and accuracy. Emphasis is on the qualitative aspects of design instead of the quantitative.

Villecco, Marguerite, Selkowitz, Stephen, and Griffith, J. W., Strategies of Daylight Design, *AIA Journal*, September 1979, pp. 1–7.

This is an excellent short presentation of daylighting strategies with simple, effective graphics. Some simplified analytical case studies showing illumination levels of various designs are also included. This article is a must for the daylighting newcomer.

Visher, Jacqueline C., Psychology of Daylighting, *Architecture*, 1987, pp. 109–112.

As more people become interested in daylighting, more questions about its benefits are being raised. The general consensus is that daylighting has many therapeutic benefits. Exactly what the benefits are is where research is needed.

Vonier, Thomas, Details, Details, *Progressive Architecture*, April 1984, pp. 94–97.

This article briefly outlines the concepts behind some passive energy conservation design strategies. Ventilation, atriums, light shelves, beam daylighting, and skylights are covered. Each topic includes a case study example and details of how it was integrated into the design of an actual building.

Watson, Donald, The Energy Within the Space Within, *Progressive Architecture*, July 1982, pp. 97–102.

Atriums can be more than just large public spaces with trees and fountains; they can also be used for passive heating, passive cooling, and daylighting applications. Each of these conservation strategies is outlined and includes a set of design goals and guidelines. A useful dot chart shows which strategies work best in the different cities throughout the United States.

Watson, Donald, Three Perspectives on Energy, *Architectural Record*, January 1979, pp. 125–128.

This is an excellent essay on the historical, technical, and social implications of energy conservation. The architectural and technical capacities are available to design buildings that save substantial amounts of energy; what is not available is an attitude that permits this. Social and cultural values must also change if we are to be successful in achieving this goal. Watson outlines three steps that must be taken to implement energy-conscious design standards. One is simple and available; the others require change on a social and cultural level.

These changes focus on the qualitative rather than the quantitative aspects of architectural design.

Where Does the Energy Really Go? *Architectural Record*, January 1981, pp. 108–111.

This is a Department of Energy study to determine exactly where energy is being consumed in high-rise buildings. The article describes proposed research on the 26-story Park Plaza Building in Trenton, NJ. It also offers a description of the controls and compliance methodology.

Wilson, Forrest, Daylight and the Human Eye, *Architecture*, June 1987, p. 112.

Architects and interior designers have long had concerns that artificial lighting deprives humans of the full spectrum of light distribution. This article contends that human visual perception did not evolve under conditions of the full spectrum. Most light enters the eye only after reflecting off of other objects. Only by staring at a light source or being inside a completely white or gray room would a person be exposed to the full spectrum.

Woodbury, Sally, Governing Energy, *Progressive Architecture*, April 1984, pp. 86–91.

This is a general review of completed state office buildings in California. This article briefly describes the master planning, design, and technology that went into these buildings. The four buildings reviewed are the Employment Development Department, the Energy Department, Water Resources, and San Jose State Office buildings. Good sectional and isometric drawings illustrate energy conservation design strategies.

INDEX